This book examines life after death and changing concepts of heaven and hell in English thought from 1650 to 1750. It explores seventeenth- and eighteenth-century images of the journey of body and soul, from Platonist accounts of pre-existence, to the intermediate state between death and the last day, to the final judgement and beyond into heaven or hell. It discloses a society in which frail and fleeting human life was lived out in the expectation of salvation or damnation, of eternal happiness or eternal torment, of heaven or hell, and depicts a world radically different from our own. Drawing on the writings not only of the elite, but also of the middling and lower classes, Almond shows how there hovered, around images of the afterlife, many classical and contemporary debates: free will and pre-destination, materialism and dualism, religion and science, Catholicism and Protestantism, religious and political radicalism, demonology and witchcraft, and so on. The picture which emerges is both representative of the age as a whole and enables us to appreciate more fully contemporary understandings of the meaning of human life and death.

HEAVEN AND HELL IN ENLIGHTENMENT ENGLAND

HEAVEN AND HELL IN ENLIGHTENMENT ENGLAND

PHILIP C. ALMOND
Associate Professor, Studies in Religion
The University of Queensland

Published by the Press Syndicate of the University of Cambridge
The Pitt Building, Trumpington Street, Cambridge CB2 1RP
40 West 20th Street, New York, NY 10011-4211, USA
10 Stamford Road, Oakleigh, Melbourne 3166, Australia

© Cambridge University Press 1994

First published 1994

Printed in Great Britain at the University Press, Cambridge

A catalogue record for this book is available from the British Library

Library of Congress cataloguing in publication data

Almond, Philip C.
    Heaven and Hell in Enlightenment England / Philip C. Almond.
        p.   cm.
    Includes bibliographical references and index.
    ISBN 0 521 45371 2 (hardback)
    1. Future life – Christianity – History of doctrines – 17th century.
    2. Future life – Christianity – History of doctrines – 18th century.
    3. Heaven – Christianity – History of doctrines.   4. Hell –
    Christianity – History of doctrines.   5. Religious thought –
    England – 17th century.   6. Religious thought – England – 18th
    century.   7. England – Intellectual life – 17th century.   8. England –
    Intellectual life – 18th century.   I. Title.
    BT832.A55   1994
    236'.2 – dc20   93-40008
                                                                                         CIP

ISBN 0 521 45371 2 hardback

UP

To Natalie

Contents

List of plates	*page* xi
Acknowledgements	xiii

	Introduction	1
1	**The journey of the soul**	4
	The pre-existence of the soul	4
	Pre-existence and human suffering	7
	The origin of souls	9
	Pre-existence and the Scriptures	13
	The transmigration of souls	17
	Free will, human and divine	24
	The vehicles of the soul	29
	A Platonic map of the world	32
2	**From the hour of death to the day of judgement**	38
	The mortality of the soul	38
	Thomas Browne and the destiny of the soul	41
	Radical mortalists	43
	Hobbes and the Kingdom of God	47
	Richard Overton and John Milton	51
	'Flying like an Eagle in the Air'	54
	Henry Dodwell and the breath of God	60
	The rejection of Purgatory	67
	Purgatory revisited	72
3	**The contours of heaven and hell**	81
	Hell's torments	81
	The dark fires of hell	87
	Punishments, body and soul	90
	Co-partners in sin	95
	Abominable fantasies	97
	Heavenly joys	100

		Heavenly bodies	105
		The symmetry of contrasts	108
4	The last day		111
		Un-Platonic fires	111
		Hell on earth	119
		From the earth to the sun	123
		Gods, suns, and comets	125
		Resurrection and persons	131
		Spiritual bodies	136
		Personal identity and the soul	140
5	Eternal torments		144
		Eternal or temporary?	144
		Reason and scripture	145
		Wrath, mercy, and justice	149
		Infinite offence	154
		Unfulfilled threatenings?	156
		The ultimate deterrent?	158

Notes — 162
Bibliography — 195
Index — 212

Plates

Between pages 114 and 115

1. Frontispiece of *Two Choice and Useful Treatises* (London, 1682), by permission of Yale University Library
2. Frontispiece of the German translation of Joseph Glanvill's *Saducismus Triumphatus*, from Alan C. Kors and Edward Peters (eds.), *Witchcraft in Europe 1100 – 1700* (London, 1973), by permission of J. M. Dent and Sons
3. Frontispiece of Joseph Glanvill's *Saducismus Triumphatus*, 3rd edn (London, 1689), by permission of The British Library
4. Title page of Richard Overton, *Man Wholly Mortal*, 2nd edn (London, 1675), by permission of The British Library
5. Title page of John Asgill, *An Argument Proving, That... Man may be translated...* (London, 1700), by permission of The British Library
6. 'The Harrowing of Hell' by Jerome Cock, from Robert Hughes, *Heaven and Hell in Western Art* (London, 1968), by permission of Weidenfeld and Nicolson
7. Illustration to [Christopher Sutton], *Disce Mori, learn to dye* (London, 1662), by permission of Cambridge University Library
8. Frontispiece of Richard Baxter, *The Saints' Everlasting Rest*, 11th edn (London, 1677), by permission of The British Library
9. The punishments of the damned, by Luca Signorelli, fresco in Orvieto Cathedral, from Robert Hughes, *Heaven and Hell in Western Art* (London, 1968), by permission of Weidenfeld and Nicolson

10 William Hogarth, 'Credulity, Superstition and Fanaticism', by permission of The British Museum
11 Henry Montagu, Earl of Manchester, *Manchester al mondo. Contemplatio Mortis, & Immortalitatis*, 6th impression (London, 1655), by permission of The British Library
12 'The Last Judgement' by Albrecht Dürer, by permission of the Boston Museum of Fine Arts, bequest of Francis Bullard
13 Frontispiece of Thomas Burnet, *The Theory of the Earth*, 3rd edn (London, 1697), by permission of Cambridge University Library
14 The medieval cosmos, Schedel's *Nuremberg Chronicle*, 1493, from Robert Hughes, *Heaven and Hell in Western Art* (London, 1968), by permission of Weidenfeld and Nicolson
15 Illustration to Tobias Swinden, *An Enquiry into the Nature and Place of Hell*, 2nd edn (London, 1727), from Robert Hughes, *Heaven and Hell in Western Art* (London, 1968), by permission of Weidenfeld and Nicolson
16 Giorgio Ghisi, 'The Resurrection of the flesh', from Richard Cavendish, *Visions of Heaven and Hell* (London, 1977), by permission of Orbis Books

Acknowledgements

For the past ten years, the Department of Studies in Religion at the University of Queensland, Australia, has provided a congenial context in which to teach and pursue research. I owe debts of gratitude to many of my colleagues. For much stimulating conversation on various aspects of this work, I am particularly indebted to my friend Dr Peter Harrison. I am most grateful too to the Administrative Officer in the Department, Ms Michelle Weil, who has always been willing to assist me with that most modern of infernal torments, the personal computer. The staff of the main library at the University of Queensland have been, as usual, unfailingly helpful. This book is dedicated to my friend and partner Natalie Bell.

Introduction

> When compared with the stretch of time unknown to us, O king, the present life of men on earth is like the flight of a single sparrow through the hall where, in winter, you sit with your captains and ministers. Entering at one door and leaving by another, while it is inside it is untouched by the wintry storm; but this brief interval of calm is over in a moment, and it returns to the winter whence it came, vanishing from your sight. Man's life is similar; and of what follows it, or what went before, we are utterly ignorant.
>
> The Venerable Bede, *Ecclesiastical History of the English People*

This book is about ignorance, ignorance of that which may have preceded our life, of that which may follow it. But images of life after death, or of its absence, *are* reflections of our lives now. Although enshrouded in our ignorance, yet they enshrine our deepest hopes and dreams, and express our greatest fears and nightmares. Life is experienced in the here and now in accord with the expectations of what it shall or shall not be after it has ended. Our beliefs and our actions in this life are permeated by images of who we shall or shall not be in the next.

This study explores ways of thinking about life after death in English thought in the seventeenth and eighteenth centuries. It attempts to show not only what people thought and felt about life after death, but to show how and why they thought about it in the way they did. To explore these is to explore the society which gave rise to them. In so doing, this book hopes to re-create, in part at least, a radically different world, a world which by virtue of its construction of life after death may be seen to be significantly discontinuous with ours, a world in which frail and evanescent human life was lived out in the expectation of salvation or damnation, of eternal happiness or eternal torment, of heaven or hell. Continuous with us in its puzzlement with mortality, it was very 'other' in its solutions to the riddle. Thus, to understand the dimensions of that society's images of life after death may serve as a reminder of the relativism of ours.

'That strange agglomeration of incongruities, the seventeenth-century mind':[1] Aldous Huxley's description is an apt one, nowhere more so than in the images of life after death constructed in both the seventeenth and eighteenth centuries. Using the map of the main highways provided by D. P. Walker in his *The Decline of Hell*, I have followed the pathways and byways that branched out from them. Thus, the more complete map which this book hopes to provide, details not only the commonplace and the average, but the eccentric and the original. It maps not only those works which still form part of the late twentieth-century canon of late seventeenth- and early eighteenth-century philosophy and theology, but the arcane, the obscure, and the forgotten. And it rediscovers parts of the canon usually ignored. It provides a guide, not only to the hopes and fears of the elite, but also to those of the middling and lower classes.

The picture which emerges is a complex one, not merely because of the range and diversity of images of the afterlife, but also because, around these, hover many classical and contemporary debates: free will and predestination, materialism and dualism, the attributes of God, reason and the Scriptures, religion and science, the origins of the soul, Catholicism and Protestantism, the nature of punishment – divine and secular, demonology and witchcraft, Parliament and people, religious and political radicalism, Puritanism and Anglicanism, enthusiasm and libertinism, the nature of personal identity, magic and Cabbalism, explanations of evil and suffering, sin, sexuality, and so on.

It remains to say something about the plan of this book. Broadly speaking, it follows the journeys of the body and soul from their beginnings to eternity. In the context of a late seventeenth-century neo-Platonic world view, chapter 1 examines the journey of the soul from its creation at the beginning of the world, to its fall from the aethereal realm into this world, to its location after death, and to its final destiny after the day of judgement. Chapter 2 investigates the life of the soul between death and its reunion with the body on the last day, whether it sleeps, dies, or retains a conscious existence in heaven, hell, or intermediate states between the two. Chapter 3 explores the symmetry of contrasts in images of heaven and hell. Chapter 4 deals with the last day and the resurrection of the body in the context of influences upon these from the new science. The final chapter discusses the ultimate destiny of the person – eternal or temporary torments, universal salvation, or the final annihilation of the wicked.

In territory as vast as this, I do not hope for comprehensiveness. The map which I have constructed is, after all, only a map and not the territory itself. Nevertheless, it is my hope that my text and the excerpts from the original texts I have provided will enable readers to experience the joy of exploring what is in many cases previously uncharted territory, and to share the excitement of opening the covers of forgotten books, of rediscovering old ideas, of resurrecting lost lives, and of re-creating the past for the present.

CHAPTER I

The journey of the soul

THE PRE-EXISTENCE OF THE SOUL

I loved not to see, what I reputed a fable and Imposture travel so confidently through the World, and everywhere vaunt itself for a genuine truth.[1]

The fable and imposture to which Edward Warren was referring in 1667 was the concept of the pre-existence of the soul in an aethereal or aerial realm prior to its embodiment in a terrestrial body. Warren was exaggerating the universality of the adoption of this concept. Certainly, in England, it remained the preserve of the intellectual elite, and in so far as it was expounded and defended, it was done with caution and some little reticence. Nevertheless, asserted and defended it was, and by several of the Restoration period's leading Platonists – the Cambridge Platonist Henry More, the Oxford Anglican cleric Joseph Glanvill, and the Anglican Bishop George Rust.

The unorthodoxy of the concept of the pre-existence of the soul was recognised by proponents and opponents alike. But by the former, it was presented as a rational opinion with scriptural assent which could be maintained without danger to the essentials of the faith. In the Preface to his *Lux Orientalis*, for example, Joseph Glanvill maintained that the Anglican Church gave latitude for speculation on matters not necessary or fundamental to the Faith, that the doctrine of pre-existence had never been excluded by the Anglican or any other church, and that he intended no innovation or disturbance to it.[2] In a letter to Robert Boyle, accompanying a copy of his *Lux Orientalis*, he wrote, 'I am secure that you will appoint no other judge of these theories, but an uninterested and impartial reason. If such as you cherish those beams of restored *Platonism*, they will shine more and more to a perfect day; otherwise this light will sneak back to its forgotten darkness, and be buried again in its old obscurity.'[3]

As we shall see, the attraction for the Restoration Platonists, like More, Glanvill, and Rust, of the doctrine of the soul's pre-existence was not merely a nostalgia for the arcane. For they believed that in this doctrine lay the key to the vindicating of the goodness of God in the face of evil and suffering in the world. Nevertheless, they were heirs of the revival of neo-Platonism in the Italian Renaissance. In the late fifteenth century, Marsilio Ficino, founder of the Florentine Academy, had translated into Latin not only all Plato's surviving works but also the *Corpus Hermeticum*, the works of Plotinus, and several works, mostly magical, of the later neo-Platonists – Porphyry, Iamblichus, and Proclus. And it was this philosophico-religious interpretation of Plato, as seen through the eyes of the AD third- to fifth-century neo-Platonists, integrated with Christian theology, that was to influence the work of the seventeenth-century English Platonists.

As Daniel Walker has pointed out, that this integration of Platonism and Christian theology could be carried out 'was largely due to the mistaken belief that behind Plato stood Moses and the Ancient Theologians'.[4] The Christian Platonists looked back, not only to Plato, but to a series of earlier ancient theologians who had themselves derived their philosophy from Moses, sometimes from Noah, Enoch, or even Adam. In short, it was believed that Platonism was God's original revelation to humankind, and Plato was but Moses speaking Greek. Thus, for example, among the ancients who accepted the pre-existence of the soul, Henry More listed the supposed author of the *Corpus Hermeticum* Hermes Trismegistus, the Indian Brahmans, the Magi, the Chaldean Oracles, the Jewish Cabbala, Moses, Zoroaster, Pythagoras, Plato, Euclid, Philo, Plotinus, Iamblichus, and Proclus.[5] A similar list was given by Joseph Glanvill, and by Christian Knorr von Rosenroth, together with Francis van Helmont, the editor of the *Kabbala Denudata*.[6]

It was, of course, a much more difficult task to discern the doctrine of the pre-existence of the soul among the early Christian Fathers, even among those with Platonic inclinations. But there was one notable exception: the third-century Alexandrian theologian, Origen. In his *De Principiis*, Origen had maintained the pre-existence of the soul, its fall from an aethereal realm as a result of its misuse of free will, and its subsequent descent into a terrestrial form. As Origen put it,

Some [souls] sinned deeply and became daemons, others less and became angels; others still less and became archangels; and thus each in turn received the reward for his individual sin. But there remained some souls who had not sinned so greatly as to become daemons, nor on the other hand so very lightly as to become angels. God therefore made the present world and bound the soul to the body as a punishment.[7]

That Origen had defended the doctrine of the soul's pre-existence was perhaps little comfort to its seventeenth-century defenders. For, among the numerous heresies which St Jerome alleged Origen to be guilty of, he included the pre-existence of the soul, and its fall into bodily existence as a result of sloth and neglect.[8] And Origen had been condemned as a heretic by the Council of Alexandria in AD 400 and the Council of Constantinople in AD 553.[9]

Be that as it may, there was a significant revival of interest in Origen during the Renaissance provoked, in part at least, by the Italian philosopher Pico della Mirandola. In his *Nongentae Conclusiones* in 1486, Pico argued that it was more reasonable to believe Origen to be saved than to believe him to be damned. Pico's work was placed on the Index, and when he reasserted his opinion in 1487 in his *Apologia* he was indicted for heresy and arrested. In 1493, this was rescinded by Pope Alexander VI, and, as Edgar Wind points out, 'the knowledge of his vindication gradually showed its effect upon humanist and theological learning'.[10] During the sixteenth century, beginning in 1503 with Aldus's edition of a number of Origen's homilies on the Old Testament, there were a further ten editions in ever increasing size, and in 1512, Jacques Merlin produced the first edition of Origen's complete works in Latin.

Still, as Walker has suggested, neither Pico, nor Erasmus, nor other Origenist sympathisers, attempted to defend Origen's opinions, either on the pre-existence of the soul or the eventual universal salvation of all humankind (and Satan and his minions). Rather, they defended him in spite of his perceived doctrinal errors.[11] But English Platonists were much more sympathetic. Henry More, for example, described him in 1659 as 'the greatest Light and Bulwark that antient Christianity had'.[12] And the anonymous 1661 work, *A Letter of Resolution concerning Origen and the chief of his Opinions*, was the first, not only to defend, but also theologically to attempt to justify the theology of Origen, and in particular the doctrines of the pre-existence of the soul and the universal restoration of all to God.

This work has been attributed – probably correctly – to George Rust. He had been a fellow of Christ's College, Cambridge, until 1659, had settled in Ireland from 1661, and was made Bishop of Dromore in succession to Jeremy Taylor.[13] Rust had certainly read

Henry More's *Immortality of the Soul* and had adopted many of its ideas. But if Rust was the author of it, More who had been his tutor at Cambridge did not know of it.[14] More himself was, as I suggested above, drawn to the theology of Origen, 'that Miracle of the Christian World', as were most of the Cambridge Platonists.[15] His reaction to *The Letter of Resolution* was sympathetic, if cautious. To Anne, Lady Conway, he wrote of it as 'a book that has witt and learning in it', although he went on to point out that the Vice-Chancellor at Cambridge, Theophilus Dillingham of Clare, looked upon it as a dangerous book.[16] Elsewhere, he described it as 'a pretty odd Book, but has some thinges very consyderable in it'.[17] One of the 'thinges very consyderable' with which More was in complete agreement was its account of the pre-existence of the soul.

PRE-EXISTENCE AND HUMAN SUFFERING

Granting that a sympathy for the doctrine of pre-existence may be seen to go hand in hand with a commitment to Platonism, what were the specific reasons for More, Glanvill, and Rust maintaining and defending, however cautiously, a doctrine which was not essential to their adoption of Platonism, and one which at best was outside of the mainstream of the Christian tradition, at worst could be construed as heretical? Essentially, it was for them the central feature of a natural theology which, by offering an explanation of human suffering, enabled them to maintain their Platonist commitment to the unequivocable goodness of God. Sins committed in pre-existent lives explained the pain and suffering of human lives in the here and now. God's righteousness and goodness can only be justified, declared George Rust, if we conclude that,

> all those wretched Souls had of old by their long *revolt* from God and the laws of his righteous Kingdome highly deserved this Scourge from him, to be so put out of his Care, as it were, and given up to the barbarous domination of the *Devil*,... and whom they by choice and affection fell off to in other regions of the world, that him and his tyranny they should here upon earth still suffer, whether with or against their wills.[18]

The theory of the soul's pre-existence explained, for example, why some people appeared to be naturally depraved from the earliest stages of life. It allowed the natures of persons in their terrestrial state to be seen as corresponding to and continuous with their pre-existent natures. As Glanvill declared,

> Let us conceive the Souls of men to have grown *degenerate* in a former *condition of life*, to have contracted strong and inveterate *habits* to vice and lewdness ... ; we may then easily apprehend, when some men's natures had so incredibly a *depraved* tincture, and such *impetuous, ungovernable, irreclaimable inclinations* to what is vitious; while others have nothing near such wretched propensions, but by good *education*, and good *discipline* are mouldable to vertue.[19]

The theory of the soul's pre-existence was therefore in conflict with that other explanation of the innate depravity of human nature, namely, the doctrine of original sin. However variously interpreted, this doctrine saw the evil inherent in human nature, not as the responsibility of the individual, but as the result of the sin of Adam. It made of humanity a *massa damnata* without free will and redeemable only by God's grace. According to John Calvin,

> All of us, therefore, descending from an impure seed, come into the world tainted with the contagion of sin. Nay, before we behold the light of the sun we are in God's sight defiled and polluted ... We thus see that the impurity of parents is transmitted to their children, so that all, without exception, are originally depraved. The commencement of this depravity will not be found until we ascend to the first parent of all as the fountain head. We must, therefore, hold it for certain that, in regard to human nature, Adam was not merely a progenitor, but, as it were, a root, and that accordingly, by his corruption, the whole human race was deservedly vitiated.[20]

While the Platonists were not unwilling to see terrestrial existence as inherently sinful, indeed as a divine punishment, they were not willing to admit that it was such as a result of the primordial sin of Adam. On the contrary, the theory of the soul's pre-existence, attributing the propensity to evil within every soul to each individual's pre-existent state, made each individual personally responsible for his sufferings in the terrestrial realm, and vindicated the divine goodness and justice. The hypothesis of the soul's pre-existence, declared Joseph Glanvill,

> clears the *divine* attributes from any shadow of harshness, or breach of equity, since it supposeth us to have sinned and deserved all the misery we suffer in this condition before we came hither: whereas the other which teacheth, that we became both guilty and miserable by the single and sole offence of Adam, whenas we were not then in being, or as to our own souls, as much as *potentially* in our great *Progenitour*, bears somewhat hardly upon the repute of the Divine perfections.[21]

The pre-existence of the soul also served to provide an explanation of human mental disorders and physical deformities. So-called monstrous births were interpreted as the consequence, not of divine providence, but as the unfortunate, albeit deserved, result of pre-existent sins. This, too, was part of a defence of the goodness of God. Late seventeenth-century Platonists were unable, unlike their sixteenth-century forebears, to view monstrous births as signs of either God's wrath or of nature's fertility; and they were unable as yet to see them in the 'natural' context of eighteenth-century embryology. They viewed them rather as the result of sin, the consequence of pre-existent lapses from godliness.[22] The divine was consequently freed from any responsibility for such prodigies.

Burgeoning knowledge of the 'savage races' during the seventeenth century also raised questions about the divine Providence. Why, wondered Rust, has Providence so arranged it that 'many whole nations both of old and at this present day were so overrun with all kinde of barbarity, ferity and bestial lust, so estranged from the knowledge of God and the love of vertue?'[23] The goodness of God could only be justified if the members of these nations were themselves responsible, a thesis only possible on the assumption of the pre-existence of souls.

For Henry More too, the members of such nations had forfeited the favour of their Creator through their actions in a prior life. Sins then committed explained 'the squalid forlornness and brutish barbarity that whole nations for many Ages have layen under ... '[24] As Jacques le Goff has pointed out, the late medieval doctrine of purgatory was an accountancy of the hereafter, the punishments of the afterlife strictly proportioned to the sins of this one.[25] In a similar way, the doctrine of pre-existence provided an accountancy of the heretofore. The evil, the suffering, and the brutishness of this life was the direct and proportionate result of the sins of a pre-existent state.

THE ORIGIN OF SOULS

The doctrine of the soul's pre-existence suggested that all human souls had come into being at, or very near, the time of the original creation of the world. In part, this was implied by the Biblical account of creation. More specifically, since according to the Biblical tradition God had ceased his creative activity on the seventh day, souls must have been created during the first six days of creation. In part too, it was a corollary of the essential goodness of God. For, granting that it was better to be than not to be, the divine goodness created us as soon as it was possible so to do:

God being *infinitely good*, and that to his *Creatures*, and therefore doing always what is *best* for them, methinks it roundly follows that our *souls lived* and 'njoy'd themselves of *old* before they came into these *bodies*. For since they were *capable* of *living*, and that in a much *better* and *happier* state long before they descended into this *region* of *death* and *misery*; and since that condition of life and self-enjoyment would have been better, than *absolute not-being*; may we not safely conclude from a due consideration of the *divine goodness*, that it was so?[26]

Such an account was at odds with two other more common theories of the origin of souls: immediate creationism and traducianism. According to the former of these, God created *ex nihilo* a fresh soul for every human individual at its conception or birth. Accepted by Jerome, by Hilary and medieval theologians in general, it was vigorously supported by Aquinas, and defended by Calvin.

According to traducianism, the soul was transmitted by one or both of the parents to the unborn child. It was traditionally associated with Tertullian, who in his *De Anima* defended it against both immediate creationism and the Pythagorean account of the transmigration of souls. According to Tertullian, there is both a body-producing seed and a soul-producing seed. At the risk of offending modesty, he asks 'whether we do not, in that very heat of extreme gratification when the generative fluid is ejected, feel that somewhat of our own soul has gone from us? And do we not experience a faintness and prostration along with a dimness of sight? This, then, must be the soul-producing seed, which arises at once from the outdrip of the soul, just as that fluid is the body-producing seed which proceeds from the drainage of the flesh.'[27]

In his *Doubt's Boundless Sea*, Don Allen has pointed out that, during the Renaissance, there were many proponents, not only of creationism and traducianism, but of many other theories of the origin of the soul. In 1601, for example, Nicholas Hill reported twenty-three theories of the soul's origin in his *Philosophia Epicurea, Democritiana, Theophrastica*.[28] Notable among seventeenth-century traducianists was Thomas Browne. In his *Religio Medici*, he admitted that both traducianism and immediate creation were compatible with religion. He himself would have been inclined to the latter theory, he suggested, except for one objection 'not wrung from speculations and subtilties, but from common sense, and observation; not pickt from the leaves of any author, but bred among the weeds and tares of mine owne braine'. He continued,

> And this is a conclusion from the equivocall and monstrous productions in the copulation of man with beast; for if the soule of man bee not transmitted and transfused in the seed of the parents, why are not those productions merely beasts, but have also an impression and tincture of reason in as high a measure as it can evidence it selfe in those improper organs?[29]

John Milton was a committed traducianist. And, like St Augustine and John Calvin, he could not see how the doctrine of original sin could be defended on the grounds of the immediate creation of souls. Moreover, he objected to the implication of creationism that God was daily involved in creating souls 'at the bidding of what is not seldom the flagitious wantonness of man'.[30] In late seventeenth-century England, while immediate creationism predominated, traducianism had one notable proponent, Henry Hills, King's printer and infamous publisher of pirated works. According to him, the whole process of propagation depended on a quintessential seed, 'a Symbolical character of the whole nature, and therefore (speaking of Man) of the soul as well as of the Body impressed in it', the passing on of which does not diminish the individual.[31]

The Platonists used the arguments of the traducianists against immediate creationists, and vice versa. Against immediate creationism, they were noticeably Manichaean. For them, the enmeshing of souls in matter was an undesirable state brought about as a result of their own misdeeds. It was inconceivable that a God who is essentially good would ever create souls in order to place them in such brutish bodies in so uncongenial a realm. Rust, for example, reminded his readers,

> For God therefore to send out of his pure and holy hands an immaculate Soul capable of living elsewhere, and fit for all virtue and heavenly wisedome, lest the lust of two brutish persons should come to nothing, and condemn it to an habitation in such parts of the earth where reigns nothing but gross ignorance and vice... what is this, saies the Father [Origen], but to betray his own offspring... unto unavoidable misery; and to put off the chief excellencies of his most blessed Nature, *goodness* and *righteousness*.[32]

That God was, through his immediate creation of souls, intimately linked to 'the lust of two brutish persons' was a matter of distaste to all the Platonists. Sexuality was an undesirable facet of terrestrial life, the consequence of a fall from more aethereal pursuits, both metaphorically and literally. And if sexuality *per se* was undesirable, except as a source of mutual comfort and for the procreation of children, illicit sexuality was abominable. Their horror of incest, adultery, and fornication was in keeping with the Catholic medieval tradition and that of the Protestant Reformation (parts of its radically libertine wing excepted). But it was undoubtedly reinforced by an English Puritanism that had led in 1650 to the Commonwealth's Act 'for suppressing the detestable sins of incest, adultery and fornication'. What had previously been considered spiritual if none the less serious misdemeanours were redefined as secular crimes.[33]

It needs to be remembered too that this was a time when the considered opinion still was that coition between members of different species could produce conception, and monstrous births. Only at the end of the seventeenth century were there in England the beginnings of the realisation that conception could not take place between the human and other species.[34] In such a context, there is a certain logic in seeing the doctrine of immediate creation as involving God, not only in sin, but also in crime, a co-conspirator if not the author of it. For More, the doctrine made God 'the chief assistant and actour... in those abominable crimes of Whoredom, Adultery, Incest, nay Buggery itself, by supplying those foul coitions with new created souls for the purpose...'[35]

The Platonists' main arguments against traducianism were directed against its incipiently materialistic nature. They saw traducianism as the thin end of a wedge leading to the denial not only of God, but also of the soul. And they were right in perceiving the link between traducianism and denials of the immortality of the soul. Thus, for example, Glanvill's criticisms of traducianism were in effect arguments against Thomas Hobbes' materialism in general. But, in particular, they were aimed at his suggestion that the notion of an 'incorporeal soul' was a logical contradiction.[36] More's criticism of traducianism assumed Descartes' definition of the soul as a non-corporeal substance incapable of division or separation.[37] Consequently, according to More, because traduction implied the divisibility of the soul, it was 'a plain contradiction to the *notion* of a Soul, and therefore of an *Indivisible*, that is of an Indiscerpible, Essence'.[38]

For those who accepted the Cartesian definition, this may have been an effective rebuttal. But for traducianists like Henry Hills who did not see the process of the birth of souls in terms of the divisibility of the souls of either (or both) of its 'parents', it would have had little effect. As we have seen, for Hills, there was a quintessential seed in every person which produced the psycho-physical unity which was the foetus. Moreover in Hills' proto-genetic theory was a theological motif which would conceptually tip the scales against both creationism and pre-existence. God, declared Hills, 'is most absolute and all sufficient of himself, yet where he hath set up nature, and ordinary wayes and means, to work by, he allwaies honoureth and useth his own ordinance...'[39] In short, therefore, explanations in terms of secondary causes were to be preferred. The Platonists, then, did have reasons to fear a traducianism which appeared to exclude any immediate role for the divine in the origin of souls. For the increasing dominance of explanations of the processes of generation in medical terms in the eighteenth century was to relegate discussions about the origins of the soul to a little-used siding, even among those who continued to hold a belief in the immortality of the soul. The question of the origin of persons was to become centred on rival physiological accounts in a developing science of embryology.[40]

PRE-EXISTENCE AND THE SCRIPTURES

But how were arguments for the soul's pre-existence to be made compatible with that repository of necessary truth, the Scriptures? On the face of it, the Biblical account of the creation and fall of man was at complete odds with the theory of the soul's pre-existence. This was not a new problem for Christian Platonists. In the second century AD Clement of Alexandria had distinguished a fourfold level of scriptural understanding: the historical, the ethical, the priestly, and the theological. Subsequently, Origen distinguished between the 'historical' meaning of the text and its 'mystical' interpretation, and identified an historical, moral, and spiritual meaning in Scriptures.

Rust's *Letter of Resolution* recognised that Origen had supported the doctrine of the pre-existence of the soul by a 'spiritual' reading of the Genesis accounts. But Rust contented himself by merely declaring that there was no direct Scriptural evidence against pre-existence, and citing several texts that were suggestive of it. Prime among these was John 9.2–3: 'And his disciples asked him, saying, Master who did sin, this man, or his parents, that he was born blind? Jesus answered, Neither this man sinned nor his parents...' For Rust, Jesus' not having ruled out the pre-existence of the man born blind was an argument in favour of it: 'our Saviour's saying nothing in so apt an occasion is one of those Cases wherein *Silence* is almost as argumentative as a positive Approbation'.[41] The argument from silence is never a strong one, a point exemplified by the fact that the same text, and the same argument from silence, were used to justify the transmigration of souls.[42] As the argumentative Samuel Parker, later Bishop of Oxford, put it in response to Rust, 'if they can infer any thing in favour of Pre-existence from our Saviours silence in so apt an occasion to have rectified the common Errour concerning it, they may with the same reason conclude his Approbation of the Transmigration of Souls'.[43]

In his *Lux Orientalis*, Glanvill was reluctant to present Scriptural evidence, primarily because of what he saw as the misuse of Scripture by enthusiasts to justify their deluded imaginings. Glanvill undoubtedly accepted Scripture as authoritative. But we find in *Lux Orientalis* an understanding of Reason as an independent and equivalent source of religious truth:

But whether what I have brought from *Scripture* prove anything or nothing, 'tis not very material, since the *Hypothesis* of *Praeexistence* stands secure enough upon those *Pillars* of *Reason*, which have their Foundation in the *Attributes* of God, and the *Phaenomena* of the world. And the *Right Reason* of a Man, is one of the *Divine* Volumes, in which are written the indeleble *Ideas* of eternal Truth: so that what it dictates, is as much the voice of God, as if in so many words it were clearly *exprest* in the *written Revelations*.[44]

It would be wrong, however, to see such an attitude to the relation of reason and Scripture as part of the inexorable march towards the Deism of the eighteenth century or as reflecting a rationalist account of the Scriptures offered by such as Hobbes or Toland. For Glanvill, and as we shall see for More, reason was that in man which reflected the Divine Reason. This was a central premiss of their Platonism. Likewise, Scripture, if read properly, could not conflict with reason, for it revealed the same Divine Reason. Thus, both Rust and Glanvill could offer rational (Platonic) readings of the creation and fall of man in terms of pre-existence.

These readings, however, were merely echoes of the much more complex 'mystical' reading of the Genesis account already developed in 1653 by Henry More in his *Conjectura Cabbalistica, or a Conjectural Essay of Interpreting the Minde of Moses, according to a Threefold Cabbala, viz., Literal, Philosophical, Mystical or Divinely Moral*. Like Glanvill, More was committed to reason in the search for divine truth, for to discourage reason was to encourage enthusiasm. And for More, because both Scripture and reason were equally sources of religious truth, their compatibility needed to be demonstrated.

According to More, the prime sources of incompatibility between Scripture and reason were science, more specifically, Copernican astronomy, and philosophy, more specifically, the Platonic doctrine of pre-existence. It is not surprising that More should have wished strongly to defend Copernicanism. Among recognised scientists, the Ptolemaic system had been unacceptable in England from the end of the first decade of the seventeenth century.[45] And as early as 1642, in his *Psychodia Platonica: or A Platonical Song of the Soul*, More praised the Copernican theory, giving arguments for it, and refuting arguments against it.[46]

What is perhaps a little surprising is that More should have defended both Copernicanism *and* pre-existence. For, on the face of it, the new science and the ancient philosophy seem as much at odds with each other as with the Scriptures. This is to be explained in part by the dominance of Platonism among scientists in Renaissance England. Francis Johnson writes, 'The mystical attitude which saw God as the great geometer and looked upon the mathematical harmonies to be found in the material world as direct revelations of the Deity, also had its roots in Platonism, and was the source of inspiration for the religious glorification of the new discoveries of science as manifestations of the wonderful workmanship of the Creator.'[47] In short, for More, both Copernicanism and pre-existence were imbedded in Platonism.

More is none the less unwilling to reject the literal understanding of the Genesis accounts of the creation and fall of man. To retain their literal truth, More adopted the theory of the twofold philosophy. The twofold philosophy has its roots in both classical and early Christian literature. Strabo, Plutarch, Cicero, Clement of Alexandria, Origen, Lactantius, and Augustine all indicate that in various ancient religions there were two distinct theologies – one for the ignorant masses, the other for the intellectual and ruling elite. Importantly, Origen had suggested this of Christianity.[48] It was, of course, a theory quite in keeping with his understanding of different levels of Scriptural interpretation.

Thus, for More, the literal interpretation not only can be accepted, but must be by those not ready to go beyond it. In the literal truth, More maintained, everything was represented 'accomodately to the apprehension of the meanest, not speaking of things according to their very essence and real nature, but according to their appearance to us, not starting of high and intricate questions, and concluding them by subtile arguments, but familiarly and condescendingly setting out the creation, according to the most easie and obvious conceits they themselves had of those things they saw in the world'.[49] But, to see the literal truth as the only truth was, for More, a cause of atheism. As he wrote to Lady Anne Conway in 1653, to see the literal truth only 'has furder'd Atheisme in the world, and made profane men secure that the whole businesse of Relligion is not better then an obvious fable'.[50]

In the second part of his *Conjectura Cabbalistica*, More took up the philosophical Cabbala. Here, he saw Moses as having expressed, beneath the simple story of the creation and fall, the conclusions of the wisest scientists and philosophers of all ages. The aim of the philosophical Cabbala was to show that both Copernicanism and pre-existence were held by Moses. Only thus could science and philosophy be freed from the suspicion of impiety and irreligion:

> Now, I say, it is a pretty priviledge of *Falshood*, (if this Hypothesis be false) and very remarkable, that it should better suite with *the Attributes of God, the visible Events of Providence*, the Phaenomena *of Nature, the Reason of Man*, and *the Holy Text itself*, where men acknowledge a mysterious *cabbala*, then that which by all means must be accounted true, *viz*. That there is no such Motion of the Earth about the Sun, nor any Praeexistency of Humane Souls.[51]

In what then did the philosophical Cabbala consist? According to More, the creation of man did not consist in the making of a being of flesh and blood. Rather, Adam was originally a wholly aethereal being, living in paradise – the aethereal realm – and charged not to eat of the Tree of Knowledge of good and evil, that is, not to misuse his free will, 'For at what time thou eatest thereof, thy Soul shall contract that languor, debility and unsettledness, that in process of time thou shalt slide into the earth, and be buried in humane flesh, and become an inhabitant of the *Region of mortality and death*.'[52] In accord with the Cabbalistic tradition, More distinguished in primordial man two qualities – masculine and feminine, active and passive, reason and the will. In an ideal world, there is a harmonious relationship between reason and the will, the latter regulated by the former. In the case of Adam, his instinct – his feminine element – overcame his reason – his masculine element, alienating himself from

God who is Supreme Reason. The expulsion of Adam and Eve from the Garden was read by More as a descent from the aethereal realm in which man was originally created to the terrestrial world. The triumph of will over reason, wrote More, 'so changed the nature of his *Vehicle* that (whereas he might have continued in an *Angelical* and *Aethereal* condition, and his *Feminine* part been brought into perfect obedience to the divine Light...) he now sunk more and more towards a mortal and terrestrial state'.[53] In sum, the theory of the soul's pre-existence was not only certified by reason, but guaranteed by an appropriately 'rational' interpretation of Scripture.

More was heir to the Christianised form of the Cabbala popularised during the Renaissance by Pico in his 900 *Theses* in 1486 and by Reuchlin in his *De Arte Cabbalistica* in 1516. He himself, however, does not seem to have had any familiarity with Cabbalistic writings at the time he wrote *Conjectura Cabbalistica*. Indeed, he admitted to Lady Conway that the conceptions in his Cabbala were the 'births of my own braine',[54] although he sought to defend them with the authority of the ancient philosophers and fathers. When, in the 1670s, he became more familiar with the Cabbalised form of Christianity propounded by Francis Mercurius van Helmont, Knorr von Rosenroth, and eventually by Lady Anne Conway, he grew decidedly unsympathetic to it; indeed, so much so, that by the end of 1675, he had completed six treatises against the Cabbalistic system of Isaac Luria.[55]

THE TRANSMIGRATION OF SOULS

Francis Mercurius van Helmont was the son of the famous Belgian physician and chemist Jean Baptista van Helmont. He arrived in England in 1670. On the twelfth of October in that year, we find him dining with Henry More in his rooms at Christ's College, Cambridge, eagerly discussing their mutual interest in Cabbalism and preexistence. More was impressed: 'a person of a very good plaine and expert humour', he wrote to Lady Conway.[56] Aware of van Helmont's reputation in medicine, he asked him to treat his friend Lady Conway, a victim of debilitating headaches. By 19 November of that year, van Helmont was at the Conway home, Ragley Hall in Warwickshire, treating Lady Conway. He was to remain there for most of the next nine years until her death in 1679. It was during this period that both van Helmont and Lady Conway became progressively more committed to the Cabbalism of Isaac Luria (1534–

72), and constructed a complex philosophical syncretism of this and Christianity which argued for the transmigration of souls and the eventual salvation of all.

For Lurianic Cabbalism, the transmigration of souls was formulated as an answer to the problem of Jewish suffering, and in particular, of the Jews' expulsion from Spain in 1492. The sufferings of those times were explained as the result of the sins committed in previous earthly lives within the context of a future millennium when all would share in the joys of salvation.[57] For van Helmont too, the problem of human suffering was resolved by a doctrine of transmigration. Only thus can the goodness and wisdom of God be reconciled with his having created 'such imperfect creatures as Fools and Naturals, Abortives and Monsters, and all those wicked and barbarous men we find in the World, which kill and afterwards feed on one another, Etc.'[58]

Van Helmont's doctrine of transmigration was set in a complex chronology of human existences leading to the final restoration of all at the millennium. Prior to the creation of this world, he argued, all souls existed in a non-terrestrial form. All these, with some notable exceptions (Moses, Elijah, Jesus), consented to the sin of Adam thus eventually assuming their terrestrial bodies. The time fixed for the revolution of the world from creation to destruction was 4,000 years.[59] In the course of this period, each person lived in terrestrial bodies for a thousand years in twelve lives, 'save only such as dying in the Faith, after once having lived in the Body, do enter into rest, and patiently wait until the first Resurrection'.[60] Between each death and subsequent life, there is an intermission of some $333\frac{1}{3}$ years (one-twelfth of 4,000 years) minus the length of the previous life.[61]

This chronology entailed that all those who had lived prior to the time of Christ have already been reborn since the resurrection of Christ. Thus all would have an opportunity for salvation: 'must not all that died before Christ was offered up, live once (at least) again in the Body, after the Death of Christ, that the Gospel may be preached unto them, and they thereby have an opportunity of believing in him as offered up, for their and our Offences ... ?'[62] Since no-one could be sure if their present life was to be their last, complacency about repentance was unwise. Moreover, if repentance was offered and rejected, there would be no second chance.[63]

During the 250 years preceding the beginning of the millennium, the good would progressively come into the world, being born of virgin mothers. The saints would live on earth during the 1,000-year millennium, being progressively perfected in heavenly bodies, together with those who had not finished their twelve lives at its beginning. During this period, children would still be born of women, not by the ordinary way of generation, 'but after some more noble, and excellent a manner, than now is done... '[64]

At the end of the millennium, the wicked would be raised to be burnt in fire, and tormented in hell. According to van Helmont, God's justice entailed severe punishment of offenders, both in quality and quantity, aggravated further by the wicked not knowing when or if it would end. Nevertheless, the wicked would not be tormented for ever. The biblical record, declared van Helmont, implied only punishment of an exceedingly long duration.[65] Crucially, out of his own experience, van Helmont had developed a philosophy of physical pain as beneficent. 'I began to love my pain', he once asserted.[66] And this is reflected in his view of divine punishment as reformative:

Is not the Nature, and end of God's vindictive justice, and indeed of all punishment, to aim at the good of those that are punished? Is not the nature of all punishment Medicinal? and ought not every Judge among Men sincerely to love those whom he condemns to punishment, and to aim at their good thereby? if God then hath placed this instinct of Justice in Men, hath he not the same infinitely more abundantly in himself?[67]

Thus, after punishment, there would be further chances for the wicked in the worlds which follow cyclically upon the creation and destruction of this one. And all, presumably, would ultimately be saved.

This combination of Lurianic transmigration of souls with Christian themes of atonement, redemption, and salvation also appeared in an anonymous work published in Latin in 1693 and in English in 1694: *Seder Olam: or, The Order of the Ages: A few questions by way of Exposition, on each chapter of the Revelation of St. John.*

Here too, as in van Helmont's work, numerological, Cabbalistic, and neo-Platonic themes are woven into a framework of Christian apocalyptic. Its authorship is obscure. Certainly it is in the style of van Helmont, and he sponsored the English translation of it. However, in a letter to Leibniz, he disclaimed authorship of it, crediting it to a physician with whom he was acquainted.[68] The translator of it from Latin, J. Clark MD, did not know who the author was, although one might be excused for thinking that he was the man who van Helmont suggested to Leibniz was the real author.

He is presumably to be identified with the 'J. C.' who translated Lady Conway's *Principles of the Most Ancient and Modern Philosophy* into English, although the *Dictionary of National Biography* identifies 'J. C.' as a Jacobus Crull.[69] Daniel Walker hazards a guess that *Seder Olam* is a work either by Lady Conway or Christian Knorr von Rosenroth, one of the most accomplished Christian Cabbalists of the seventeenth century, and the editor, with van Helmont, of the *Kabbala Denudata*, the largest collection of Cabbalist treatises in Latin up to that time.[70] The English edition contains an appendix not in the Latin. Since, in this appendix, corrections to the main body of the text are made to fit suggestions in the *Two Hundred Queries*, van Helmont was probably the author of the appendix.

Seder Olam suggested, like van Helmont, a plurality of worlds, in this case, of 7,000 years' duration, the seventh being the millennium (one week of seven days).[71] After seven weeks of worlds (that is, after 49,000 years), 'many Souls are to be saved and reconciled to God by Christ, which as yet could not obtain Salvation in the preceding weeks of Worlds, but suffered for their Impieties the most just Judgmnet [sic] of God the execrable torments of Hell Fire'.[72] Some may be saved earlier, some later. Nevertheless, after a year of such days (that is, 365,000 years), all would be saved: 'because God is infinite Goodness, therefore God's Will to forgive Sins is as necessary as his Will to punish it'.[73] One fifty-second of all souls ought to be saved, on this chronology, in each 7,000-year age, a calculation reinforced in *Seder Olam* by the same ratio being calculable from the size of the Holy City in the Book of Revelation to the area of the whole earth.

Another complex chronology gave more detailed information on the progress of this present age. *Seder Olam* calculated the period from the creation to the Crucifixion of Christ to be 3,996 years. This would suggest a beginning to the millennium in AD 2004. During this period, each individual soul would have a maximum of twelve terrestrial lives in which to perfect itself. These twelve revolutions could not be completed in less than 4,000 years, and all would be completed at the end of the millennium. Moreover, until its perfection, each soul would come three times into the world in a carnal body in each millennium. Thus, no soul could have reached perfection before the death of Christ. Salvation of all, including the heathen, was crucially linked, as it was in van Helmont's work, to 'Christ's coming in the Flesh, and Faith in him'.[74]

Seder Olam presented two somewhat confused pictures of the millennial period. On the one hand, at the millennium (or during the 260 years preceding it), all would be raised up to live upon the earth for a thousand years in a terrestrial body not needful of food or drink. Until 260 years after the beginning of the millennium, the saints would marry and have children. Those who were alive at the beginning of the millennium would live on, the wicked only for a hundred years, the good for its duration. The good would bear children who were the Saints who had lived before: 'all the Sons and Daughters of the Saints in the future Millennium, are the Souls of all the Saints that ever have liv'd in a carnal Body since the beginning of the World, and finally raised up to Life in a Body of Flesh, and born of Fathers and Mothers into the world...'[75] The conflict in this account on the means of the Saints' resurrections was rectified in the Appendix. It declared that the raised saints would not marry and have children, only those who were alive at the millennium would so do, and these children would not be the deceased saints reincarnate.[76]

At the end of the millennium, the Saints would receive spiritual, celestial bodies and ascend into heaven. The wicked would be raised up to be sent into hell for 7,000 years. At the completion of their punishment, they were to be sent forth again into a new world 'for a fresh Tryal of their Obedience'.[77]

While both van Helmont and the author of *Seder Olam* endorsed the transmigration of souls into a series of human bodies, they seem not to have envisaged the possibility of the transmigration of souls into the bodies of animals. In the seventeenth century generally, this found little support. 'I cannot beleeve the wisedome of *Pythagoras* did ever positively, and in a literall sense, affirme his *Metempsychosis*, or impossible transmigration of the soules of men into beasts'..., declared Thomas Browne.[78] Henry More rejected it outright: 'those that suppose the Transmigration of humane Souls into the Bodies of Beasts, I look upon as Fables...'[79] Ralph Cudworth in his *True Intellectual System of the Universe* described the notion of the descent of souls into brutes, trees, and plants as 'a most prodigious extravagancy'.[80] *The Athenian Gazette* in 1691 saw transmigration in general as so ridiculous a doctrine as to be 'scarce worth the refutation'. Although it recognised that Plato, Pythagoras, and Plotinus had taught it, it suggested that they had not personally believed it.[81]

Origen too was a proponent of the transmigration of souls into animals as one possible consequence of the fall of the soul into evil.[82]

Origen's commitment to it may well have inspired Joseph Glanvill seriously to consider transmigration both into human and animal forms. In a letter in 1661 to the author of *A Letter of Resolution concerning Origen*, he noted that the theory of pre-existence suggested the possibility of a fall into an animal body:

For (1) the divine goodness which regardes all his creatures seems to require it, otherwise some will bee faultlessly miserable; for what account els can be given of the state of beasts who some of them are all their lives subject to the tyrannical tastes of merciless man, except wee suppose them to have deserv'd this severe discipline by some former delinquencyes. (2) Some men seem naturally prepar'd for a descent into bruite bodyes, by the bruitish dispositions, and have almost nothing to speak them better while in humane flesh but speech and their external persons ... (3) The next state is a state of punishment to the wicked, and therefore worse than this, and therefore they will have worse bodyes ... [83]

As we have seen, Glanvill's commitment to the pre-existence of the soul was motivated by his desire to explain human suffering. In his later work, however, he did not develop further his recognition in the letter above that animal suffering too needed to be squared with the goodness of God.

The most radical account of transmigration into a non-human form, or rather of the transmutation of species, was that of Lady Anne Conway. Influenced by the Cabbalism of van Helmont and Rosenroth, and by the Platonism of Henry More, Lady Conway proposed a monistic vitalism in the context of a critique of Descartes, Hobbes, and Spinoza.

In her only work, *Principles of the Most Ancient and Modern Philosophy*, she recognised only three classes of Substance: God, who is wholly spirit; and Christ, and the created substances, both of which share spirituality and corporeality (although there is no ultimate distinction between spirit and matter). Since all created beings share in the one substance, their essence is mutable. Thus, human substances can change – are really changed – into different kinds of things, sometimes into animals, eventually into aethereal beings. Things may transmute upwards or downwards, according to the justice of God and their moral deserts:

And so here is a certain Justice in all these, as in all the Transmutation of Things from one *Species* into another, whether it be by ascending from the Ignobler or Baser unto the Nobler, or by descending into the contrary, there may be found the same Justice: For Example: Is it not just and equitable, if a Man on Earth liveth a pure and Holy Life, like unto the Heavenly Angels, that he should be exalted to an Angelical Dignity after Death, and be like unto them, over whom also the Angels rejoice? But if a Man here on Earth lives so wickedly and perversly, that he is more like a Devil raised from Hell than any other Creature, if he dies in such a State without Repentance, Shall not the same Justice tumble him down to Hell? And shall not such deservedly become like Devils, even as those who led an Angelical Life are made equal with the Angels? But if a Man hath neither lived an Angelical or Diabolical, but a Brutish, or at least-wise an Animal or Sensual Life on Earth; so that his Spirit is more like the Spirit of a Beast than any other thing: Shall not the same Justice most justly cause, that as he is become a Brute, as to his Spirit ... that he also ... should be changed into that *Species* of Beasts, to whom he was inwardly most like, in Qualities and Conditions of Mind?[84]

Crucially, a high moral value was attached, for Lady Conway, to punishment and human suffering, a view she undoubtedly derived from van Helmont and the Cabbala. All punishment and suffering was ultimately curative. 'Every pain and Torment', she declared, 'excites or stirs up an operating Spirit and life in everything which suffers ... through Pain, and the enduring thereof ... and so the Spirit ... is made more Spiritual, and consequently more Active and Operative through suffering.'[85]

No doubt, this optimistic view of human suffering reflected her own nobility of character in enduring increasingly severe and debilitating headaches from the age of twelve until her death at the age of forty-seven. For she lived in an age in which severe suffering was seen as more conducive to the embitterment of human souls than to its glorification. However that may be, her view of human suffering was philosophically supported by her Platonic view of God. For her, God was infinitely and unchangeably good. And because there was no Being infinitely and unchangeably evil, there was a limit to evil, but none to good. Thus, a point could be reached below which a creature could not go. Because it was unable to sink into mere inactivity, it must at length return to the Good, that is, to God. Consequently, the torments of hell can only be temporary. As she put it, 'Now seeing a Creature cannot proceed infinitely to Evil, nor slide down into Inactivity or Silence, nor yet also into mere eternal Passion, it uncontestably follows, that it must at length return unto Good; and by how much greater its Sufferings are, so much the sooner shall it return and be restored.'[86]

FREE WILL, HUMAN AND DIVINE

Whether committed to metempsychosis or pre-existence (or both), Platonists in the late seventeenth century, with few exceptions, explained the problem of human suffering in terms of the human misuse of will in previous human lives and/or in a pre-existent life.[87] Origen provided the defenders of the pre-existence of the soul with an ancient authority for the misuse of free will as the cause of the fall of all persons into terrestrial life.[88] But there were pressing seventeenth-century reasons for a vigorous defence of free will, and not only among those who supported the pre-existence of the soul.

Prime among these was the perceived need to combat the determinism of Thomas Hobbes, itself an outcome of his materialism. Hobbes adopted a position which, in modern times, is known as soft determinism: the view that, while persons may be compelled to act by inner forces or constraints, their act will remain free as long as no *external* force or constraint compels them. As Hobbes expressed it,

> *Liberty* and *Necessity* are Consistent: As in the water, that hath not only *liberty*, but a *necessity* of descending by the Channel; so likewise in the Actions which men voluntarily doe; which, because they proceed from their will, proceed from *liberty*; and yet, because every act of mans will, and every desire, and inclination proceedeth from some cause, and that from another cause, in a continuall chaine, (whose first link is the hand of God the first of all causes,) proceed from *necessity*. So that to him that could see the connexion of those causes, the *necessity* of all mens voluntary actions, would appeare manifest.[89]

The Platonists were strongly libertarian, committed to the incompatibility between being determined to act in such and such a way and being free so to do. Consequently, Hobbes' position was anathema to them, not only because it denied any human responsibility for moral misdeeds, thus denying the development of an autonomous moral life, but also because it appeared to lay upon God the ultimate responsibility for all human misdeeds, thus denying the essential goodness of God. John Bramhall, Archbishop of Armagh, was no Platonist. More sympathetic than many of the Platonists to Hobbes, he none the less truly expressed their sentiments:

> Though I honour T. H. for his person and for his learning, yet I must confess ingenuously, I hate [his] doctrine from my heart. And I believe both I have reason so to do, and all others who shall seriously ponder the horrid consequences which flow from it. It destroys liberty, and dishonours the

nature of man. It makes the second causes and outward objects to be the rackets, and men to be but the tennis-balls of destiny. It makes the first cause, that is God Almighty to be the introducer of all evil and sin into the world, as much as man, yea, more than man... Excuse me if I hate this doctrine with a perfect hatred, which is so dishonourable both to God and man; which makes men to blaspheme of necessity, to steal of necessity, to be hanged of necessity, and to be damned of necessity... It were better to be a Manichee, to believe two gods, a God of good and a God of evil; or with the heathens to believe thirty thousand Gods: than thus to charge the true God to be the proper cause and the true author of all the sins and evils which are in the world.[90]

The commitment to a libertarian version of free will was also directed against the theological counterpart of Hobbes' determinism, namely Calvinistic predestination. For Hobbes, as we have seen, God's role was as the initiator of a course of events which then proceeded from natural causes. For Calvinism, all events proceeded from the sovereign will of God. Be that as it may, the God of Hobbes and the God of Calvinism were equally rejected. The God who could predestine persons to eternal damnation irrespective of their moral deserts came to be despised.[91] Joseph Mede, teacher both of John Milton and Henry More, could not tolerate that 'black doctrine of Absolute Reprobation'.[92] Samuel Hoard was not untypical of the drift away from predestination. Described as 'a zealous Calvinist in the beginning, but a greater Arminian afterwards',[93] he became convinced of the untruth of predestination because it charged God alone with the responsibility for eternal torments in hell: 'it maketh him to bee the prime, principall and invincible cause of the damnation of millions of miserable soules... '[94] We know too, from Richard Ward's life of Henry More, that as a youth, More rejected 'that hard Doctrine concerning *Fate*':

I did... very stoutly, and earnestly for my Years dispute against this *Fate* or *Calvinistick Predestination*, as it is usually call'd: and that my *Uncle*, when he came to know it, chid me severely; adding menaces withall of Correction, and a Rod for my immature Forwardness in *Philosophizing* concerning such Matters: Moreover, that I had such a deep Aversion in my Temper to this Opinion, and so firm and unshaken a Perswasion of the *Divine Justice* and *Goodness*, that on a certain Day, in a Ground belonging to *Aeton* College, where the Boys us'd to play, and exercise themselves, *musing* concerning these Things with myself, viz. If I am one of those that are predestinated unto Hell, where all Things are full of nothing but Cursing and Blasphemy, yet will I behave my self there patiently and submissively towards God; and if there be any one thing more than another, that is acceptable to him, that will I set my self to do with a sincere Heart, and to the utmost of my Power: Being certainly persuaded, that if I thus demeaned my self, he would hardly keep me long in that Place.[95]

Calvinism appeared however not only to deny free will but also to empty the divine goodness of meaning. From the perspective of Calvinism, the sovereign will of God was central. Thus, in effect, in spite of the fact that predestination to damnation might offend our moral sense, it cannot count against the goodness of God – what God wills is necessarily good. George Rust suggested that if God could be primarily defined as sovereign will, then to all intents and purposes, God could be a devil.[96] Glanvill saw the equation of divine goodness with divine will as the major error in Calvinism:

> For the first Errour, which is the ground of the rest is, That things are good and just, because God Wills them so to be; and if that be granted, we are disabled from using the arguments taken from natural notions ... If there be no settled Good and Evil, Immutable and Independent of any Will or Understanding, then God may have made his reasonable Creatures on purpose to damn them forever.[97]

In sharp contrast to Calvinism, it was essential to the Platonist cause that goodness was capable of being defined independently of the will of God, and of being determinable through the use of reason. That it was so capable was because right reason was the image of God in man. Thus, what was determined as the good by right reason was so universally. As Henry Hallywell put it, 'This harmony therefore and agreeableness of Moral Objects to our Intellectual parts, is antecedent to the things themselves, so that they are not good because God for example commands them, but therefore they are injoyned, because there is an innate Goodness in them.'[98] And therefore, according to Hallywell, the notions of good and evil, justice and injustice were unalterable, even by God himself.

For the Platonists then, God was *essentially* good. Moreover, the argument for the *essential* nature of the divine goodness was a key element in the argument for the soul's pre-existence. That God was essentially good entailed that God always acted necessarily for the best. Consequently, since it is better for souls to exist than not to exist, God must have created all souls at the time of the original creation. According to Joseph Glanvill,

> *God* being *infinitely good*, and that to his *Creatures*, and therefore doing always what is *best* for them, methinks it roundly follows that our *souls lived* and

'njoy'd themselves of *old* before they came into these *bodies*. For since they were *capable* of *living*, and that in a much *better* and *happier* state long before they descended into this *region* of *death* and *misery*; and since that condition of life and self-enjoyment would have been better, than *absolute not-being*; may we not safely conclude from a due consideration of the *divine goodness*, that it was so?[99]

However, among those who agreed with the Platonists that 'goodness' was determinable independently of the will of God were some who denied that God did always and necessarily act according to the good. Samuel Parker, for example, pointed to instances of God's acting out of anger and severity. For Parker, God's goodness was not at all essential: it 'rather approaches to the nature of a habit seated in the Divine will, then to the condition of an Essential faculty'.[100] Edward Warren argued that God's will dominated his goodness. Somewhat oddly though, he does argue that goodness is of the essence of God, for otherwise he would be 'but a prodigious Feind, and plenipotentiary Devil...'[101] Warren's God certainly does give the appearance of being such. Eternal torments are his warrant for the claim that though essentially good, God cannot always do what is best: 'the Goodness of *God* was not left to it self in meting out the punitive sorrows of delinquent Spirits; but by the authority of his Will, was lead to a permission of the extreamist severities upon them, and made to give way to their eternal sufferings'.[102]

A stronger argument advanced by Warren and Parker was to the effect that, if God could not but do the good, there was no divine freedom of the will, and that consequently God was lacking in power and in perfection.[103] This implied that God's freedom was a *libertas indifferentiae*: that God could only be free to perform or not to perform an act if he had no inclination either to perform it or not to perform it. The Platonist response was to argue that God's freedom was not of this sort. George Rust, for example, argued that the power to do evil was not a perfection; Henry Hallywell suggested that God *was* free to act conformably to his nature; More declared that God's anger and severity *were* expressions of his nature.[104]

As we have seen, with respect to human free will, the Platonists were decidedly libertarian; if persons could not but act in certain ways, they could not be deemed to be free in those actions. But, with respect to the divine freedom, they were clearly soft determinists. For Hallywell, More, and Lady Conway, the divine freedom was primarily defined as entailing the absence of any external restraint.

God was essentially good by virtue of his always and necessarily having to do what was best, but also free in that nothing external could restrain him from so acting. 'God', wrote Lady Conway, 'is the most free Agent, and yet of all the most necessary.' She continued,

> if the aforementioned Attributes of God be duly considered, and especially these two; to wit, his Wisdom and Goodness, that Indifferency of Will, which the Schoolmen, and Philosophers falsly so called, have imagined to be in God, will be utterly refuted, and wholly turned out of Doors; which also they have improperly called Free-Will; for although the Will of God be most free, so that whatsoever he doth in behalf of his Creatures, he doth freely without any external Violence, Compulsion, or any Cause coming from them: Whatsoever he doth, he doth of his own accord: Yet that Indifferency of acting, or not acting, can by no means be said to be in God; because this were an Imperfection, and would make God like corruptible Creatures; for this Indifference of Will is the Foundation of all Change, and Corruptibility in Creatures ...[105]

In spite of the Platonists' attempts to construe divine freedom in such a way as to make it compatible with God's essential goodness, they were unable to avoid the admission that divine (libertarian) freedom was curtailed by God's inability to do evil. This was seized upon by Parker. He argued that 'goodness' could only be attributed to free agents, that is, to those who could do other than the good; and that consequently, the denial of the freedom of God to do evil entailed the denial of the predicate 'goodness' to God.[106] In essence, Parker's argument was an attack on the logical coherence of the concept of essential goodness, namely, that the concept of goodness only had meaning when predicated of an agent who could do other than good.

Henry More responded in two ways. First, he quite simply admitted that, granted God could not do other than the good, his actions could not be described as 'moral'. But, he reasoned, that they could not be so described did not entail they could not be described as 'good'. Second, he suggested that even Parker would admit that God cannot act from a purely evil will, and therefore must admit there was no incoherence in the notion of God's acting from a purely good will.[107]

We can now perceive the way in which the theory of the soul's pre-existence was part of an attempt to formulate a Christian Platonist theodicy. For Calvinism, the problem of evil and suffering was resolved, or rather dissolved, into the inscrutable divine sovereign will. For Warren and Parker, for example, the problem was solved by a God who can and does do evil. In these cases, to all intents and purposes, the essential goodness of God was denied. For the Platonists, the problem was to reconcile the exigencies of the human situation with the existence of a God who was both essentially good and all-powerful. The pre-existence of the soul was an *expression* of the essential goodness of God. Human suffering was a consequence of the misuse of free will by pre-existent souls – thus excusing, indeed *vindicating*, God's essential goodness.

There were weaknesses in this theodicy. Edward Warren, for example, inquired why, if God were good, he had not made men immutably blessed. He suggested that God would have acted more for the best if persons had been created without the possibility of their misusing their free will.[108] Against this argument More resorted to ridicule:

> that the mere making of such an Order of Beings as have a freedom of Will, and choice of their Actions, that this is misbecoming the Goodness of God, is as dull and idiotical a conceit, and such as implies that God should have made but one kind of Creature, and that the most absolutely and immutably happy that can be, or else did not act according to his Goodness, or for the best: Which is so obvious a Falshood, that I will not confute it.[109]

Hallywell, for one, did not think it so obvious a falsehood. Indeed, his response was an inchoate version of what has now come to be called the free-will defence of the problem of suffering. For Hallywell, in spite of the fact that the having of free will has brought moral evils into the world, the good inherent in persons having free will, rather than their being merely good-doing *automata*, is greater than the amount of evil and suffering that results from the misuse of human freedom. God foresaw, declared Hallywell, 'that the calamity which many of them were like to undergo by deserting their primitive Happiness, was not sufficient to out-ballance the good which might accrue to themselves and the rest of the Creation in their production; for albeit they were made lapsable, yet it was no wayes necessary that they should actually recede from their blessed life...'[110]

THE VEHICLES OF THE SOUL

For the seventeenth-century Platonists, the journey of the soul was a temporal one: for van Helmont and Lady Conway, from eternity to eternity; for More, Glanvill, and Rust, from the time of the creation until eternity. But it was also a spatial one. For souls had been, and always would be located in this spatio-temporal realm whether in its aethereal, aerial or terrestrial parts. That it was necessarily so located was the result of its being, at least in so far as it was conscious, connected with a body appropriate to these regions.

The belief in the vehicles of the soul was an inheritance from neo-Platonism. Although difficult to discern in Plato, the theory played an important part in neo-Platonic thought, particularly among those neo-Platonists most interested in ritual magic. For Origen, too, all rational creatures appropriated bodies suitable to the regions into which they descended.[111] As Ralph Cudworth summed it up, the ancient philosophers generally conceived the soul in its pre-existent state 'to have had a lucid and aethereal body... as its chariot or vehicle; which being incorruptible, did always inseparably adhere to the soul, in its after-lapses and descents, into an aerial first, and then a terrestrial body... '[112]

According to Joseph Glanvill, souls were initially created with the highest intellectual and spiritual faculties, and were united with the most subtle matter in a pure and aethereal body. He was uncertain about the location of these pure souls, although he considered 'those *immense* tracts of *pure* and *quiet aether* that are above *Saturn*' more likely than the sun.[113] There was also uncertainty about the temporal duration of souls in the aethereal realm, although Rust hazarded the guess that the aerial life far exceeded the terrestrial, and 'the *aereal period* falls as far short of the celestial as the blended Atmosphere of the pure lucid *Aether*'.[114]

Having fallen from its aethereal state, the soul assumed an aerial vehicle. For More, the placement of souls in particular bodies was the responsibility of the Spirit of Nature, that entity which superintended God's work in the aerial and terrestrial regions.[115] Glanvill imagined souls as allocated under an impersonal spiritual law (albeit with angelic assistance on occasion), and God effectively played no role from the time of the creation on:

it seems to me very becoming the wise Author of all things so to have made them [souls] in the beginning, as that by their own *internal spring and wheels*, they should orderly bring about whatever he intended them for, without his often *immediate* interposal. For this looks like a more magnificent apprehension of the *Divine Power* and *Prescience*, since it supposeth him from everlasting ages to have seen and constituted the great *machina* of the *world*, that the infinite variety of *motions* therein, should effect nothing but what in his *eternal wisdom* he had concluded *fit* and *decorous*...[116]

The vehicles of the soul

For most souls, a further descent was necessary, from the aerial to the terrestrial. At times, there being more souls ready for terrestrial vehicles than there were vehicles available, the soul may lie in a state of inactivity and silence until '*awakened* into *life* and *operation* in such *bodies* and *places* of the earth, as by their dispositions they are fitted for...'[117]

At death, the soul left its terrestrial vehicle, according to More, either through the mouth or one of the other openings in the head.[118] A few souls resumed their aethereal vehicles in the heavenly realm; but most were allotted vehicles of air, where they appeared in 'the ordinary form of Angels, such a countenance, and so cloathed, as they'.[119] The soul in its aerial (and aethereal) form had enhanced hearing, sight and touch. Its moral quality was reflected in its physical form. According to More,

> For if vertue and Vice can be ever seen with outward eyes, it must be in these aerial Vehicles, which yield so to the Will and Idea of good and pure affections, that the Soule in a manner becomes perfectly transparent through them, discovering her lovely beauty in all the efflorescencies thereof, to the ineffable enravishment of the beholder.[120]

While there was no sexual desire, nor essential difference of sex, between aerial beings, there was a formal discrimination of beauty into male and female. This was an Elysian realm of friendship and love, a realm where 'kind converse and amorous eloquence warm their chast minds into the highest sense of Heav'nly Love...'[121]

Virtuous souls were envisaged by both More and Glanvill in the upper regions of the air, closer to the aethereal realm: ''tis very likely', explained Glanvill, 'that *these Regions* [viz., near the earth] are very *unsuitable*, and *disproportion'd* to the *frame* and *temper* of their *Senses* and *Bodies*;... Nor can the *pure* and *better* any more endure the *noisom steams* and *poysonous reeks* of this *Dunghil* Earth, than the *delicate* can bear a confinement in *nasty Dungeons*, and the foul *squalid Caverns* of uncomfortable Darkness.' [122] Because virtuous souls were located in the upper reaches of the air, they seldom appeared. Moreover, in the upper regions of the air, the virtuous were safe from the assaults of demons. More argued that the aerial realm, about fifty miles high, had three dimensions. Thus,

> though the souls of good men after death be detained within the Atmosphere of the Air... yet there is no necessity at all that they should be put to those inconveniences... from the company of devils, or incommodious changes and disturbances of the Air. For suppose such inconveniencies in the middle

and lowest Region, yet the upper Region, which is also part of the third Heaven, those parts are ever calm and serene. And the Devils Principality reaching no further than through the lowest Region next the earth ... the souls of the departed that are good, are not liable to be pester'd and haunted with the ungrateful Presence or Occursions of the deformed and grim Retinue, or of the vagrant vassals of that foul Feind, that is Prince of the Air ...[123]

In contrast to virtuous souls, wicked souls were confined by More to regions close to the earth in company with aerial demons. The pangs of conscience brought the aerial body into 'intolerable distempers, worse than death it self'; those without conscience were exposed to the torments of demonic ministers of justice who 'satiate their lascivient cruelty with all manner of abuses and torments they can imagine'.[124] Glanvill was disturbed by the presence in the air of wicked souls, believing them to be less miserable there than in their terrestrial bodies when they ought to be more so. Consequently, in *Lux Orientalis*, he placed the wicked after death within the earth. In the cavities beneath the earth's surface, they did severe penances for their wickedness. Contained in gross and foetid bodies of air, variously tormented and persecuted by demons, they awaited the day of judgement 'no more able to abide the *clear* and *lightsome* Air; than the *Bat* or the *Owl* are able to bear the Suns noon-day beams ... '[125]

A PLATONIC MAP OF THE WORLD

What then were the factors which motivated the Platonists to construct such elaborate accounts of the journeys of souls? In part, it was a reaction against Christian mortalism – the view that the soul died or slept between death and the day of judgement. Mortalism had been a recurring element in English religion from the time of the Reformation and was particularly common among the radical sects during the Commonwealth period.[126] Cudworth, More, and Glanvill all assumed that any spirit without a body could not be involved in the affairs of the world for it would be 'asleep' or at least insensate. So the theory of the vehicles of the soul enabled persons to retain a continuity of consciousness by guaranteeing a conscious post-mortem existence and a memory of their earthly lives.[127] But if the notion of disembodied souls was accepted, More maintained,

It is easy for the Psychopannychites to support their opinion of the Sleep of the Soul, for the Soul being utterly rescinded from all that is corporeal, and having no vital union therewith at all, they will be very prone to infer, that it is impossible she should know anything *ad extra*, if she can so much as dream. For even that power may also seem incompatible to her in such a state, she having such an essential aptitude for vital union with Matter.[128]

The notion of the soul's vehicles, by ensuring the temporal continuity of the soul, ruled out even the possibility of the sleep of the soul.

The same theory also ensured the spatial location of the soul. Descartes had defined the soul as an unextended, non-corporeal substance. For More, the non-extension of the soul entailed that it was nowhere, 'it being the very essence of whatever is, to have parts of extension in some manner or other. For, to take away all extension, is to reduce a thing only to a Mathematical point, which is nothing else but pure negation or non-entity; and there being no medium betwixt entity and non-entity, it is plain that if a thing be at all, it must be extended.'[129] More's concept of the soul as extended was meant to avoid what he saw as the implicit materialism of Cartesianism which, in denying any extension to the soul, effectively denied its existence. It was a high cost for More to pay. As John Henry remarks, 'The result is so materialistic in its major details as virtually to belie its author's professed beliefs in immaterial souls.'[130] That may well be so. But crucially, it did entail that the realm of soul and spirit could not be removed from a progressively mechanically interpreted world. As an extended entity, spirit was inextricably located within the world of space and time.

While the notion of the soul's extension ensured that it was somewhere in the universe, it failed to allow for the possibility of its being at any specific location. For one implication of its being *extended* was that it was (like God) everywhere at the one time, that is, co-extensive with the universe. Thus, the theory of the soul's vehicles allowed a *specific* location for the soul. The vehicle of the soul – whether aethereal, aerial, or terrestrial – limited the soul's potentially infinite extension. The vehicle 'contained' the soul, while the shape and form of the soul, by virtue of its innate capacity to penetrate the body it possessed, was determined by the shape and form of its vehicle.[131] Thus could a plurality of spirits – angelic, demonic, and human – co-exist within the same universe.

The vehement defence of spirits was a consequence not only of what was perceived as Descartes' incipient materialism but of Hobbes' materialism. Certainly, materialism with its consequent denial of the reality of souls and spirits was seen as the thin end of a wedge leading inexorably to atheism. As early as 1653, More was convinced

> that a contemptuous misbelief of such like Narratives concerning *Spirits*, and an endeavour of making them all ridiculous and incredible is a dangerous Prelude to *Atheisme* it self, or else a more close and crafty Profession or Insinuation of it. For assuredly that Saying was nothing so true in Politicks, *No Bishop, no King*; as this is in Metaphysicks, *No Spirit, no God*.[132]

Glanvill believed that those without sufficient courage to commit themselves to atheism 'content themselves for a fair *step*, and *Introduction* to deny there are SPIRITS, or WITCHES'.[133] This was a common theme, and not only among Platonists. The Anglican Benjamin Camfield, for example, observed that the antipathy of many to the existence of spirits 'hath carried them on (and naturally doth so) to the dethroning of God, the supreme Spirit, and Father of Spirits'.[134]

Hobbes' materialism was seen as leading, through its denial of spirit, not only to a denial of God but also to libertinism. After the Restoration in 1660, 'libertinism' as 'Hobbesian free-thinking' and 'libertinism' as 'dissolute behaviour' were conflated. As Charles Wolseley remarked,

> Irreligion 'tis true in its practice hath been still the companion of every Age, but its open and publick defence seems the peculiar of this; 'Tis but of late that men come to defend ill living and secure themselves against their own guilt, by an open defyance to all the great maxims of Piety and Virtue ... and most of the bad Principles of this Age are of no earlier a date then one very ill Book, are indeed but the spawn of the Leviathan.[135]

Thus, for example, Thomas Bromhall in his *A Treatise of Specters* saw the denial of spirits as leading, not only to the denial of God, but also to the denial of good and evil and to all kinds of 'iniquity, impiety, and dissolute living'.[136] George Sinclair, philosopher and mathematician in Glasgow, saw scepticism about spirits as an excuse for men to 'live as they list'.[137]

These many related concerns – atheism, materialism, and libertinism – help to explain the passion with which many sought out credible stories of the activities of deceased souls, angels, demons, and witches, and the proliferation of collections of stories about them. The credibility of these 'Relations' was perceived as the strongest bulwark against the atheist: 'if there be once any visible ghosts or spirits acknowledged as things permanent, it will not be easy for any to give a reason why there might not be one supreme ghost also, presiding over them all and the whole world', wrote Ralph Cudworth.[138] In correspondence with Joseph Glanvill in 1677, Robert Boyle showed his awareness of the number of fraudulent stories in circulation. And he exhorted Glanvill to examine all accounts meticulously, 'for we live in an age, and a place, wherein all stories of witchcrafts, or other magical feats, are by many, even of the wise, suspected; and by too many, that would pass for wits, derided and exploded'.[139] Glanvill, for his part, was convinced that the methods of natural science could be utilised to verify the reality of soul and spirit. Science was for him the preferred weapon against the onslaught of materialism, and the key to the defence of the co-existence of spirit and matter, the angelic and the demonic. To the Royal Society, he wrote,

Indeed, as things are for the present, the LAND OF ESPIRITS is a kind of *America*, and not well discover'd *Region*; yea, it stands in the *Map* of *humane Science* like *unknown Tracts*, fill'd up with *Mountains*, *Seas*, *and Monsters*... For we know not anything of the world we live in, but by *experiment* and the *Phaenomena*; and there is the same way of *speculating immaterial* nature, by *extraordinary Events* and *Apparitions*, which possibly might be improved to *notices* not *contemptible*, were there a *Cautious*, and *Faithful History* made of those *certain* and *uncommon appearances*. At least it would be a *standing evidence* against SADDUCISM, to which the present Age is so *unhappily* disposed, and a *sensible Argument* of our *Immortality*.[140]

These deep-seated fears of the collapse of religion and morality help to explain the credulity with which were accepted, in late seventeenth-century England, the worst excesses of European demonological theory. Only in the late Middle Ages was there added to the European notion of witchcraft that of a compact between Satan and witches, together with that of the Sabbath at which witches gathered to worship Satan and to copulate with him. From the end of the sixteenth century this European concept was disseminated in England.[141] The Witch of Endor conjuring the spirit of Samuel for Saul provided Biblical verification of the reality of witches.

More and Glanvill did not cavil at basic demonological assumptions, indeed they vehemently supported them. But they did try to place demonology on a scientific footing.[142] Glanvill, for one, was willing to defend the abilities of witches to fly out of windows, to transform themselves into animals, raise tempests, be sucked by their familiar spirits, and so on; and this on the dubious grounds that their high unlikelihood suggested the probability of their truth. But he did argue for a scientific scepticism which refused to rule out such occurrences without investigation in the hope that 'we may give an account how 'tis *possible* and not *unlikely*, that such things (though somewhat varying from the common *rode* of *Nature*) may be acted'.[143]

The theory of the vehicles of the soul was to play a crucial role in Glanvill's explanation. It did so in a general way by providing for the corporeality of spirits, human, demonic and angelic. This was particularly directed against the scepticism of Reginald Scot who, along with Thomas Hobbes and John Webster, was Glanvill's main target.[144] Scot's 1584 work, *The Discoverie of Witchcraft*, was republished in 1665. In the appendix to this work, Scot had maintained that 'Devils are spirits and no bodies.'[145] Stuart Clark has pointed out this was Scot's most telling argument for it reduced 'all demonic agents to a noncorporeal condition, thus removing them from physical nature altogether'.[146] The theory of the vehicles of the soul was a bulwark against this. It kept spirits, demons, and angels within the 'physical' realm and thus capable of scientific investigation.

More particularly, the vehicles of the soul provided a 'natural' explanation for many of the activities of witches. It explained, for example, how witches were able to travel long distances to congregate at Sabbaths, for they travelled there in their aerial vehicles. It explained too the ability of witches to transform themselves into animals, since the aerial body was more pliable than the terrestrial.[147] Moreover, Glanvill suggested, the sucking familiar breathes a vapour into the body of the witch allowing the witch to effect transformations: ' 'tis very likely that this *ferment* disposeth the *imagination* of the *Sorceress* to cause the ... *separation* of the *soul* from the *body*, and may keep the *body* in fit temper for its re-entry; as also it may facilitate *transformation* ... '[148]

For the seventeenth-century Platonists, no great gulf was fixed between the living and the dead. Those yet to be born, those still living, those who had died were all to be located in the same spatio-temporal realm. The spiritual and the material, the angelic and the demonic, the natural and the supernatural, were part of the one universe – a universe which operated according to fixed laws both spiritual and material, though one in which the preternatural could periodically manifest itself.

For the Platonists, it was essentially a vertical universe of two levels: of the aethereal heavenly Kingdom where dwelt God, the saints, the angels, and the souls of the blessed; and an aerial Kingdom, to the higher levels of which evil could not penetrate, in the lowest levels of which in the cavities within the earth and in the air around the earth dwelt Satan, his minions, and the souls of the wicked, always threatening to forestall the return of souls to the divine. The earthly life was perched precariously both in time and space between the hopes of an eternal blessedness and the possibilities of torments severe, long-lasting if not eternal.

CHAPTER 2

From the hour of death to the day of judgement

THE MORTALITY OF THE SOUL

> About the same time others arose in Arabia, putting forward a doctrine foreign to the truth. They said that during the present time the human soul dies and perishes with the body, but that at the time of resurrection they will be renewed together.
>
> Eusebius, *The Church History*

In 1646, Edmund Calamy the Elder discerned two radical views among the sectarians of his time. 'Some believe', he wrote, 'that the *Soul dyeth with the Body*, and that both shall rise again at the Last Day. Others begin to say, they believe that the *Soul* is mortal, as well as the *Body*, and that there is no resurrection neither of Soul nor Body.'[1]

Such views were certainly radical, but they were not new. On the contrary, mortalist views – particularly of the sort which affirmed that the soul slept or died – were widespread in the Reformation period. George Williams has shown how prevalent mortalism was among the Reformation radicals.[2] The early writings of Luther strongly supported it. He was firmly committed to a dualism between body and soul and therefore to the continued existence of the soul between death and the resurrection of the body. Nevertheless, for Luther, all the emphasis was on the final day of judgement when bodies would rise from the dead, as did Christ's on Easter morning, and be reunited with their souls. Thus, the question of the state of souls between death and the resurrection was of little importance. The intermediate state, then, was not that of a conscious existence but of a deep and dreamless sleep without consciousness and feeling. On the last day, the soul would reawaken unaware of the time that had passed since it had fallen asleep at the point of death:

For just as a man who falls asleep and sleeps soundly until morning does not know what has happened to him when he wakes up, so we shall suddenly rise on the Last Day; and we shall know neither what death has been like or how we have come through it.³

Later Lutheran theology did not follow Luther on this issue and returned to the notion of an intermediate state in which, before the resurrection, souls lived a conscious life with Christ. In part, this was to do with the adoption of mortalism, with its stress on the imminence of the Kingdom of God and the general resurrection of the dead, by the radical wing of the Reformation. John Calvin's attack upon mortalism was certainly motivated by its adoption by the radicals. In 1542, in the Preface to his *Psychopannychia*, his first theological writing, Calvin saw the Anabaptists as the heirs of Eusebius' Arabians who had begun 'To blow abroad certain sparkes thereof: which, sparkling farre and wide, in the end, fell out into hoat [*sic*] fiery flames ... '⁴

As a Platonist, Calvin found it easier than Luther to envisage the continued conscious existence of the soul after death. For a Reformer committed to the establishment of an enduring church, the immediacy of the Kingdom of God held little appeal. For both reasons, he was passionately opposed to those who advocated the sleep or the death of the soul. At the same time, he studiously avoided any suggestions of purgation or spiritual development beyond the grave. The state between death and the last judgement was a static one, the souls of the elect awaiting the perfection of their happiness in Abraham's bosom, the reprobate awaiting in chains their ultimate and eternal punishment:

> When the abode of blessed spirits is designated as the *bosom* of *Abraham*, it is plain that, on quitting this pilgrimage, they are received by the common father of the faithful, who imparts to them the fruit of his faith. Still, since Scripture uniformly enjoins us to look with expectation to the advent of Christ, and delays the crown of glory till that period, let us be contented with the limits divinely prescribed to us – viz. that the souls of the righteous, after their warfare is ended, obtain blessed rest where in joy they wait for the fruition of promised glory, and that thus the final result is suspended till Christ the Redeemer appear. There can be no doubt that the reprobate have the same doom as that which Jude assigns to the devils, they are 'reserved in everlasting chains under darkness, unto the error of the great day'.⁵

Essentially, Anglicans were to follow this position. The last judgement was still expected, though not in the immediate future. In the meantime, souls were kept in a half-way house, so to say, of either happiness or misery. Only thus could sense be made of the two

Scriptural passages most suggestive of continued life immediately after death: namely, Jesus' words to the thief crucified with him, 'Today thou shalt be with me in Paradise' (Luke 23.43); and Dives' vision of Lazarus comforted after his death in the bosom of Abraham (Luke 16.22).

Calvin's concerns about mortalists were shared by Henry Bullinger, Zwingli's successor as chief pastor of Zurich. His attacks on the mortalists were particularly influential in England. The tenth dialogue of his *An Holsome Antidotus of counter-poysen, agaynst the pestylent heresye and secte of the Anabaptistes*, published in English in 1548, was primarily a Scriptural argument against soul-sleeping. But it also provided philosophical reasons for the immortality and incorruptibility of the soul.[6] His major contribution occurred in *The Second Helvetic Confession* in 1566, a creed for which he was primarily responsible, and one which was endorsed by all the Reformed Churches. 'We say', declared Bullinger,

that man doth consist of two, and those diverse substances in one person; of a soul immortal (as that which being separated from his body doth neither sleep nor die), and a body mortal, which, notwithstanding, at the last judgment shall be raised again from the dead, that from henceforth the whole man may continue forever in life or in death.

We condemn all those who mock at, or by subtle disputation call into doubt, the immortality of the soul, or say that the soul sleeps, or that it is part of God.[7]

That mortalism was a matter of concern in Britain from the time of the English Reformation onwards is demonstrated by indictments of mortalism in various confessions of faith.[8] The fortieth of the articles of religion of the Church of England in 1553,[9] the Scotch Confession of Faith in 1560, and the Westminster Confession of Faith in 1647 outlawed it. As the Scotch Confession put it,

The Elect departed are in peace and rest fra their labours: Not that they sleep, and come to a certaine oblivion, as some Phantastickes do affirme; bot that they are delivered fra all feare and torment, and all temptatioun, to quhilk we and all Goddis Elect are subject in this life, and therfore do bear the name of the *Kirk Militant*: as contrariwise, the reprobate and unfaithfull departed have anguish, torment, and paine that cannot be expressed. Sa that nouther are the ane nor the uther in sik sleepe that they feel not joy or torment.[10]

In his important work, *Christian Mortalism from Tyndale to Milton*, Norman Burns has shown the extent to which mortalist ideas were present in the first century after the English Reformation. While such notions were current in the time of Henry VIII and Edward VI, they appear to have subsided until late in the reign of Elizabeth I. We know, for example, that on 11 January, 1589, the Arian John Kett was burnt at the stake for his heresies among which, according to one source, was his belief that 'the soules of all men are reserved in a sweate sleape untill the revelation of joye... '[11] No doubt, the complaint of John Hull was exaggerated, but it does bear witness to the fears which the radicals generated among their contemporaries in the early part of the seventeenth century:

Men are secure, scoffers increase, Epicures abound, Atheisme is ripe. The creation is accounted a figment: the deluge a fable: the worlds burning a tale: the Scriptures but humanity: and religion but policy: Christs comming is derided: the day of iudgement despised: the resurrection not beleeued: nor the immortality regarded. Christ is refused, Christianity contemned, Gods prouidence reiected. Men seeke not saluation, make a scorne of the Prophets, minde not repentance, flie not from hell, neither walke vnto heauen. Good Lord, amend vs.[12]

THOMAS BROWNE AND THE DESTINY OF THE SOUL

Thomas Browne was no 'soul sleeper'. But he does admit that, in what he called his 'greener studies', he was attracted by it, along with Origenistic universalism, and prayers for the dead. It was an attraction motivated as much by the consideration of his own unworthy existence as by any tendencies to sectarian beliefs.[13] It is unclear why he should have rejected the possibility of soul-sleeping. Undoubtedly, his tolerant Calvinism played a role, committing him to the belief in an intermediate state. Perhaps, too, he saw mortalism as a step in the direction of atheism. For, although he rejected the extremes of demonological theory, he accepted the reality of witches and spirits: 'for my [owne] part', he wrote, 'I have ever beleeved, and doe now know, that there are Witches; they that doubt of these, doe not onely deny them, but Spirits; and are obliquely and upon consequence a sort, not of Infidels, but Atheists'.[14] Even so, Browne's mature position did give intimations of a view of heaven and hell which would have struck chords among his mortalist contemporaries who denied both an intermediate state of the soul and any final day of judgement. To be sure, Browne foresaw the day when God should gather the scattered parts of individuals and restore their bodies to their natural immortality. And he recognised too that the habitations of those restored selves would be heaven and hell. But he was quite unwilling to fix heaven or hell in any physical location after the final resurrection. On the contrary, to be in heaven was to be in the presence of God and to be in hell was to live apart from him. Consequently, heaven and hell were in the here and now, as much as in the hereafter:

> Briefely therefore, where the soule hath the full measure, and complement of happinesse, where the boundless appetites of that spirit remaine compleatly satisfied, that it cannot desire either alteration or addition, that I thinke is truely Heaven: and this can onely be in the enjoyment of that essence, whose infinite goodnesse is able to terminate the desires of itselfe, and the insatiable wishes of ours; wherever God will thus manifest himselfe, there is Heaven, though within the circle of this sensible world. Thus the soule of man may bee in Heaven any where, even within the limits of his owne proper body ... And thus wee may say that Saint *Paul*, whether in the body or out of the body, was yet in Heaven.[15]

Browne's view of heaven and hell, both now and in the hereafter, stemmed from his neo-Platonism. For Browne, the natural world was not only a created order maintained by its creator. It was also an emanation of the divine, which manifested its divine source. 'I am sure', he wrote, 'there is a common Spirit that playes within us, yet makes no part of us, and that is the Spirit of God, the fire and scintillation of that noble and mighty Essence, which is the life and radicall heat of spirits ... this is that irradiation that dispells the mists of Hell, the clouds of horrour, fear, sorrow, [and] despaire; and preserves the region of the mind in serenity.'[16] Thus, the way to real knowledge of God, to an awareness of the divine presence, was through contemplation of the divine spirit within one's self, and of its ultimate source. Thus could heaven be attained now, and its opposite, hell – the absence of the divine – could be avoided:

> I THANKE God, and with joy I mention it, I was never afraid of Hell, nor ever grew pale at the description of that place; I have so fixed my contemplations on Heaven, that I have almost forgot the Idea of Hell, and am afraid rather to lose the joyes of the one than endure the misery of the other; to be deprived of them is a perfect hell, & needs me thinkes no addition to compleate our afflictions; ... they goe the surest way to Heaven, who would serve God without a Hell; other Mercenaries that crouch unto him in feare of Hell, though they terme themselves the servants, are indeed but the slaves of the Almighty.[17]

RADICAL MORTALISTS

All this suggests that mortalism, and the fear of it, was widespread in England in the century after the Reformation. But the English Revolution, in particular, was a crucible out of which radical new ideas boiled. Mortalist ideas multiplied rapidly in the 1640s with the decline of censorship and greater liberty of the Press. Books abounded. As Barry Reay reports, 'there was a deluge of pamphlet literature. The London bookseller, George Thomason... collected over 700 publications in 1641, 2,000 in 1642; in all some 22,000 items (tracts and news-books) during the Revolution.'[18] Further, the large numbers of people named as mortalists in contemporary sources, who, as far as we know, did not commit their theories to writing, suggests the significant extent to which mortalist ideas were transmitted orally.[19] The Act of 1650 which committed those convicted of denying heaven and hell to prison for six months appears to have had little effect, although it indicates the degree of concern at the government level.[20] Concern was expressed too at a popular level. As one pamphleteer remarked in 1651,

it is no new work of Satan to sow heresies, and breede Heretickes, but they never came up so thick as in these latter times. They were wont to peep up by one and one, but now they sprout out by huddless and clusters (like locusts out of the bottomlesse pit). They now come thronging upon us in swarmes, as the Caterpillars of Aegypt.[21]

Thomas Edwards was concerned. 'You have made a Reformation', he told Parliament, 'but with the Reformation have we not a Deformation, and worse things come in upon us than we ever had before?'[22] In his *Gangraena*, he listed some 267 heresies current in 1646. Of these, eleven related to mortalism. Following Calamy's division of mortalists into 'soul sleepers' and 'annihilationists', Norman Burns has grouped these as follows:

HERESIES THAT TEACH THE SLEEP OF THE SOUL
83. That the soul of man is mortall as the soul of a beast, and dies with the body [I, 26]. 84. That the souls of the faithfull after death, do sleep till the day of judgement and are not in a capacity of acting any thing for God, but 'tis with them as 'tis with a man that is in some pleasing dream [I, 26–7]. 88. That none of the souls of the Saints go to Heaven where Christ is, but Heaven is empty of the Saints till the resurrection of the dead [I, 27]. 173. No man is yet in hell, neither shall there be any there untill the judgement;

for God doth not hang first, and judge after [I, 36]. 10. That it is injustice in God to punish the souls of the wicked in Hell while their bodies lie at rest in their graves, for seeing both were sinners together, both must be sufferers together; if God should punish the soul of *Cain* in Hell five or six thousand years before he punisheth the body of *Cain*, he then would show himself partiall in his distribution of justice [III, 8–9].

HERESIES THAT TEACH THE ANNIHILATION OF THE PERSONAL SOUL
15. That man had life before God breathed into him, and that which God breathed into him was part of the divine Essence, and shall return into God again [I, 20]. 21. That the soul dies with the body, and all things shall have an end, but God only shall remain forever [I, 20–1]. 22. Every creature in the first estate of creation was God, and every creature is God, every creature that hath life and breath being an efflux from God, and shall return into God again, be swallowed up in him as a drop is in the ocean [I, 21]. 89. There is no resurrection at all of the bodies of men after this life, nor no heaven nor hell after this life, nor no devils [I, 27]. 91. There is no hell, but in this life, and that's the legal terrours and fears which men have in their consciences. [I, 27].[23]

The errors identified by Edwards reflected a number of deapseated concerns in the seventeenth century. The extinction of all life at the moment of death was a more comforting prospect to many than eternal punishment or even temporary punishment to be followed by extinction. The thought that one was predestined to eternal torments was an appalling one. Henry More as a youth was tormented by the prospect of being predestined to hell. John Rogers, the future Fifth Monarchist, reported that, as a boy, he suffered terribly from the fear of hell and the devils.[24] Many were brought to despair. The author of *Tyranipocrit Discovered* saw the doctrine of predestination as leading to 'the quintessence of hell, I mean despair'.[25] Lodowick Muggleton spoke passionately of his youthful fear of being cast into hell after his death, and there being tormented by the Devil, eternally and without respite, and this perhaps irrespective of any righteous earthly life. 'These things', he wrote, 'wrought in my mind exceeding great Fear, and stir'd me up to a more exceeding Righteousness of life, thinking thereby that my Righteous Life would have cast out those tormenting Fears, but it did not.'[26]

Many radicals avoided Muggleton's dilemma by rejecting the doctrine of predestination, or by rejecting all notions of heaven and hell, or both. Muggleton rejected the annihilation of the individual at the moment of death, accepting the desirability of some day of judgement on which the good would be rewarded and the wicked punished. He and John Reeve were to solve the problem of predestination by pronouncing themselves to be the Lord's last two witnesses and prophets, thus assuring salvation to those who believed their doctrines, and damnation to those who did not. This, at least, would have mitigated Muggleton's own fears of hell, if not the fears of those unpersuaded by his and Reeves' prophetic pretensions. For them, little mercy would be shown. On the day of resurrection, hell would be located in the bodies of the disbelievers on an infernal earth. Their *Joyful News from Heaven* was not joyful for the wicked. The bodies of the wicked

> shall be fiery bodies, of spiritual darknesse, yea bodies of all unrighteousness, having all their wicked deeds of their former bodies conveyed into these bodies, as fewell to kindle the fire of new sorrows: In these bodies of Hell and utter darknesse, and their spirits in these bodies shall be fiery Devils; so their Bodies shall be their Kingdome of Hell and their proud spirits, that had pleasure in unrighteousnesse shall be the Devils, that shall be barr'd in close prisoners within their bodies, from all motioning or thinking of any former comforts, either spiritual, or natural ... ; then ... shall their spirits and bodies burn together like a flame of fire, that is all as dark as pitch, they never stirring from the place of their resurrection.[27]

Reeve and Muggleton were not millenarians in the strict sense. That is to say, they expected neither a one-thousand-year reign of Christ at the beginning of the millennium, nor the coming of Christ at its completion. Rather, as the above passage suggests, this earth would be, from the time of the coming of Christ, a hell for unbelievers, and the believers would be removed to a heaven, located above the stars, on the day of resurrection. But they did share with millenarians an expectation of the imminence of the end time. And they shared with other mortalists a material view of human nature, and a scepticism about the existence of spirits. For Muggleton and Reeve, the only difference between men and beasts was that the latter would remain in the dust for ever, the former would arise on judgement day.

For mortalists who argued for the annihilation of the individual soul at death, there was no difference between humans and animals. Ecclesiastes 3.9 was a favourite text: 'For that which befalleth the sons of men befalleth beasts; even one thing befalleth them: as the one dieth, so dieth the other; yea, they have all one breath; so that a man hath no preeminence above a beast.'

But such plebeian materialism was often uneasily combined with a pantheism which saw God in all things. Pantheism was central to the doctrines of the Ranters. Richard Coppin saw God in everything: 'The same God which dwels in one dwels in another, even in all; and in the same fulness as he is in one, he is in everyone.'[28] Joseph Salmon believed that 'God is that pure and perfect being in whom we all are, move and live; that secret blood, breath and life, that silently courseth through the hidden veins and close arteries of the whole creation.'[29]

It is difficult to discern the specific sources of the pantheism of the radicals. Many works on mystical religion were published in the 1640s, any of which may have played roles in the development of pantheism. Translations of some of the works of the Dutch founder of the Family of Love, Henry Nicholas, began to be published from 1646. From 1645 the better known books of the Protestant mystic Jacob Boehme began to appear in English translations. Nicholas of Cusa's *The Vision of God* was published in 1646, the late fourteenth-century mystical work *Theologia Germanica* in 1648, and the Lutheran mystic Valentine Weigel's *The Vision of God* in 1648.

We may also look to such mystical writings as the sources, direct or indirect, of radical views of heaven and hell among the annihilationists. For the Familists, for Weigel, and for Boehme, heaven and hell were in the here and now, within individual human souls. Such views were common among the radicals. For the Ranter William Bond, 'There was neither heaven nor hell except in a man's conscience, for if he had a good fortune and did live well, that was heaven: and if he lived poor and miserable, that was hell, for then he would die like a cow or a horse.'[30] For Richard Coppin, heaven and hell were internal states, the one of the saints, the other of the wicked:

...in the persons of wicked men there may be the chambers of hell, the Synagogue of Satan, where all this wicked abomination, death, and hell shall be tormented and ended; for as in the Saints there are the chambers of heaven, the temple of God, where all good things, holy things, upright things, divine apprehensions of God shall be kept and preserved in a discovery of light and glory in God to all eternity; so in wicked men there are the chambers of hell, the habitations of devills, where all evill things, vain thoughts, humane inventions, shall be gathered into a body of confusion and darkness, as in hell, to be tormented, separated and ended.[31]

Christopher Hill makes the point that doubts about a localised heaven and hell may also have been influenced by the popularisation of Copernican astronomy, and that this too led to the internalisation of heaven and hell.[32] Jacob Bauthumley, for example, in 1650 in his *The Light and Dark Sides of God* claimed to be able to make little sense of God as dwelling in a localised heaven, seeing him rather as an omnipresent Spirit 'in low and dark appearances, as well as in the most glorious'. And his image of God as equally in everything motivated his mortalism. 'I am willing', he declared, 'to let fall any carnall apprehension of a visible or corporeal enjoyment of God, or any expectation of a happy condition out of God after this life and dayes are ended, being willing to resign and give up to God what he is in me in flesh, that so God may be all, and advanced above all in the spirit.'[33]

That we, as human beings, are psycho-physical unities and are not composed of a mortal body and an immortal soul is a relatively modern idea. And it is tempting to see the mortalists among the radicals as precursors of it, as further evidence of the way in which the seventeenth century cast off medieval ideas and moved into the scientific future. But their materialism was often united to their pantheism. Spirit and matter, God and nature co-mingled. And they looked back to Old Testament images of the unity of the individual rather than forward to science. Thus, their doctrines, like their religious allegiances, were fluid. This is particularly exemplified in Laurence Clarkson – an Anglican, a Presbyterian, a Dipper, a Seeker, a Ranter, and finally a Muggletonian. On the one hand, Clarkson appears to be a committed materialist. The body, he wrote, after it is laid in the grave, 'is buried in its heaven, glory and happiness, where it shall rot and consume into its own nature for ever and ever'.[34] On the other hand, he used the common radical image of the spirit returning into the ocean of the divine: 'even as a stream from the Ocean was distinct in itself while it was a stream, but when returned to the Ocean, was therein swallowed and become one with the Ocean; so the spirit of man while in the body, was distinct from God, but when death came it returned to God, and so became one with God, yea God itself'.[35]

HOBBES AND THE KINGDOM OF GOD

The mortalism of Thomas Hobbes was also linked to his materialism. For Hobbes, the concept of the soul as a substance incorporeal was a nonsense. Because, according to him, 'substance' and 'body' meant the same thing, then '*Substance incorporeall* are words which, when they are joined together, destroy one another, as if a man should say, an *Incorporeall Body*.'[36] Moreover, he viewed the notion of the soul's existence independently of the body as the cause of religious errors – of the doctrine of eternal torments, of the ghosts of the dead walking abroad, of exorcisms, of the invocation of saints, of purgatory and of indulgences – 'of exemption for a time, or for ever, from the fire of purgatory, wherein these Incorporeall Substances are pretended by burning to be cleansed, and made fit for heaven'.[37] Consequently, he saw the denial of incorporeal substance as entailing an end to what he saw as these abuses.

Crucial to Hobbes' critique of the soul was his denial of its *natural* immortality. That the souls of men were substances distinct from their bodies which subsisted after death by virtue of their intrinsic nature was, Hobbes argued, a disease caught by the Church from the daemonology of the Greeks. For Hobbes, Scripture was decidedly against any notion of natural immortality: 'That the Soul of man is in its own nature Eternall, and a living Creature independent on the body; or that any meer man is Immortall, otherwise than by the Resurrection in the last day,... is a doctrine not apparent in Scripture.'[38] According to the Scriptures, argued Hobbes, 'soul' and 'life' mean the same thing. Thus, 'eternal life' can only mean the revivifying of the body on the day of resurrection. That is to say, for Hobbes, immortality was not the soul's natural right to an existence outside of time, but was a supernatural divine gift conferred upon the bodies of the elect in a future time.[39]

Basil Willey has suggested that Hobbes' account of the day of judgement was part of a cynical attempt to undermine the Christian religion: 'to say that dead men awake', he wrote, 'on the Day of Judgement is, for him, as good as to say that they wake up never, only it has the advantage of sounding much more orthodox'.[40] Willey appears to have been unaware that, in the seventeenth century, the sort of eschatology advocated by Hobbes appealed to many. Moreover, as we shall see, Willey does not appear to have been aware that, in holding that the wicked would be annihilated after a period of suffering, Hobbes was decidedly unorthodox. And although, at this distance, we cannot possibly determine the extent to which Hobbes was a sincere if somewhat unusual Christian, there is little doubt of his determination to develop his account of the last judgement on scriptural grounds. More importantly, that Hobbes' eschatology is no mere hollow sham, but a central feature of his thought, is suggested by the role it plays in his political theory.

For Hobbes, the Kingdom of God can only be a Kingdom on this earth. The Biblical type of the Kingdom of God was the civil kingdom inaugurated by God in the covenant made between him and the people of Israel. And moreover, it was one in which ecclesiastical power on the one hand, and civil power on the other, could not be separated. Thus, Hobbes' interpretation of the Biblical notion of the Kingdom of God as an earthly kingdom under the rule of one sovereign with no distinction between his spiritual and temporal powers was a direct criticism, not only of the Catholic Church's belief that *it* was the existing Kingdom of God, but also of its belief that the Kingdom of God was a spiritual and not a temporal matter. As J. G. A. Pocock writes,

The tactic of combining apocalyptic with mortalism served, as it always had, to destroy the claim that the Church possessed the keys to an individual's salvation at the hour of his death; he could be saved or damned only by an action which God was to take in the future, and the church was merely a community of faithful expectant of that future act.[41]

The denial of an intermediate state together with an emphasis on the expectation of the Kingdom of God in the future served also as a critique of the Calvinist view that the Kingdom of God had begun with the resurrection of Christ, and that, consequently, the Calvinists, as the representatives of the true Kingdom of God on earth, had authority over civil sovereigns. Against the Calvinists, Hobbes argued that the overall weight of Scriptural evidence indicated that the Kingdom of God did not begin with the resurrection, but would do so only on the day of judgement. For Hobbes, therefore, both Catholic and Presbyterian doctrines of the Kingdom of God were designed to usurp legitimate sovereign power: 'This power Regal under Christ, being challenged, universally by the Pope, and in particular Common-wealths by Assemblies of the Pastors of the place, (when the Scripture gives it to none but Civill Soveraigns), comes to be so passionately disputed, that it putteth out the Light of Nature, and causeth so great a Darknesse in mens understanding, that they see not who it is to whom they have engaged their obedience.'[42]

The sovereignty of the King was therefore a precursor of the sovereignty of Christ when he returned to earth to usher in the

Kingdom of God. As Hobbes rejected the notion of a heavenly existence in the intermediate state, so also he rejected the concept of the righteous, on the day of judgement, being carried from the earth into heaven.[43] Rather, on this earth, Christ in his risen body would reign for ever over the elect into the infinite future. On that day, 'the Faithfull shall rise again, with glorious, and spirituall Bodies, and bee his Subjects in that his Kingdome, which shall be Eternall: That they shall neither marry, nor be given in marriage, nor eate and drink, as they did in their naturall bodies; but live for ever in their individual persons...'[44]

The wicked too would arise on the day of judgement to be punished, both spiritually and physically, in the sight of their sovereign. The wicked would be in the state they were in after the sin of Adam; they would 'marry, and be given in marriage; that is, corrupt, and generate successively; which is an immortality of the Kind, but not of the Persons of men...'[45] But they would also face the certainty of a second and eternal death having received the punishment for their wickedness, 'For though the Scripture bee clear for an universall Resurrection; yet wee do not read, that to any of the Reprobate is promised an Eternall life.'[46]

Hobbes was hard put to it to avoid the clear implications of those Scriptural passages that imply everlasting torments in eternal fire to be the ultimate fate of the damned. But, as we shall see later, he foreshadowed John Locke's solution to the same quandary by arguing that everlasting fire does not entail the eternal survival of those within it. Although the fire is everlasting, he argued, 'it cannot thence be inferred, that hee who shall be cast into that fire, or be tormented with those torments, shall endure, and resist them so, as to be eternally burnt, and tortured, and yet never be destroyed, nor die'.[47]

The ultimate annihilation of the wicked was philosophically made possible by Hobbes' denial of natural immortality and his understanding of it as a supernatural gift. Thus the wicked could – logically would – die a second death. Although he intimated that a sovereign could justly condemn the wicked to eternal torments, theologically he saw the final annihilation of the wicked as a result of the mercy and, I think, of the justice of God:

it seemeth hard, to say, that God who is the Father of Mercies, that doth in Heaven and Earth all that hee will; that hath the hearts of all men in his disposing; that worketh in men both to doe, and to will; and without whose free gift a man hath neither inclination to good, nor repentance of evil, should punish mens transgressions without any end of time, and with all the extremity of torture, that men can imagine, and more.[48]

RICHARD OVERTON AND JOHN MILTON

Eight years before the publication of Hobbes' *Leviathan*, the mortalist position which he exemplified had been popularised (or perhaps unpopularised) in a work by the Leveller Richard Overton. The title page of the second edition in 1655 gives us a clear indication of its contents: *Man wholly Mortal. Or, a Treatise Wherein 'Tis proved, both Theologically and Philosophically, That as whole man sinned, so whole man died; contrary to that common distinction of Soul and Body: and that the present going of the Soul into heaven or hell, is a meer Fiction: And that at the Resurrection is the beginning of our immortality; and then actual Condemnation and Salvation, and not before.* Ecclesiastes 3.19 provided the proof-text for the work.

Philosophically, Overton attempted to reduce the concept of the immortality of the soul to absurdity, on the overall assumption that 'Man is but a creature whose several parts and members are endowed with proper natures or faculties, each subservient to other, to make him a living Rational Creature; whose degrees or excellences of natural Faculties make him in his kind more excellent than the Beasts...'[49] But the overall weight of his argument for the soul's mortality is Scriptural and within the context of the Christian doctrines of Creation, Fall, and Redemption.[50]

Crucial to his argument was Genesis 2.7: 'God breathed in his [Adam's] face the breath of life, and man became a living soul.' For Overton, as for Hobbes after him, this could not mean 'an Angelical Entitie; a supernatural, spiritual, infinite Existence to be couched in the flesh, or mens corpulency; whose being doth not depend on it, but is proper and peculiar to it self',[51] but rather and merely a living being, who as such would have lived for ever had he not sinned. Thus, for Overton, the Fall did not entail only the mortality of the body but of the whole being. Moreover, he maintained, on the supposition of the immortality of the soul, no coherent sense could be made of the resurrection on the day of judgement. As he put it in his typically ebullient way,

If the soul (as they say) be the very life, or have all life in it self, and the body but its instrument; then the body now hath no more life in it, then when it is reduced to the earth; but is [now] as dead as a dore-naile: And so at the Resurrection cannot be raised from death; for that which never had life, cannot be raised from death; and the union of it to the Soul at the Resurrection they Fabulate on, is but an addition of corpulency or gross matter to the Soul; which in truth is no Resurrection at all from the dead, no more then the restoration of flesh lost by Famine, sickness, &c. For Resurrection from the death, is not the addition of gross matter to life, but the Restoration of life from death ... [52]

It was virtually impossible in the seventeenth century for the orthodox to contemplate the possibility that sound Christian doctrine should not include a belief in the immortality of the soul. And there was a firmly held conviction that the denial of the soul's immortality would result in the collapse of all law and order. The pugnacious Alexander Ross, for example, declared, 'These *Arabian Pygmies* will never be able with such *engines* to overthrow the soules *immortalitie*, which is the strong Fort and *Citadell* of every good Christian in his afflictions. Let there be but way given to this doctrine of the *Saducees*, wee must bid farewell to *lawes* and *civility*, nay to *Religion* and *Christianity*.'[53] And he went on to describe mortalists as Cynics and Epicureans 'whose souls are fitter to dwell with Nebuchadnezzars in a beasts body, then in their owne ... [54] But, in historical retrospect, we can recognise that Hobbes' and Overton's denial of the immortality of the soul and an intermediate state between death and the last judgement, and their advocacy of the psycho-physical unity of the human individual together with their emphasis on the resurrection of the body were quite in accord with both the Old and New Testaments. And their Scriptural interpretations should not be read as the result of a disguised and disingenuous philosophical naturalism.

The same must be said of the mortalism of John Milton.[55] Milton's conviction that individuals shall only arise on the day of resurrection was totally based on Scripture.[56] We do not know when Milton came to his mortalist position. It is clearly stated for the first time in his *De Doctrina Christiana* written around 1658–60. As with Overton, so also with Milton, Genesis 2.7 was central:

Nor has the word 'spirit' any other meaning in the sacred writings, but that breath of life which we inspire, or the vital or sensitive, or rational faculty, or some action or affection belonging to those faculties. Man having been created after this manner, it is said, as a consequence that 'man became a living soul'; whence it may be inferred (unless we had rather take the heathen writers for our teachers respecting that nature of the soul) that man is a living being, intrinsically and properly one and individual, not compound or separable, not, according to the common opinion, made up and framed of two different natures, as of soul and body, but that the whole man is soul, and the soul man, that is to say, a body, or substance individual, animated, sensitive, and rational; and that the breath of life was neither a part of the divine essence, nor the soul itself, but as it were an inspiration of some divine virtue fitted for the exercise of life and reason, and infused into the organic body; for man himself, the whole man, when finally created, is called in express terms a living soul.[57]

It is unnecessary to follow Milton's mortalism further, for it is of a piece with that of Overton's, albeit much more rhetorically reserved, and the Scriptural passages cited are part of the mortalists' stock-in-trade. But it is necessary to emphasise that Milton, Overton, and Hobbes believed in a post-resurrection immortality in which the righteous would be rewarded and the wicked punished. And, unlike the radical sectarians who preached the eternal death of the soul at the end of this life, they held firmly to the central features of traditional Christian eschatology – judgement, resurrection, heaven and hell – in the conviction that Scripture, above all, had the authority in matters of faith.

Mortalism of the annihilationist kind was itself not to survive the Restoration in 1660. The return of the Monarchy and Episcopacy, of strict censorship laws, and the imposition of uniformity in religion served to suppress the sectarian base upon which mortalist ideas depended. As Christopher Hill puts it, after the Restoration, 'Preaching tinkers returned to their villages, or like Bunyan went to gaol. Levellers, Diggers, Ranters and Fifth Monarchists disappeared, leaving hardly a trace... Property triumphed. Bishops returned to a state church, the universities and tithes survived... The island of Great Bedlam became the island of Great Britain, God's confusion yielding place to man's order.'[58] And if the Glorious Revolution of 1688, and the new spirit of toleration after it, resulted in an outburst of nonconformist religious activity, religious enthusiasm was not to be encouraged, even among those persuaded to reason and latitude in matters religious.

But mortalist themes did emerge in the early part of the eighteenth century. Although not directly derived from sectarianism, they undoubtedly reflected ideas in popular religion which were sectarian in origin. And those with memories of the connections between mortalism, enthusiasm, and a world turned upside down viewed them with apprehension.

'FLYING LIKE AN EAGLE IN THE AIR'

> All my disciples must be airy,
> And dance as nimble as a Fairy,
> Must never think of sordid Dying
> But practise must the Art of Flying.[59]

Mortalist themes and suspicions of enthusiasm are well illustrated in the bizarre case of John Asgill. On 18 December, 1707, John Asgill, lawyer, member of Parliament, and amateur theologian was expelled from the first Parliament of the House of Commons of Great Britain. The cause of his exclusion was the discerning of 'many profane and blasphemous Expressions, highly reflecting upon the Christian Religion',[60] in a work which Asgill had published anonymously in 1700. The work was entitled, *An Argument proving that according to the Covenant of Eternal Life revealed in the Scriptures, Man may be translated from hence into that Eternal Life without passing through Death, although the Humane Nature of Christ himself could not be thus translated till he had passed through Death.*

Asgill's work and the eschatology contained within it was something of a *cause célèbre* during the first decade of the eighteenth century. Unlike the controversies surrounding William Whiston and Henry Sacheverell during this same time, the case of Asgill has been forgotten for the past century.[61] But it is a case worth resurrecting. For it well demonstrates that, if men of a 'rational persuasion' allowed and were given some latitude in matters doctrinal, any hint of enthusiasm was to be suppressed. Asgill was, in the final analysis, a martyr to the pursuit of social stability.

In his *Defence*, after his expulsion from the British House of Commons, Asgill gave an explanation of the circumstances which led to his work, 'having been ask'd more than twice (with Admiration of Friends and Foes) how such a thing could come into my Head?'[62] He tells us that, having lost a lot of money around the time of his admission to the Bar in 1692, he confined himself to his chambers with his law books and a Bible for some years. In his reading of the New Testament, he was particularly struck by the verses, 'I am the resurrection, and the life: he that believeth in me, though he were dead, yet shall he live: And whosoever liveth and believeth in me shall never die.'[63] After much meditation upon these verses, he committed his ideas to writing, and paid a printer to produce a few copies in secret. The printer, presumably seeing a market for the work, asked to print an edition at his own expense, 'saying, He thought some of the Anabaptists would believe it first'.[64]

Asgill undoubtedly believed that his interpretation of the Scriptures was a totally original one. He was later to argue that he never wrote to undermine the Scriptures.[65] But his reading of the Bible was certainly idiosyncratic and brought upon him only charges of blasphemy, and ridicule or pity. As Daniel Defoe remarked of it in 1704, 'When Men Pore upon the Sacred Mysteries of Religion with the Mathematical Engines of Reason, they make such incoherent stuff of it, as would make one pity them...'[66]

Asgill's theology depended upon a legal argument for the impossibility of death on the basis of a penal substitutionary theory of the meaning of Christ's death. Simply put, that is to say, through Adam came death, Christ overcame the law of death, and therefore, men need never die. According to Asgill, as a result of the Fall of Man, death reigned from Adam to Moses over all people; and from Moses until the time of Christ, death was inevitable for all, with the two exceptions of Enoch and Elijah, who were translated to heaven prior to their deaths. But the Law of Death was annulled by the death of Christ, and the legal power of death was removed. In his resurrection, Christ regained life by conquest. After breaking the Law of Death, and having arisen, Christ 'stood perfectly qualified to make his *Exit* by way of Translation... And thereupon God sent him down one of the Chariots of Heaven to convey him thither...'[67]

The remarkable consequence of Christ's death, resurrection, and ascension was that death, and therefore resurrection (either immediately *post mortem* or on the last day), was no longer a necessity for mortals. Those who have faith that Christ has overcome the inexorability of death need not die but can be translated to heaven. On the face of it then, since the death and resurrection of Christ, there ought not to have been death. Asgill's explanation of its continuation was a psychological one. In part, men died because they expected to; the custom of the world to die has predisposed us, he argued, to the necessity of death. But, he continued, 'Custom itself, without a reason for it, is an argument only to fools.'[68] In part, too, men died because of their fear of death: '*the Dominion of Death is supported by our fear of it*, by which it hath bullied the World to this day'.[69] For those who, like Asgill, had faith in translation, the precedent of death was broken, the fear of death was removed. Thus, of his own future, he declared,

> I shall not go hence *by returning unto the Dust*, ... But that I shall *make* my Exit by way of *Translation*, which I claim as a dignity belonging to that Degree in the Science of Eternal Life, of which I profess my self a graduat, according to the true intent and meaning of the Covenant of Eternal Life revealed in the Scriptures. And if after this, I die like other Men, I declare my self to die of no religion.[70]

The Kingdom of Heaven, then, would be an instantaneous reality for those who had faith in translation. Like Enoch, Elijah, and (presumably) John Asgill, they would ascend to paradise in a heavenly chariot. But what of those who would die or had died without the benefit of Asgill's salvific faith in translation? His millennial scenario gives us a number of clues, albeit inchoately.

It is clear that, logically, Asgill's theology has no role for an intermediate state of existence between death and the day of resurrection. For, on that final day, those who are to be saved will be *translated* from earth to heaven. An intermediate state of existence would entail those already in the heavenly realm redescending to earth in order to be translated thence back to heaven – a clearly illogical state of affairs. Thus, Asgill was logically committed to some form of mortalism.

Like Overton, Milton, and Hobbes, Asgill denied the immateriality and immortality of the soul. For him, the conscious life of individuals was the consequence of God's having breathed life into them. As a result, body and spirit were inseparable: 'in this Composition', Asgill wrote, ' the Spirit is so perfectly mixed with, and diffused through the whole Body, that we can't now say which is *Spirit*, nor which is Earth, but the whole is *one intire living Creature*'.[71] Consequently, the death of the body entails the cessation of conscious existence until such time as the body is raised up. This view was particularly prevalent among Anabaptists, and this was the reason why Asgill's printer saw a market for his work among the sectarian remnants of post-Restoration England.

Asgill's mortalism also reflected the pantheism so prevalent among the Ranters. Ranter beliefs did survive the Restoration. In 1684, for example, the Quaker Steven Crisp warned the Quakers of Ranters in their midst who believed ' the Soul shall dye with the Body, and suffer an annihilation as well as the Body, or shall be swallowed up out of all particularity, as a drop of Water into the Sea and so then what matter'.[72] Whether Asgill's pantheism was the result of direct Ranter influence cannot be shown. But his pantheism was of a kind with the pantheism of the radicals. Those who have died without faith in Translation, he maintained, neither die nor sleep between death and the resurrection. Rather their bodies are reabsorbed into matter, their spirits into God. God can extract the spirit leaving 'the lump to the Elements of which it was first composed ... ' The individual spirit maintains no self-existence 'having surrendered it self into the Ocean of Life, from whence it first flowed' as rivers are 'merged in the Ocean of their original Fountain'.[73]

However, unlike the radical sectarians, Asgill did not envisage the reabsorption of spirits back into God as continuing to eternity. On the contrary, the dwelling within the divine of such spirits who died without faith in translation would last only until the day of resurrection. Fortuitously, God had retained in his memory the character and ideas of every spirit and body, 'whence (in the day of the restitution of all things) every Body shall have its own Spirit, and every Spirit its own Body'.[74]

Asgill believed that, by the time of the day of resurrection, Translation without death would be the rule rather than the exception. Still, on that Day, the just would arise, after which there would be a period of time for the perfecting of the Faith of Translation, 'And by that very Faith they shall be then convinced, that if they had that Faith before, they need not have died.'[75] When both the resurrected and those that were still alive on the day of resurrection had learnt this Faith, the general resurrection of the dead would follow, the just 'to be caught up together in the Air'.[76]

Asgill was fully aware of the possible danger to him that could result from the views he expressed. For, as he informs us, he left the title page anonymous in order to protect himself. And he recognised that, should anyone be incensed sufficiently to kill him, his faith would be falsified:

But if any one hath spight enough to give me a polt thinking to falsify my Faith, by taking away my Life, I only desire them first to qualify themselves for my Executioners, by taking this short *Test* in their own Consciences. Whoever thinks that any thing herein contained is not fair dealing with God and Man (and giving the Devil himself his due) let him, or her, burn this Book, and cast a Stone at him that wrote it.[77]

There were many willing to take up Asgill's challenge to burn his work (literally) and to bury him beneath an avalanche of stones (metaphorically, at least). He was denounced for his pride and conceit, and lampooned mercilessly.[78] Still, even if, on occasion, perhaps not untypically for a member of the legal profession, the pleasure he gained from the presentation of an argument exceeded the intensity of his belief in it, he was without doubt seriously committed to the central tenet of his theology – translation.[79]

Daniel Defoe was one who treated his views seriously, and published his response, addressed to the Irish House of Commons, in 1704. Although he recognised that Asgill's account was thought of as 'an Enthusiasm or pious Lunacy',[80] he thought it deserved an enquiry, especially in the light of Asgill's claim that, if wrong, he would die of no religion. Asgill, declared Defoe, 'ought never to be so positive as to renounce his Religion upon the Certainty of a thing, which has any room left for a miscarriage; wherefore I cannot but be concerned for him as a Desperado...'[81]

Defoe's tactic was to show both the inconsequence and incoherence of Asgill's views. For example, he argued that if Christ had taken away the Law of Death, there was no necessity for a translation: 'we may as well *save God Almighty the Trouble*, abide where we are, and go all to Heaven at once'.[82] Moreover, he questioned whether the terrestrial body was a subject fit for heaven. Drawing on 1 Corinthians 15, he argued that Asgill's view was either unscriptural or incoherent:

Now if you allow Translation to be a direct passage from Earth to Heaven without a change... the Scripture is directly against it. If there is a Change made in the passage, then *you are where we all are*; you dye and are raised again, for Death and Resurrection are both necessary in order to a change.[83]

Indeed, he went on to say, such a change is not only necessary but desirable else, in contrast to those who died and were raised, 'you would be out of the Fashion there, and look like none of the Company'.[84]

Defoe's own position on the Fall of Man is relatively clear. The Fall brought about two kinds of death – death eternal and death temporal, the former the punishment for Adam's transgression, the latter the consequence of his nature. Eternal death was removed by the promise of Christ, upon the conditions of faith and repentance. 'Death therefore', he declared, 'is considered *in a double Capacity*, as a

Consequence, and as a *Curse*; as *a Curse* I allow all that is alleadged, that it is taken away by the Death of Christ; but as *a Consequence*, it remains to Nature.'[85] Only if man had eaten of the Tree of Life would temporal death have been overcome, God adding to the human frame and constitution some matter thus qualifying it for duration.[86] The work of Christ, consequently, was relevant only to that which had been lost, that is, death eternal, and not to that which might have been gained, that is, the negation of death temporal.

On 24 April 1707 the first Imperial Parliament was constituted, members for England and Scotland being transferred to the House of Commons for Great Britain. On 23 October the new Parliament assembled. But the member for Bramber, John Asgill, was absent, having been detained in the Fleet Prison for debt. On 10 November at Asgill's request, a committee was established to determine whether Parliament could exercise its privilege to have him released. But before this was done, a committee was established to investigate whether a work signed 'J. Asgill' and entitled *An Argument*... was heretical. Its final report was considered on 18 December, and Asgill was brought before the House. The substance of the report consisted of a dozen or so passages culled from Asgill's book.[87] Surprisingly, except for Asgill's declaration that he would be translated, the passages quoted in the Commons Journal cannot be deemed atheistic, blasphemous, or heretical. Asgill's refusal to retract his opinions in his oral defence before the House sealed his fate. His book was ordered to be burnt and he was expelled from the House and returned to prison. With no one willing to pay his debts, he spent the next thirty years of his life as a prisoner in the King's Bench. No doubt to his eternal chagrin, John Asgill died, untranslated, in 1738.

The causes of his downfall were perhaps many – Irish interests, his Hanoverianism, the new Scottish members – all these have been suggested.[88] Victim of personal or political malice he may well have been, but his theology undoubtedly contributed to his downfall. Asgill's age was not an intolerant one, nor especially fervently religious. But what fervour there was, was directed against what Roland Stromberg has called 'the slavish authoritarianism of Popery and the weird anarchy of private enthusiasm'.[89] Asgill gave all the signs of a dangerous enthusiast. His jocularity, his inwardly-guided interpretation of the Scriptures, his mortalist tendencies, and, above all, his arrogant confidence in the truth of *his* understanding of the Faith – of translation into heaven – all were frightening echoes of a world only recently turned right side up from the terrors of sectarianism and the fears of papal domination. Asgill was a victim of these alarums.

HENRY DODWELL AND THE BREATH OF GOD

If not as bizarre an eschatology as that of John Asgill, the views of Henry Dodwell were met with as much astonishment by his contemporaries, particularly because he was the most erudite of the first generation of non-jurors.[90] Dodwell was an Irishman, educated at Trinity College, Dublin, but settled in Oxford where he was appointed Camden Praelector of Ancient History. Having resigned from this position on account of his non-juring principles, he moved to nearby Shottesbrooke where he remained until his death in 1711.[91]

He was renowned both for his learning and for his eccentricities of belief. Thomas Macaulay thought him a pious and sincere man, but suggested that some of his books seemed to have been written in a madhouse. Certainly, his eschatology was unusual. But his defence of the uses of instrumental music in public worship to counteract the influence of devils on the spinal marrow of human beings, and his belief that the spinal marrow when decomposed became a serpent were, to say the least, eccentric, even in his times.[92]

However that may be, his work on the mortality of the soul in 1706 brought upon him almost universal opprobrium. 'He disgusted those who had hitherto been his greatest admirers', reported the *Biographia Britannica* in 1793.[93] The Anglican divine Edmund Chishull asked Dodwell's forgiveness for ranking him 'in that lower Class of Learned Men, who are indeed fitted for the collecting of Materials, but are unqualified to judge rightly of, and to reason upon what they shall collect'.[94] The Anglican vicar of Greenwich, John Turner, was especially severe. He likened Dodwell to a glutton with a bad digestion: 'Such a one', he announced, 'is sure to Eat more than he can well dispose of, more than what will turn to sound Nourishment and a healthful Constitution; and by that means he must either disgorge himself, to the very great Offence and Displeasure of all those that are round about him, or else keep the undigested Load to breed filthy Humours and bad Distempers, to his own great Uneasiness and Vexation.'[95]

The modern reader, like Dodwell's contemporaries, will certainly find Dodwell's arguments difficult to swallow and his literary style difficult to digest. But at least the title is plain: *An Epistolary Discourse, proving from the Scriptures and the First Fathers, that the Soul is a Principle naturally Mortal, but Immortalized actually by the Pleasure of God to Punishment or to Reward, by its Union with the Divine Baptismal Spirit, wherein is proved that none have the Power of giving this Divine Immortalizing Spirit since the Apostles but only the Bishops.*

Tentatively, Dodwell's eschatology can be reconstructed along the following lines. God created Adam out of the Dust, and added his *Afflatus* – his breath (*pneuma*) of life – so that man became a 'living soul'. God also added his divine breath (*pnoe*) to man which qualified him for immortality. At the Fall, the *Afflatus* was lost and man became mortal. But man retained the divine breath (*pnoe*) so long as God was pleased to continue his breathing. Thus, as a result of the Fall, man lost his natural immortality, but was not thereby put into a state of non-existence at death. For God supernaturally maintained souls in existence in a *post-mortem* state. As he put it more clearly in his 1707 work *A Preliminary Defence of the Epistolary Discourse*, the breath of God (*pnoe*) 'seems to be the *Principle* that enables *Humane Souls* to subsist in *Hades* in their *separate* State'.[96]

The place of separate souls, both righteous and wicked, after death was in the air (Hades), the middle Place between heaven and hell. The righteous and the wicked had different residences. Souls survived their bodies in vehicles of the same shape as those in which they formerly lived.[97] The good and the wicked had different residences as a result of the varying grossness of their new vehicles 'occasioned by their *Aversion* to *Heavenly* things in this *Life*, and their having preferred *Material* Enjoyment before them'.[98] But, although there was a grading of souls, there was no conversation between the happy and the unhappy. The least unhappy were confined below the moon, and the least happy just above it, the moon being the outer limit of the devils of the air. In the lowermost parts of heaven, the less perfect suffered expiatory pains to prepare them for the higher regions. On the day of resurrection, the bodies would be raised out of their graves on earth into the air to be united to their souls already there. Then, Dodwell maintained, 'our *Bodies* also will by him be made *Pneumatical*, when they are *fashioned like his glorious* Body, and fitted for the *Wings* of the *Spirit*, which will then translate them to the *highest Heavens*...'[99]

In his assertion of the natural mortality of the soul, Dodwell was clearly aligned with the mortalists. But his commitment to the intermediate state of the soul between death and the last judgement, through his assertion of its survival through the pneumatic activity of God, was quite out of keeping with the mortalist tradition. He was none the less accused of being a mortalist. Edmund Chishull, for example, aligned him with the Arabians of Eusebius, and invoked Articles 39 and 40 of the so-called Edwardine Articles of 1553.[100] This was a misreading of Dodwell on the part of Chishull. In his *Epistolary Discourse*, he had specifically rejected the error of the Arabians.[101] And he had done so, he later claimed, to distinguish his position from that of two latter-day Arabians, namely, William Coward and Henry Layton.[102]

Between 1692 and 1706, Henry Layton had produced a series of pamphlets which, while endorsing the notion of a general resurrection on the last day, had asserted the mortality of the soul primarily on physiological grounds though with the aid of Scripture.[103] Similarly, William Coward wrote a series of works from 1702 to 1706 in which he argued for the mortality of the soul and the resurrection of the dead on the last day.[104] For Coward, not only was the mortality of the soul in accord with reason, tradition and the Scriptures, but also the immortality of the soul was a heathenish invention. Thus, for Coward,

> there is no such Spiritual Substance [i.e. immaterial soul] in Man, but that all those Operations of Reason, Motion, &c. may be and are perform'd by an extraordinary or supereminent Power; First at the Creation implanted by God, in Matter or Material Man, ... which Power ceases to be, when the Body dies, and will not be renew'd again, or Reimplanted in the same Matter, until the Day of the Resurrection ...[105]

Not only did Dodwell's views on the intermediate state differ from those of Layton and Coward, but his vision of the day of judgement was also quite unique. Those who had heard the Gospel and responded to it would be raised on the last day and granted eternal happiness. Those who had heard it and rejected it would incur eternal punishment. Those who had remained ignorant of it, having been rewarded or punished in the intermediate state for their merits or demerits, would be raised on the last day and be annihilated shortly afterwards.[106] Thus, the heathen would on the last day have the divine breath withdrawn from them because they merited neither eternal happiness nor eternal torment and because there cannot be 'any *Third* Eternal State suitable to the *Nature* of a Rational Soul'.[107]

It would be incorrect to see Dodwell as punishing the heathen for their ignorance. On the contrary, Dodwell saw God's annihilation of them as the lesser of two evils, the greater being that they should be eternally tormented for their ignorance. His opponents saw it differently. The Platonist John Norris, for example, saw it as incompatible with the love of a God who himself expresses his perfections in the making of his creatures. For Norris,

> the striking off so vast a number of Human souls, as the whole Pagan World with many others which you are pleased to put upon the same *File*, from the list of the Creation, would make a strange Havock, I had almost said *Desolation*, among the Works of God. It would be a kind of a *Massacre* in the Intellectual World, for which it would be hard to give any good Account.[108]

Moreover, it followed from the nature of human beings that *all* should be at the final judgement. For Norris it was not so much a question of having heard the Gospel, but of being rational and moral: 'are they [the heathen] not Rational Creatures?', he asked. 'Have they not a Principle of Reason to know Good from Evil? And have they not Liberty of Will to avoid the one, and to chuse the other?... And have they not Consciences within them accusing or excusing, approving or condemning them according as their Actions agree or disagree to this internal Rule?'[109] So for Norris, as for the Cambridge Platonists of whom he was a late disciple, there was hope for the virtuous heathen. At the very least, whether virtuous or unvirtuous, they were to be accorded the privilege of being judged.

For the Newtonian rationalist Samuel Clarke, to whom the essence of true religion was obedience to the moral and eternal law of God, the crucial question was not the heathens' ignorance of the Gospel but their 'having obeyed or disobeyed the Law of Nature'.[110] And with Clarke, there is the suggestion that, not only does their obedience or disobedience to the law of nature qualify them for judgement, but it also qualifies them for salvation or damnation: 'Is not the Universe large enough, for God to dispose of all his Creatures into States suitable to their Natures? Are there not in God's *House many Mansions*?'[111]

The scriptures were also invoked against Dodwell's suggestion that the ignorant would be annihilated. The crucial text was John 5.28–9: '... the hour is coming, in the which all that are in the graves shall hear his voice, And shall come forth; they that have done good, unto the Resurrection of life; and they that have done evil, unto the Resurrection of damnation.' Dodwell argued that this did not imply that all would be judged for salvation or damnation, and saw it as a piece of Oriental exaggeration: 'It is usual with these Eastern writers especially, to use these *large* expressions, when they mean no more by them than was requisite for the *occasion* on which they use them.'[112] Clarke simply denied that the text was intended only for that occasion.[113] Thomas Milles, Bishop of Waterford, maintained he could find nowhere in Scripture where a universal statement was ever intended to be taken in a limited way.[114] Daniel Whitby saw Dodwell's argument merely as expedient.[115]

There was, however, another aspect of Dodwell's thought which implied that, by the time of the day of resurrection, no one could be in ignorance of the Gospel, and therefore that, on that day, all would be judged anyway. For Dodwell made much of the traditional doctrine of Christ's harrowing of hell.

Orthodox Christian doctrine held that the key to salvation was faith in Jesus Christ. But this seemed to imply that all those who had lived before Christ, noble pagans and Jews alike, were doomed to eternal punishment. The doctrine of Christ's harrowing of hell developed as a means of making possible their salvation. It was primarily based on 1 Peter 3.18–20: 'For Christ also hath once suffered for sins, the just for the unjust, that he might bring us to God, being put to death in the flesh, but quickened by the Spirit: By which also he went and preached unto the spirits in prison; Which sometime were disobedient...'

By the middle of the second century, the belief that, between his death and his resurrection, Christ had descended into Hades to preach to and/or to baptise those there was beginning to develop. The Alexandrian theologian Clement was among the first to link the salvation of the ancients with 1 Peter 3.19. In his *Stromateis*, he maintained that Christ had preached the Gospel to souls in hell. A just God could not but do so: 'If, then, he [Christ] preached the gospel to those in the flesh in order that they might not be condemned unjustly, how is it conceivable that he did not for the same reason preach the Gospel to those who had departed this life before his coming?'[116] The subject was a central theme in many medieval mystery plays, its popularity reinforced by the medieval genre of visions of hell. Literal understandings of Christ's descent into hell waned during the Reformation period, and from the beginning of the seventeenth century it progressively disappeared as a dominant theme of Christian symbolism.[117]

Be that as it may, we find the traditional and literal understanding of the doctrine in Dodwell. Influenced by the early Church Fathers and by Clement of Alexandria in particular, Dodwell did suggest in *The Epistolary Discourse* that, by virtue of Christ's harrowing of hell, all who were ignorant of the Gospel would have a chance to become immortalised for reward or punishment on the day of judgement.[118] Samuel Clarke missed this point but can be forgiven for doing so. Whitby noted that Dodwell supported it, but he went on to reject the whole doctrine.[119] Turner believed that Dodwell was simply confused and unable to see the conflict between his acceptance of both the annihilation of the ignorant and the harrowing of hell.[120] Dodwell himself, it would seem, wanted the best of both worlds. On the one hand, if the harrowing of hell were true, he suggested, then his adversaries' complaints against his notion of the annihilation of the ignorant were irrelevant, for all would be judged. That is to say, 'on supposition that they, who never heard of the *Gospel* in this *Life*, may have it *Preached* to them in *Hades*, and may there be admitted to *Baptism*... This will *qualifie* the compliers for the *Rewards* of *Heaven*, and expose those, who shall prove Refractory, to a just Sentence of *partaking* in the *Fire prepared for the Devil and his Angels*...'[121] But, on the other hand, although he accepted that God might admit '*all* (if he pleases) to this *Option*',[122] he remained convinced that the Scriptures did argue for the ultimate annihilation of at least some.

Dodwell's opponents were also disturbed by his notion of God's immortalising persons *solely* to punish them eternally. Daniel Whitby, for one, was no opponent of the doctrine of eternal torments, but he did question the rationality of God's making a mortal soul immortal only to torment it for ever. 'How much more rational is it', he inquired, 'to conceive, that the Evils which the Wicked are to suffer in the World to come, as far as they relate to the Soul, arise from its Natural Immortality?'[123] Samuel Clarke was opposed to the eternity of hell's torments. For him, the crucial issue was not which persons would be involved in such punishments, but rather, whether it was reconcilable with the goodness of God in any circumstances 'to put *any Persons* at all upon a necessity of making such an Option, wherein if they chuse amiss, the Misery they incur must be irrecoverable'.[124] For Dodwell, on the contrary, as for most supporters of eternal torments, the divine goodness was vindicated in the allocation of equal (eternal) time for both rewards and punishments.[125]

His critics also saw his eschatology as politically divisive. They drew the implication that, in the final analysis, it was informed by his non-juring principles, and that, more importantly, only those who had received baptism from non-juring clergy would attain immortality. Even though, in 1705, Dodwell had written a discourse to argue that, when all the non-juring bishops had either died or resigned their Sees, non-jurors ought to return to the Church, there were sufficient hints in his *Epistolary Discourse* to incense his adversaries. John Turner's fury was evident:

I have a very great Regard to those Honest and sincerely Consciencious Men who merely out of Scruple could not take the Oaths: And carrying themselves Wisely and Discreetly, they are to be pity'd, I think, in all their Sufferings on that Account. But to run this so high, as not only to condemn our Communion as Unlawful, to Reflect severely on the Conduct of the State, to Censure the whole Episcopacy and Clergy as Schismaticks ... and in short, to put us into such a State as destroys all our hope of Immortality, I think it does shew such a Man to understand Perverseness much better than the rest of Mankind.[126]

Attacked for his lack of tolerance on the one hand, he was accused of encouraging libertinism and atheism on the other. All his critics agreed that the possibility of annihilation was an incentive to disbelief and an encouragement to moral decline. Chishull's response was typical: 'that he should be so far sunk in the very Dregs of Heresy; that he should go so far hand in hand with the Atheists and the Libertines of the Age: Is what no considering Person can ever wonder or deplore enough.'[127] Dodwell's not unreasonable response was that, after all, only those who were ignorant of the Gospel were candidates for annihilation, that none of these were likely to have read his book, and that those who had read it would have already accepted or rejected the Gospel, and would therefore be judged on the last day.[128]

But this was an argument unlikely to be heard in a decade in which there was a growing despondency over the country's morals. One determined effort to stamp out permissiveness and 'evil-living' had led to the formation of the Society for the Reformation of Manners with the aim of enforcing the criminal laws on Sabbath observance, gaming, drinking, cursing, and profanities in general.[129] But even so, the high Churchmen who wrote *The Presentation of the Present State of Religion* in 1711 affirmed that 'we cannot without unspeakable grief reflect on that deluge of impiety and licentiousness which hath broken in upon us and overspread the face of this church and kingdom'.[130] Any eschatology, therefore, which seemed not sufficiently a deterrent to sin was not to be encouraged.

THE REJECTION OF PURGATORY

One of the chief attractions of mortalism and the denial of any intermediate state of the soul was its implicit denial of the Catholic doctrine of purgatory. Thomas Hobbes noted with obvious satisfaction that his view of the soul destroyed the philosophical base of many Catholic beliefs and practices – the belief in purgatory, ghosts, indulgences, and the invocation of the saints.[131] The Socinian mortalist Joseph Stegmann argued that any notion of an intermediate state between death and the day of judgement opened the door for Catholic abuses: '[the papists] beleeve in effect that the dead live... Now this is the foundation not only of Purgatory, but also of that horrible Idolatry practised amongst the Papists, whilest they invocate the Saints that are dead. Take this away and there will be no place left for the others.'[132] Henry More was, as we have seen, no mortalist. But he linked the rise of mortalism to the 'affrightful Figment of Purgatory':

the grand Mischief of this cheating invention is a blasphemous affront to the Merits and Satisfaction of our dear Saviour, and a Tyrannical oppression of the consciences of the simple; but so great a scandal to the more nasute, that it were a strong temptation to them to misbelieve the whole summe of Religion, or any state at all of the Soul after death, but that she is mortal and perishes; these false Apostles having abused the Doctrine of her survival after the death of the Body so grossely and rancidly, merely to the advancing of their own estates in this life, and to the wallowing in wealth, honour and sensual pleasures.[133]

The notion of purgatory as a place, in which between death and the last judgement those who have died in the grace of God could be purged of their venial sins or continue their penances for mortal sins committed, confessed and forgiven before death, arose in the latter part of the twelfth century. In his seminal work *The Birth of Purgatory*, Jacques le Goff has argued that the noun *purgatorium* entered the lexicon only around AD 1170. At the same time, spatial terms began to be applied to the world beyond the grave. Thus, from this time on, there were three possible destinations for souls immediately after death who had sinned as individuals with varying degrees of responsibility. Simply put, the wicked would go to hell, the good to heaven, and those who were neither totally good nor totally wicked to purgatory, there to be purified for their eventual heavenly destiny.

Thus, crucially, the traditional dual system of heaven (or paradise) and hell (or Hades) after death and before the last judgement was replaced by a triple system of heaven, purgatory, and hell until the last day when all would receive either eternal rewards or eternal punishments. With the extension of life beyond the grave into purgatory, the world of the dead and the world of the living became intimately related. Death, less the final frontier, became an extension of earthly life. 'Purgatory', remarks le Goff, 'gave rise to citizenship of the other world, to citizens of the time between death and the last judgement.'[134] The indefinite time of waiting after death for judgement on the last day was replaced by a judgement immediately after death. This immediate *post-mortem* judgement created an accountancy of the hereafter, a complex system of proportionality by which the punishments in purgatory could judicially reflect the nature of the sins committed on earth.

Purgatory was, however, a passive state. The individual soul could do nothing by itself to alter its fate. As the Catholic Nicholas Caussin put it, 'it is the impossibility of impossibilities, that in the other world not capable of merit or demerit, he [the soul] may change himself'.[135] But, the soul could win a reprieve or early release from punishment, not only through God's mercy and from merits accrued during its life, but also by suffrages exercised by the Church at the behest of those still living.

Most importantly, the time of purgatory, for individual souls, was not seen as lasting until the day of judgement. Punishment was inevitable, but hope of salvation before the last day was created. As le Goff points out, the exact time of deliverance depended on 'the quantity and quality of sins remaining to be purged and the intensity of suffrages offered by the living. Thus, there came to be established in the hereafter a variable, measurable, and, even more important, manipulable time-scale.'[136] The Church, in the ecclesiastical sense, was in charge of the calculations. And it was the political and financial beneficiary of the new system of the hereafter through its administration of the affairs of the living on behalf of the dead – prayers, alms, masses, offerings of all kinds, and of course indulgences.

Luther's response to what he saw as the abuses of the purgatorial system was, as we have seen, to deny the intermediate state altogether.

For Calvin, the state of souls was fixed at death. In a very important sense, for Calvinism, the last judgement became something of a formality: those in Abraham's bosom (or paradise) could rest assured that their blessedness would be ratified, those who were confined and bound in chains could not hope for any reprieve.[137]

For English Protestantism also, following Calvin, the state of souls was fixed at death, and there was no possibility of souls' improving their state either in the intermediate state or after the final judgement. If we look broadly across the period of the English Enlightenment, from 1660 to 1750, this remained the orthodox opinion. The independent divine William Strong put it quite bluntly:

There is a great Gulfe set that is by a divine decree stablished and fixed, a mans state is set for eternity, and there is no hope of a change, a passage here there is from death to life, but there is none hereafter; for there is a great Gulfe that God has set between, that there can be no passage, no change of a mans condition, there can be no translation ...[138]

William Sherlock, Dean of St Paul's and Chaplain to the King in 1696, was uncertain about the nature of life after death, but of the finality of death he had no doubts: 'Tho the Happiness or Miseries of the next world may increase, yet the state can never alter ... '[139] To Richard Jenks, because the next state was an unchangeable one, and because 'men of vicious sensual Tempers, cannot have their Souls new moulded there',[140] the punishments threatened as the wages of sin were necessarily eternal. For the Anglican Tobias Swinden in 1714, no inward change was possible in the afterlife. While the damned would retain their reason, understanding, and memory, those faculties remained to increase and aggravate their misery, 'and not as a means to lead them to a better Life, or to bring them out of their sharp and never ceasing Torments'.[141] Matthew Horbery of Magdalen College, Oxford, invoked the Scriptures. The Bible, he argued, 'never represents this State of Misery as a State of Purgation, or Purification, or anything like, or analogous to a State of Trial, where they may fit and qualify themselves for some better State of Existence'.[142]

Others admitted the possibility that the damned could change, but only for the worse. Edward Warren in 1667, for example, in his work against the pre-existence of souls, maintained that, not only did the wicked in hell not become better, they actually became worse. The pains of hell, he declared, would provoke the wicked to rage and swell, with anger and impatience; to fret and fume against the providence of *God*, and to curse and blaspheme the Majesty of Heaven for afflicting them; and so will sink them lower, and Chain them faster into that sulphureous Lake and flaming dungeon, rather than any way capacitate them for deliverance ...[143]

William Dawes, reputedly the best preacher of his day, believed the wicked would continue sinning in hell, thus meriting further punishment.[144] In a sermon preached in 1706 on Matthew 25.46, Bishop William Lupton found the wicked 'Unalterably confirmed and established in the Habits of sin', and therefore deserving of punishment as long as they continued so. And that, he proclaimed, 'is for ever and ever'.[145]

Interestingly, although ignored by Protestant theologians,[146] a philosophical basis for the unchanging nature of the soul after death was laid by two Catholics – Sir Kenelm Digby in 1644 in his *Two Treatises*,[147] and his mentor, the Catholic priest Thomas White in his *De Medio animarum statu* in 1653.[148] The overall aim of Digby and White, in all their writings, was to gain toleration for Catholics by developing a reformed Catholic theology reconcilable with English Protestant thought, and more conformable to what they believed to be the true Catholic faith. With respect to eschatology, they were committed to establishing an account of life after death which avoided the dangers of mortalism. Thus, for example, in his *Obervations upon Religio Medici*, Digby remarked, 'I shall observe how if hee [Sir Thomas Browne] had traced the nature of the soule from its first principles, hee could not have suspected it should sleepe in the grave till the Resurrection of the body.'[149] But, more importantly, they were at pains to exclude the Catholic doctrine of purgatory.

Crucial to Digby's *Two Treatises*, the one on body, the other on soul, was the notion that change and decay could only happen to material entities, for all change was ultimately the result of the rearrangement in space of the constituent parts of bodies, that is, atoms. Because souls were incorporeal in the disembodied state, they were exempted from both place and time, and were consequently incapable of change: 'there can bee no change made in her, after the first instant of her parting from her body ...'[150] The implicit denial of purgatory is clear. Thus, from the time of death onwards, the soul would be miserable or happy according to the virtues or vices of this life: 'what happiness or misery betideth her [the soul] in that instant [of death] continueth with her for all eternity'.[151] God was, to all intents and purposes, exempted from charges of injustice for his imposing eternal torments for sins committed in such a short space of earthly time. Eternal punishment followed inexorably, almost automatically. God's part in the torments of the afterlife was virtually denied; and the damned themselves were seen as responsible for their misfortunes. Thus, declared Digby, we can dispose of the objection 'how God, can in justice impose eternal paines upon a soule, for one sinne acted in a short space of time. For we see it followeth by the necessary course of nature, that if a man die in a disorderly affection to any thing, as to his chiefe good, hee remaineth by the necessity of his owne nature, in the same affection: and there is no imparity, that to eternal sinne, there should bee imposed eternall punishment.'[152] In sum, as John Henry argues, 'the earliest fully worked-out system of mechanical philosophy in English was written to provide a philosophical basis on which to erect a new eschatology'.[153]

This eschatology was elaborated by Thomas White. White explicitly rejected purgatory as an innovation in the Church and not a part of true tradition. Following Digby, he believed that no change in the soul was possible after death, and therefore he dismissed the purgatorial notion that souls could be purged by pain inflicted by an external agent. After death, then, the soul could not physically suffer in the flames of purgatory or hell.[154] Rather, between death and the day of resurrection, the wicked soul could only suffer psychological torment, while the good soul waited patiently with inner gladness for the last day:

Being therefore by the operation of death, as it were new moulded and minted into a purely spiritual substance, he carries inseparably with him the matter of his torment in the like manner as he also doth who takes leave of the body with his affections only venially disordered. We have no occasion here to employ *infernal* Architects to invent strange *racks* and *dungeons*, since the innate, and intimately inhering strife and fury of the affections bent against reason, perform alone that execution; which is therefore proportioned to the sins because springing and resulting from them, nor ever otherwise possibly capable to cease and determine, unless the soul by a new conjunction with the body, become again susceptible of contrary impressions.[155]

On the day of resurrection, the soul would be reunited with its body, be judged by God for eternal punishment or eternal reward, be admitted to a localised heaven (after being finally purged) or hell, there to be rewarded or punished both physically in the body and spiritually in the soul. Thus, on the basis of his analysis of the Scriptures and tradition, White concluded,

first, that some souls *already* enjoy God; secondly, that none are yet *locally* in heaven (since to be *in place* requires a body), thirdly that all the faithful *expect* the day of Judgment, that they may receive the *reward* of what they acted in their life-time, wherein all their works are to be try'd by fire ... From whence we may with the same constancy pronounce, that since those who dye in sin ... are in the last day to suffer purging flames, there can be no other material ones after this life, but they.[156]

PURGATORY REVISITED

To seventeenth-century believers, the prospect of eternal torment was a frightening one. But contemporary descriptions of purgatory would also have offered little comfort. Although a large geographical space existed between purgatory and hell, there was little rhetorical distance. The seventeenth-century Genovese General of the Barnabite Order, Romolo Marchelli, for example, described purgatory as 'a slaughter-house in which the sheep chosen by the evangelical shepherd, having been separated from the reprobate goats, taken from the sheep-folds of the world and massacred by death, were cruelly cut to pieces by the barbaric butchers of hell, on the chopping block of the crimes which they had committed, by axes, flames, and with piercingly painful blows'.[157] English Catholic readers of Thomas White would have found little unusual in his account of purgatory as 'a subterraneous *cave*, fill'd with *flames* and horrid *instruments* of torture, which his there confined and imprison'd soul must, till expiated endure. And these pains ... are inflicted by *extrinsical* Agents and *against* the will of the patient.'[158]

Purgatory, then, was never contemplated as a mitigation of the torments of hell. Nevertheless, although the punishments of purgatory were quantitatively and qualitatively indistinguishable from the torments of hell, the existence of purgatory between heaven and hell did provide a hope for many Catholics that, in spite of their sins, they might finally reach heaven before the day of judgement. For Protestants, on the other hand, there was, quite simply, no hope. The state of the soul was fixed at death, and eternal happiness or eternal misery were the only two possibilities.

Moreover, there was the frightening expectation that the number to be damned would greatly exceed the number to be saved. The small number of the latter was strongly asserted in the Gospels: 'strait is the gate and narrow is the way, which leadeth unto life, and few there be that find it' (Matthew 7.14; Luke 13.24), and 'many are called, but few chosen' (Matthew 20.16; 22.14). The clear implication of these texts was hard to avoid. Few dared to deny that the majority would be damned. A few vehemently asserted it.

One such was the nonconformist and controversialist Lewis du Moulin. The title of his last work eloquently suggests its author as a man who could be described as 'a cross and ill-natured man':[159] *Moral Reflections upon the Number of the Elect, proving plainly from Scripture Evidence, &c. that not One in a Hundred Thousand (nay probably not One in a Million) from Adam down to our Times shall be saved.*[160] The nonconformist divine John Shower was convinced that only a very few would be saved, in comparison to the many that would perish. And he warned his readers not to think that a death-bed repentance would have any effect: ''Tis almost as reasonable to expect that the Sun should cross the order of Nature, and rise in the West, as that the Son of Righteousness should arise with Healing in his Wings upon an habitual, obstinate Sinner at the last Hour.'[161]

The Anglican Tobias Swinden in his *An Enquiry into the Nature and Place of Hell* in 1714 was angry at the suggestion of Drexelius that there would be 100,000,000,000 of the damned in a hell one German mile square. 'It is a poor, mean and narrow Conception both of the Numbers of the Damned, and of the Dimensions of Hell...', he declared.[162] And one of his main reasons for transferring the location of hell from beneath the earth to the Sun was that the inside of the earth could not contain the vast number of lapsed angels and damned souls.[163]

The zealous Puritan Christopher Love, in his fifth sermon on the terrors of hell, divided the world into thirty-one parts, nineteen possessed by the doomed Turks and Jews, seven by the heathen similarly fated to hell, the remainder populated by Papists and Protestants, the former likewise damned.[164] In this, he was opposed by Pierre Cuppé, a *vicaire* of the diocese of Saintes, a disciple of John Locke, and the anonymous author of *Heaven Open to all Men*.[165] Cuppé's mind could not comprehend the notion of a God who would create thirty persons to eternally damn twenty-nine of them. To Cuppé, who hoped for the eventual salvation of all humankind through the love of God, the great numbers damned by the God of Love 'diffuses over the Conduct of God an Air of Cruelty that is no way suitable to him, he being infinitely good, and his Mercy surpassing all his other Works'.[166]

The Anglican Matthew Horbery, unlike Cuppé a firm believer in the eternity of the torments of hell, was also troubled by the numbers of the damned. He believed that the opponents of the torments of hell greatly exaggerated these numbers, and he reinterpreted the New Testament texts to suggest that half would be saved and half damned. Not unreasonably for the middle of the eighteenth century, he estimated infant mortality at 50 per cent, and since 'One half of our Species die, perhaps, before they have actually committed any Sin to deserve the Damnation of Hell ... it may be reasonably hoped that they will *escape* it.'[167] This was no doubt of comfort to infants, previously doomed to damnation by Augustine if unbaptised, or at best deprived of the Beatific Vision in an eternal limbo. Adults may have felt less comforted. For Horbery's statistics suggested that the population of heaven would consist largely of babies, the majority of adults having been consigned to the infernal regions.

One could speculate that the high probability of being among the damned rather than the saved, and this from the point of death, must have been a great psychological weight for many Protestants to bear. The morally static nature of life after death undoubtedly led to a greater emphasis on living morally and religiously on this side of the grave to ensure, as far as possible, that one was among the elect. As Max Weber remarked, 'without its power [the idea of the afterlife], overshadowing everything else, no moral awakening which seriously influenced practical life came into being in that period'.[168] And this was true whether one was inclined to Predestinarianism or Arminianism.

Be that as it may, there were a number who questioned the static nature of the afterlife. As we saw in the last chapter, Francis van Helmont and Lady Conway argued that, although souls could do nothing for themselves, they could be purged by God. This was a Protestant version of purgatory in which the mercy and justice of God replaced the suffrages of those still living to mitigate the sufferings of souls after death by means of purifying them. The reason for *postmortem* punishments, for Lady Conway, was medicinal, 'that by them these diseased creatures may be cured and restored to a better condition than before they enjoyed'.[169]

Like Lady Conway, the Cambridge Platonist Peter Sterry was committed to the ultimate salvation of all, though unlike her and many of his Platonist colleagues, he was also a believer in predestination. But the harshness of predestination was tempered for Sterry by the fact that all could look forward to an ultimate happiness: 'the rain will be over; the storm pass't away. The sweet, the clear, the Golden, the glorious smiles of Love will return after the Storm, and Rain...Wrath is but for a moment; at longest the moment of this Life, this Shadow, this short Dream of Lifes. The Truth of Life, the Perpetuity of Life, Eternity is for Love.'[170]

Sterry's most detailed account of life after death is contained in a small manuscript entitled 'That the state of wicked men after this Life is mixt of evill, and good things.' The saints were gathered immediately at death into the unity of the eternal Spirit.[171] The damned were 'empty, deformed Shades' who went into a shadowy world of darkness. There, they were tormented by deep regrets for their wickedness: 'Thus the sense of their losse, restlesse desyres, and pursuites, perpetuall frustrations, and disappointments with the feares, cares, anguishes, and torments that accompany these, are the knawings of that worm which never dies in them.'[172]

The wicked would also suffer in the flames of hell fire. But, for Sterry, the flames of hell fire were identified with the love of God: 'If he [God] meet with any pure and sweet Spirit, like himself; he closeth with it, in all manner of gentleness, and softness, as *Two Flames* embrace one another. But where he meets with opposition he rageth. He burns upon dark, unclear, intractable Hearts, as *Fire* in the *Ironworks*; till he hath poured them forth into the Temper, and Mold of his Spirit and Image.'[173] Thus, in the outermost darkness, the wicked would none the less feel their ultimate unity with God, and would come to realise that, through their sufferings, they would pass into eternal rest, joy, and glory. The suffering of evil spirits after death, Sterry wrote, 'is as the work of a goldsmith trying, and refining the Gold by fire, untill the drosse be entyrely consumed, that it may come forth pure, shining, and incorruptible'.[174]

The afterlife envisaged by Sterry was, like that in purgatory, morally static. Individuals could do nothing themselves to alter their posthumous status or ultimate destiny; all depended finally on the grace of God. But others, similarly dissatisfied with the fixing of the destiny of the soul at death, opted for a morally dynamic state between death and the day of judgement. That is to say, the possibilities of individual repentance, of moral and religious development, and consequently of divine forgiveness and the gift of salvation, were extended beyond the grave. This was perhaps the most significant development in conceptions of life after death in the seventeenth century. For it was an innovation in the history of Christian thought about the afterlife, which was to reach its zenith in Immanuel Kant's argument that, not only was moral development possible in the afterlife, but the demand of the human reason for moral perfection could only be satisfied by the postulation of a *post-mortem* eternity in which the self could become morally perfect.

A clear example of this was offered by the Platonist Henry Hallywell in his *A Private Letter of Satisfaction to a Friend* in 1667.[175] In this work, Hallywell argued against the notion of the sleep of the soul until the day of resurrection on two grounds. First, he argued, if the soul slept until the last day, it would lose all memory of its earthly life and be unaware of why, after the last judgement, it was being rewarded or punished. Second, he put forward the familiar argument linking mortalism with libertinism. Sensuality, he maintained, 'is the great Patronesse of this heartless and dull fancy, of the Soul's Sleep after death'.[176]

According to Hallywell, therefore, there were rewards for the good immediately after death, and shame and misery for the impious. But he was not convinced that the Scriptures made it clear that the good went to heaven and the wicked to hell. Rather, he suggested, on rational grounds, it would be more appropriate for all to go to an intermediate state after death until the resurrection. He was careful to distinguish it from purgatory, primarily because, whereas purgatory was penitential, his intermediate state was purificatory and morally dynamic:

by this middle State I mean no such condition of Being, as that wherein a man from his impious transactions in this life, shall undergo very sharp and acute torments, the protraction or abbreviation of which yet, depend upon the will and pleasure of his Holiness and mercenary Priests... but, such a state, wherein, by a due purification of their minds, and subjugation of those stubborn lusts and desires which exalt themselves against the life of God... the Soul of Man becomes wholly dead to every inordinate affection.[177]

In particular, Hallywell found it unsatisfactory that, granted that most do not perfect themselves in piety during their life-times, 'the infinitely far greater part of men are damned'.[178] And, as a Platonist, he found it inconsistent with the goodness of God to allow the majority to be born into circumstances where there would be little hope of recovering the image of God in their souls and everlasting misery the inevitable outcome. Consequently, free will was extended beyond the grave, and souls in the middle state were thus able morally to improve themselves: 'surely it would be a great eye-sore and blemish in heavens righteous Oeconomy and dispensation in the World, if there were really no time or means allowed for the recovery of these lapsed souls'.[179]

Hallywell's doctrine of a morally dynamic life after death opened up the possibility of salvation not only for those who had heard the Gospel and had responded appropriately or otherwise, but also for those who had lived in ignorance of it. For the possibility of salvation now extended beyond the hour of death. To be sure, all this did not imply that all would ultimately be saved. And Hallywell did not argue against the possibility of eternal torments after the day of resurrection. But nevertheless, his vision of a morally dynamic middle state, although it did not ensure that all would be saved, made it possible that all *could* be saved.

The belief that, in getting rid of the doctrine of purgatory, the Protestant Reformation may have thrown out the baby with the bathwater was also held by Bishop Archibald Campbell of Aberdeen. He held that Protestantism had failed to distinguish what was popish from what was primitive. And like Hallywell, he detested the notion that only those who were without any sin at the moment of their deaths were to be saved, since this meant so many were inevitably to be damned. 'This attacks', he declared, 'the *Love* of God, and wounds the *Charity* of Man, for thus we must Despair of the *Salvation* of almost *all Mankind*... Therefore I abominate and abhor this *Doctrine*, as *Cruel*, as *Barbarous*, as *Unbecoming* the *Infinite Goodness, Love*, and *Mercy of God*...'[180] His task, as he saw it, was to re-establish the doctrine of the middle state of souls as it was taught by the early Church Fathers. His account of the state of souls after death was especially reminiscent of Augustine.[181]

According to Campbell, at death, souls proceeded to Hades where they remained until the resurrection. Hades was divided into two sides with a series of mansions within each: one for righteous souls that would ultimately be admitted into the Beatific Vision; and the other for the wicked who, after reunion with their bodies on the day of judgement, would proceed to hell. Between these a great gulf was fixed so that 'none of the *Souls* which are upon the *Right Hand Side* are in any manner of *Danger* of falling into the *Prison of Gehenna*, or can any on the Left Hand *Side* penetrate into that of the *Right*'.[182] For those on the right-hand side of Hades, progress from mansion to mansion towards paradise proper was possible, though the gulf between the mansions of paradise and the lower mansions could not be entered until the soul had been purified and purged: 'This *Gulf* hinders those who are in the *Mansions* of *Purgation* and *Purification* from entering into the *proper Paradise* until they are duly *Qualified* for such *Admission*, in the *Lower Mansions*, by *Purgation* and *Purification* ...'[183]

As for Hallywell, so also for Campbell, for those being purified, the flames of hell were the purging flames of the Divine Love. And although they were in pain, it was to them a pleasure, because the soul 'is *Resigned* most Humbly to *God*, and therefore is well satisfied with it, and also it is *Sensible* that this *Purification* is *Necessary*, and will *Effectually* make it Pure, Holy, and perfectly *Happy*'.[184] So also in paradise, souls were active in making advances in perfection and improving their happiness, just as in this life souls increased their piety and happiness.

Nevertheless, in spite of the morally dynamic nature of the middle state, both Hallywell and Campbell did want to suggest that the prayers of those on this side of the grave could assist souls on the other. As Hallywell suggested, if the dead are in a state of being bettered, 'they may likewise receive good and advantage by our prayers'.[185]

Prayers for the dead were, as we have seen, part of the medieval doctrine of purgatory. But Campbell attempted to legitimate them as a part of primitive Christianity. And he was right to do so. Christians appear to have prayed for the dead from a very early period. There is ample evidence of the practice in the inscriptions of the Catacombs, and early liturgies commonly contained commemorations of the dead. A number of the early Church Fathers were familiar with it. Consider Augustine's heartfelt prayer for his mother after her death: 'I know that she dealt mercifully, and from her heart forgave those who trespassed against her: do Thou also forgive such trespasses as she may have been guilty of in all the years since her baptism, forgive them, Lord, forgive them, I beseech Thee: enter not into judgement with her.'[186] Later, in *The City of God*, Augustine again took up the issue of prayers for the dead. While he believed that prayer could do nothing for the damned, he suggested they were of help to those persons who were neither particularly good nor particularly evil: 'on behalf of certain dead the prayer of the Church, or of certain pious men, is heard, but only on behalf of those who were born again in

Christ and whose life on earth was not so badly lived that they are judged unworthy of such mercy, nor yet so well lived that they are found to have no need of such mercy'.[187]

Archibald Campbell stood in this Augustinian tradition. He distinguished four classes among the departed. First were those who died without repentance who went straight to the left-hand side of Hades to await final punishment. Second, there were those who, having repented on their death-beds, went to the lower mansions on the right-hand side. These would remain uncertain of their fate on the day of judgement. Among the third class were those who repented but died before their lives were sufficiently grounded in habits of virtue. This group 'shall be carried by the *Holy Angels*, upon their *Exodos*, their *Death*, into some or other of the *Mansions* on the *Right Hand side* of *Hades*, and their go through such *Purgations* as are necessary for their *Purification* ... '[188] The final group consisted of those pure souls who would proceed directly into the uppermost places of paradise.

Prayers for the dead should be directed, suggested Campbell, to these three last groups: to the second group, more out of charity than in any expectation of their salvation; to the third group, in the hope of their being refreshed while in the purifying fire of God's love; and, since we on this side of the grave cannot fix any individual to any of these classes, even to those who had apparently died '*in the Sign of Faith*, in *the Peace of the Church*'.[189] And if, ultimately, all were finally left in the hands of a loving and merciful God, Campbell's reassertion of prayers for the dead at least allowed the living a hope for and a charity towards those who, not paragons of virtue on this side of the grave, were presumed to be progressing through the labyrinthine mansions of the middle state towards the Beatific Vision after the day of judgement.

The principle that the punishments of the state of the soul from the hour of death to the day of judgement were curative or medicinal, or that the state of the soul was not fixed at death but could morally progress in the afterlife, effectively created a Protestant purgatory, although with the differences we have noted. The rejection of the Catholic doctrine had created a harsh either/or at the moment of death – either eternal happiness or eternal punishment. Those dissatisfied with this did not reintroduce a purgatorial system in which the release from punishment depended upon the initiatives of those on this side of the grave with all its attendant ecclesiastical abuses. But, by suggesting that individuals could find release from *post-mortem* punishments either through their own repentance or by virtue of divine curative graces, the abuses of the Catholic tradition were perceived as having been avoided, and the major strength of the purgatorial system – that for most of us our ultimate destiny need not be determined at the moment of death – could be embraced.

CHAPTER 3

The contours of heaven and hell

HELL'S TORMENTS

We have heard ... of some who have endured breaking on the Wheel, ripping up of their Bowels, fleaing alive, racking of Joynts, burning of Flesh, pounding in a Mortar, tearing in pieces with Flesh-hooks, boyling in Oyl, roasting on hot fiery Gridirons, etc. And yet all these, tho' you should superad thereto all Diseases, such as the Plague, Stone, Gout, Strangury, or whatever else you can name most torturing to the Body ... they would all come short ... of that Wrath, that Horror, that unconceivable Anguish which the Damned must inevitably suffer every Moment, without any Intermission of their Pains, in Hellish Flames.[1]

Readers of John Shower in 1700 would have been quite familiar with the spectacle of sufferings inflicted publicly on the bodies of those convicted of crime. Public punishments, corporal and capital, were dramatic representations of the power of life and death which the body politic held over its subjects. Capital punishment was intended to deter, and to terrify those who witnessed it. And the farewell speech of the convicted was intended for the admonishment and betterment of its listeners. In 1680 for example, John Marketman, convicted of the murder of his wife, made a typical speech, declaring

That he had been very disobedient to his too indulgent parents, and that he had spent his youthful days in profanation of the Sabbath and licentious evils of debaucheries beyond expression, and that he had been over penurious in his narrow observance of his wive's ways, desirous that all should pray to the Eternal God for his everlasting welfare, and with many pious expressions ended this mortal life.[2]

Shower's readers also lived intimately with pain and disease. Bubonic plague and smallpox were the biggest killers. But dysentery, intestinal worms, malarial fevers, and tuberculosis were also rife. Considering the sanitary conditions in cities and towns in seventeenth- and eighteenth-century England, this was inevitable. Contemporary descriptions of eighteenth century towns are, to the modern reader, like descriptions of hell. As Lawrence Stone describes them,

> the city ditches, now often filled with stagnant water, were commonly used as latrines; butchers killed animals in their shops and threw the offal of the carcases into the streets; dead animals were left to decay and fester where they lay; latrine pits were dug close to wells... Decomposing bodies of the rich in burial vaults beneath the church often stank out parson and congregation; urban cemeteries became overcrowded as the population grew, and the decaying bodies... began to pollute the air of the neighbourhood.[3]

However much intensified, the punishments of the damned reflected those with which Shower's contemporaries were all too familiar in their every-day lives.

The nature and extent of hell's torments were a familiar feature of any account of the afterlife – whether of the period before the last judgement or that which followed it. The Puritan divine Richard Baxter's *The Saints' Everlasting Rest*, a work written as he put it 'with one foot in the grave, by a man that was betwixt living and dead', was typical. While the major part of his book was an exposition of the reward of the godly, the sufferings of the wicked were not neglected. Like Shower's, Baxter's descriptions of hell's torments were intensifications of suffering on this side of the divide. Both the soul and the body would suffer:

> If it be an intolerable thing to suffer the heat of the fire for a year, or a day, or an hour, what will it be to suffer ten thousand times more for ever? What if thou wert to suffer Lawrence's death, to be roasted upon a gridiron; or to be scraped or pricked to death as other martyrs were; or if thou wert to feed upon toads for a year together? If thou couldst not endure such things as these, how wilt thou endure the eternal flames?[4]

Baxter's hell was a world of social reversal – a Puritan's revenge for what he saw as the sins of the social elite. The rich man in hell would not be a gorgeous, well-dressed gallant; there would be no powdering or curling of the hair, no expectations of admiring glances. The social activities of which Baxter disapproved would be absent – no cards, dice, hunting, dancing, stage plays, nor drinking; neither lascivious discourse, amorous songs, nor wanton dalliance: 'Oh that sinners would remember this in the midst of their pleasure and jollity, and say to one another, We must shortly reckon for this before the jealous God.'[5] The preacher would have his reward for the laughter and derision he had suffered. Baxter's fantasy of the laughing God is sadistic and cruel: 'Is it not a terrible thing to a wretched soul, when it shall lie roaring perpetually in the flames of hell, and the God of mercy himself shall laugh at them; when ... God shall mock them instead of relieving them; when none in heaven or earth can help them but God, and he shall rejoice over them in their calamity.'[6] Baxter's God was an executioner, insensible to mercy, the avenger of sweet-smelling voluptuousness, of hedonistic delights, of the pleasures of town and countryside. The inaptly named Puritan Christopher Love similarly rejoiced in the prospect of the laughter of God at the sufferings of the damned: 'when thou art scorching in thy flames, when thou art howling in thy torments, then shall God laugh at thy destruction, and then the Saints of God shall sing and rejoyce, that thou art a vessel of his justice, and so his power and wrath are made known in thee'.[7]

On the one hand, then, the sufferings of hell were magnifications of the pains of illness and disease with which the seventeenth century was all too familiar. Thomas Vincent reminded his readers of the pains they had already experienced in their heads, bowels, legs and teeth. These were nothing, he argued, in contrast to the pains of hell. 'You shall be extreamly and eternally tortured', he wrote, 'with pain in every part, your eyes shall be full of pain, your tongues full of pain, your heads full of pain, your backs full of pain, your bellies full of pain, your feet full of pain ... no part shall be free; your bodies shall roul and tumble in flames, and there burn with horrible pain, and yet never be consumed.'[8] Richard Younge was a Calvinist well known for his view that this world was the hell of the godly, the next that of the ungodly. Like Shower and Vincent, he maintained that the pains of hell would be worse than the pangs of death and childbirth, scalding lead, drinks of gall and wormwood, griping of chest worms, fits of the stone, gout, and strangury: 'Are these, and all other pains that can be named put together, but *shadows*, and *flea-bitings* to it?'[9] To Richard Stafford, all the evils, pains, fears, diseases, and afflictions throughout the whole earth 'do not make up the ten thousandth part so bad as the Torments of Hell'.[10] Christopher Love emphasised not only the variety of sufferings but the universality of them:

Upon earth, you have diseases haply; but though some parts are afflicted, other parts are free; though you be ill in your body, yet your head may be free; though ill in your head, yet vitals free; though ill in your vitals, yet arms and legs free; there is no disease that puts the whole body in pain at once: but in hell it is not so, in hell all the parts of your bodies, and powers of your souls shall be tormented ... [11]

On the other hand, the sufferings of the damned were magnifications of the sufferings of criminals. The penal system of the damned was a projection of the early modern penal system. Sadism and piety combined. The divine Judge was an omnipotent replica of earthly judges. For Baxter, as for his contemporaries, the purpose of punishment for those convicted of crime was retributive, and the conscious infliction of physical suffering in a public context was central. Descriptions of the sufferings of the damned functioned as linguistic correlates to the visual spectacle of the punishments of criminals. Like these, they were intended both to admonish and to terrify. For John Bunyan, a sense of guilt was necessary to the reception of grace. And Bunyan's emphasis on the terrors of hell was meant to prepare the sinner for repentance. Bunyan's God was a vengeful one, and one whose punishments in hell justified the brutal sentences handed down in the criminal courts – 'those petty judgments among men, as putting in the stocks, whipping or burning in the hand'.[12] The worst tortures imaginable on this earth, maintained Bunyan, were as flea-bites to the sufferings of those who go down into hell fire. 'I will give you the scope of them in a similitude', he wrote:

Set case you should take a man, and tie him to a stake, and with red hot Pincers pinch off his flesh by little pieces for two or three years together, and at last, when the poor man cryes out for ease and help, the tormentors answer, Nay but besides all this you must be handled worse. We will serve you thus these 20. years together, and after that we will fill your mangled body full of scalding lead, and run you through with a red hot spit, would not this be lamentable? ... But he that goes to hell shall suffer ten thousand times worse torments then these, and yet shall never be quite dead under them.[13]

Hell was an assault upon the senses. According to Christopher Love,

The eye it shall be tormented with the sight of Divels. The ear shall be tormented with the yellings and hideous outcries of the damned in flames. The nostrils shall be smothered with brimstone, to choak you: the tongue with a flame; the whole body (in a word) shall be tormented in flames of fire; there is no part of the body, neither hand, foot, tongue, nor eye, but shall be subjects of those flames.[14]

Thus, the eyes would be affronted by horrible sights. 'Did lust enter at the Eye from corporeall Beauties?' asked Robert Sharrock of Winchester Cathedral. 'In Hell', he wrote, 'Horror shall more abundantly enter there from ghastly sights.'[15] The nose would be assaulted by smells, far worse than those of the early modern town and city. 'Your dainty delicate persons', declared the Anglican William Gearing, 'that now cannot brook the least savoury smell, shall lie down in a stinking dungeon, in a loathsome lake, that burns with fire and brimstone for ever.'[16] The stench of the foetid damned was a physical manifestation of the stench of sin. The sense of smell, argued Thomas Vincent, would be affronted by 'suffocating odours and nasty stench, worse than of Carrion, or that which cometh out of an open sepulchre'.[17]

In the early modern period, the ceremony of secular justice demanded that the guilty should cry and moan in their punishments.[18] The cries of the damned similarly punctuated the divine justice in hell. The damned 'shall ever be whining, pining, weeping, mourning, ever tormented without ease', wrote Bunyan.[19] According to Thomas Vincent, the ear would be afflicted 'with hideous noises, shreeks and yellings of fellow damned sinners'.[20] The terrors of hell were multiplied for Baxter by the shrieks and cries of one's companions, by children crying out against their parents, husbands against wives and wives against husbands, masters and servants, ministers and people, magistrates and subjects, cursing and recriminating with each other into the infinite future.[21] The ear that laughed at religion, wrote William Sharrock, will take its farewell of ancient pleasures and 'content itself if it can with the variety of Noises that shall be found in the howlings and drummings of *Tophet*'.[22]

The horrors of this eternal cacophony of misery and blame were augmented by the screams of devils. The damned, imagined Gearing, would be affronted by the horrid noise of damned ghosts, 'crying and roaring out with doleful shriekings...'[23] In this world, suggested John Bunyan, the very thought of devils appearing was sufficient to make the flesh tremble and the hair stand up on end. The spirits of the wicked would be daunted by hobgoblin and foul fiend. What will you do, he asked, 'when not onely the supposition of the devils appearing, but the reall society of all the devils in hell to be with thee howling and roaring, screeching and yelling in such a hideous manner, that thou wilt be even at thy wits end, and be ready to run starke madde again for anguish and torment'.[24] Christopher Love cited St Anselm to the effect that he 'would rather endure all the torments that art or nature can devise, then see the Divel with my bodily eyes; then see him as he afflicts and torments the damned in hell'.[25]

In hell, one's companions were both the wicked and devils. Men and devils descended to the bestial. One could expect nothing from such company, remarked William Dawes, in a sermon to King William and Queen Anne, 'but continual jangling, hatred, anger, snarling, and biting at one another, nothing but the most terrible Fears and jealousies of, the most malicious and spiteful bickerings, against each other'.[26] The devils were both tormenting and tormented.[27] To William Bates the title 'him who has the power of death' signified the Devil's 'tormenting Sinners with unrelenting Cruelty in Hell, which is the second Death'.[28] According to Henry More, wicked souls would be exposed to grim and remorseless officers of Justice as devoid of any sense of good as those that they would punish. These demons 'satiate their lascivient cruelty with all manner of abuses and torments they can imagine...'[29] These demons themselves would be tortured in ways far above 'what the cruellest Tyranny has inflicted here, either upon the guilty or innocent'.[30] Christopher Love made the analogy between the sadism of devils in hell and the mercy of earthly executioners:

Beloved, it would somewhat lessen a mans torments, though a man were condemned to endure some punishment, if the man that was to be his executioner, were a mercifull man; if he would spare him what he might: If a man were to be burnt in the hand, if the man that was to burn him would spare him, and hardly touch him, he would count it a great happiness: it would somewhat lessen your torments were they but mercifull creatures in hell. But who are your tormenters? Your tormenters are Divels, in whom is no pity, who will not spare, but will torment you as much as they are able to inflict, or you to bear: Be sure your tormenters will have no mercy; but they will load you with rivers of brimstone, and mountaines of fire to the utmost...[31]

The punishments inflicted by the devils upon the wicked were at God's behest. They were God's executioners. They manifested the glory and justice of God. In demonological theory, demons had only as much power as God allowed them to exercise. God could not be excused the malevolence of devils. They were tormenters and executioners to wicked men, wrote Thomas Bromhall in his *Treatise of Specters*, 'that so his Justice might shine the more glorious, to the comfort of the Godly, and of his Elect ... '[32] Thus, God was ultimately responsible for the activities of demons on this side of the grave and the other. Let no man imagine, declared the Calvinist Thomas Goodwin, 'that Devils are the greatest Tormenters of Men, or of their Consciences in Hell: or if any would affirm it, I would demand, who it is that torments the Consciences of Devils themselves? Certainly none but God.'[33]

It is important to note that, from the end of the seventeenth century, at least among the literate, hell's population became significantly depleted. References to devils, their presence in hell, and their tormenting of the wicked disappeared from the literature. And, one might add, the role that the devil and his minions played in the everyday world went into a similar decline. The baroque fantasy of Satanic compacts, of witches' Sabbaths, and devil worship began to lose its purchase in the mental furniture of the European mind. The philosophical naturalism of such as Hobbes and Descartes banished demons from the natural world. The progressive assumption of the orderly regular universe of the new science made increasingly untenable the capricious intervention of demons.

The intervention of demons, and their power in earthly and aerial regions, implied a view of nature which was looking increasingly absurd. And with their role minimised in the natural world, their part in the infernal realm correspondingly declined. In a hell which some at least were coming to see as reformative rather than retributive, the demonic ministers of retributive justice became redundant. But even among those who remained convinced that hell torments were retributive, the geography of hell changed, and the sufferings of the damned were no longer superintended by the dark King of the infernal regions, but only by the effulgent divine and heavenly King, whose dark, flaming wrath engulfed the wicked.

THE DARK FIRES OF HELL

A variety of biblical images served to emphasise hell's horrors. It was a bottomless pit of darkness, utter darkness, a furnace of fire, a lake that burned with fire and brimstone, a dark and tormenting prison, the blackness of darkness, chains of darkness. All were agreed that the wicked would be punished with fire, though the description of Joseph Trapp, Oxford University's first Professor of Poetry, was more fevered than many in its collation of fiery metaphors:

> Doom'd to live death and never to expire;
> In floods and whirlwinds of tempestuous fire
> The damn'd shall groan, – fire of all kinds and forms,
> In rain and hail, in hurricanes and storms,
> Liquid and solid, livid, red and pale,
> A flaming mountain here, and there a flaming vale,
> The liquid fire makes seas; the solid, shores:
> Arch'd o'er with flames the horrid concave roars.
> In bubbling eddies rolls the fiery tide,
> And sulphurous surges on each other ride.
> The hollow winding vaults, and dens and caves,
> Bellow like furnaces with flaming waves.
> Pillars of flame in spiral volume rise,
> Like fiery snakes, and lick the infernal skies.
> Sulphur, the eternal fuel unconsumed,
> Vomits redounding smoke, thick, unillumed.[34]

But there was some debate about the quality of hell fire. Some, like the Baptist Samuel Richardson in his *A Discourse of the Torments of Hell*, argued that the notion of a corporeal fire was incoherent. He suggested that since hell was a place of darkness, and a real corporeal fire would provide light, the fire of hell could not be real. Any corporeal fire, he argued, was extinguishable, and since the fires of hell were not, they could not be physical fires. Moreover, he suggested a corporeal fire could not work on spirits. He refused to sanction the argument that God's omnipotence would overcome such obstacles: 'to say God is able to make corporal Fire work upon a Spirit, and able to make to live without food or refreshment to eternity, and to make fire burn without wood, is no proof that he will do so, and is as silly a kind of reasoning, as to say God is able to do all things, ... therefore he will do all things.'[35]

Most held to the view that the flames of hell were real. John Brandon, for example, in his response to Richardson, maintained that hell fire was real although it contained unique properties by virtue of divine power. 'I see no reason at all to the contrary', he declared, 'but that we may suppose the Fire that shall torment the Bodies of the wicked to be real and corporal fire, as ours is, though perhaps not of the same kind.'[36] Thomas Vincent in 1670 clearly had the Great Fire of London in his mind in his suggestion that, although

corporeal, the dark, fierce, irresistible, unquenchable, everlasting
fires of hell would far exceed experience of earthly fire – which was
like the biting of a flea or the prick of a pin in comparison. In the vast
bottomless pit, the wicked would see 'themselves on Fire, Head,
Back, Breast, Belly, Hands, Arms, Legs, Feet, every part on fire, and
that such a fire though it doth torment them, yet that shall not be
able to consume them'.[37]

Apart from the fires of hell, its major characteristic was darkness.
'...in Hell there is utter darkness', remarked Richard Stafford in
1697.[38] For Thomas Vincent, 'Hell is called by the name of utter
darkness.'[39] The darkness of hell emphasised its penal quality – its
dungeon-like nature and demonic ambience. The torments of hell
were increased by the absence of any consolatory light. The greatest
part of the dead, claimed Bishop William Beveridge in a sermon
before the Queen in 1690, 'live with the fiends of Hell, in the infernal
pit, where they have no light, nothing but darkness and horrour to
the utmost extremity round about them'.[40]

Even the fires of hell were dark. The natural order was overturned.
While the righteous enjoyed light without heat, the damned suffered
heat without light. As Thomas Goodwin put it in 1680, 'the same
God, who appears all in Flames, and as a devouring Fire, unto
Hypocrites in Hell; is all light and Beauty to the Upright in
Heaven'.[41] The darkness of hell fire was a traditional part of the
Christian image of hell. John Milton's description of hell in *Paradise
Lost* as

> A Dungeon horrible, on all sides round
> As one great Furnace flam'd, yet from those flames
> No light, but rather darkness visible
> Serv'd onely to discover sights of woe... [42]

stood in a tradition developed by the Church Fathers, utilised by the
scholastic philosophers, and articulated by Chaucer.[43] Robert
Sharrock's warnings of the lowermost hell, of the labyrinth of
darkness from which there was no escape, of the 'burning allwaies
but never shining fire',[44] and of the torments of a 'black and dark
fire'[45] were familiar images to his readers. But although there would
be no light from the flames of hell, visions of horror would remain.
To Thomas Vincent,

the fire itself will give no light, all will be dark and black, black Devils,
black Bodies, black Souls, and they may without light have perceivance one

of another, as devils have now unto whom light is no use; or if there be a duskish light there, to represent one anothers ruful countenances, and other frightful spectacles, be sure there will be no refreshing light, there the damned will be in a place and state of darkness for ever.[46]

PUNISHMENTS, BODY AND SOUL

Still, there was at least one mitigating factor in all this, namely, that the torments of the damned would be proportionate to their sins. While it was not much discussed, it was generally unquestioned. The proportionality of punishment and sin was inherited by English Protestantism from the medieval consensus. As we saw in the last chapter, the doctrine of purgatory assumed such a proportionality, though one which took into account both the quality and the time of suffering. That the torments of hell were graded was endorsed by the Councils of Lyons in AD 1274 and Florence in AD 1439. Dante's works intricately depicted the grading of both rewards and punishments in the heavenly and infernal realms. And in spite of their commitment to the doctrine of justification by faith, which implied that the joys of heaven were independent of the merits of the righteous and were a divine gift, neither Luther nor Calvin rejected the gradation of pains and joys.[47]

The gradation of hell's torments reflected a belief in the gradation of sins. N. Orchard in 1676 saw a strict proportionality of sin and punishment: 'There are without doubt degrees of sin here, and will be of Torments in that infernal Tophet... according to the Dimensions and Aggravation of the Sins...'[48] To William Bates in 1691, all the damned would be equally miserable in their despair, yet the degrees of their torment would be different: 'Sins of Ignorance are extenuated in comparison of rebellious Sins against Knowledge... and as they incur greater Guilt will expose to greater Punishment.'[49] That sufferings were to be graded in hell reflected too a commitment to retributive justice. William Dodwell was a strong believer in the eternity of hell's torments, but he recognised that the concept of God's justice required that the punishments fitted the crime: 'the positive degrees of misery shall be inflicted in exact proportion to the Demerit of the Offenders'.[50]

In her discussion of the degrees of glory, Emma Disley makes the point that, while a proportionality between sin and punishment was rendered possible by the understanding that such punishments were deserved, it was far more difficult to argue that there were degrees of glory for the righteous, because it suggested that they had merited their rewards. Nevertheless, during the century after the English Reformation with which she is primarily concerned, she concludes that the majority of Protestants retained the concept of the gradation of rewards for the righteous.[51] The same must be said of the following century, although in a period less committed to the doctrine of predestination and more inclined to assertions of the freedom of the will, there were fewer difficulties in aligning rewards for virtue with God's gift of salvation. Biblical precedents, for gradations of both reward and punishment, remained important.

Crucial was the necessity of maintaining a symmetry of contrasts between heaven and hell. If the sufferings of hell were graded, so too were the joys of heaven. Justice entailed a proportionate distribution of both rewards and punishments. In response to the question, 'Are all equally happy in heaven?', *The Athenian Gazette* remarked, 'If degrees of Punishment in Hell, there must be of Happiness in Heaven: One there is, or else all sins were equal; the other consequently there must be, for there is a right unto, and justice in Rewards as well as Punishments...'[52]

The question of degrees of suffering in hell was also intimately connected to the scholastic distinction between the punishment of loss (*poena damni*) and the punishment of the senses (*poena sensus*). The former of these was the pain which consisted in deprivation of the Beatific Vision and the consequent sense of grief, loss, and anguish; the latter, the physical punishments primarily inflicted by fire. To Milton, 'the second death, or the punishment of the damned, seems to consist partly in the loss of the chief good, namely, the favor and protection of God, and the beatific vision of his presence, which is commonly called the punishment of loss, and partly in eternal torment, which is called the punishment of sense'.[53] The Scriptural justification for this distinction arose from Isaiah 66.24: 'And they shall go forth, and look upon the carcases of the men that have transgressed against me: for their worm shall not die, neither shall their fire be quenched; and they shall be an abhorring unto all flesh.'

During the period of the Counter-Reformation, the worm that dieth not, the ever-gnawing worm, was often read as a literal punishment to be undergone in hell.[54] The popular belief that worms spontaneously generated from putrefying flesh was the direct impetus for this interpretation.[55] But, although it did little perhaps to lessen the horror, generally, in both Catholicism and Protestantism, the worm, and its power to breed spontaneously amid decay, was interpreted figuratively as the torments of grief and envy. The Independent divine William Strong used the metaphor of the eternal worm in a sermon on Mark 9.48, and its description of hell as the place where the worm dieth not and the fire is never quenched. Worms, he declared, are something despicable, tormenting, and continually vexing. If worms, he preached,

> should breed in a man, and feed upon him whilst he were alive, it would be much more terrible; as it was a torment invented by a Tyrant to keep a man in a Coffin, and feed him, till by his own filth he breed worms, and these worms devoured his flesh, and he dyed from them... but what will it be for a worm to be gnawing upon the soul for ever?[56]

Conscience, he declared, was the worm that ever gnaws: 'a Worm is bred out of the putrefaction of the subject in which it is; now in the conscience of men there is much corruption, the conscience is as it were the sink where all the evil in a man is...'[57]

The body was physically punished by fire. The fire was seldom interpreted metaphorically. Among the Church Fathers, only a few, amongst whom was Origen, interpreted the fire of hell as equivalent to remorse, regret, and so on.[58] Calvin's suggestion that the plain meaning of Isaiah 66.24 was 'that the wicked shall have a bad conscience as an executioner, to torment them without end, and that torment awaits them greater than all other torments; and finally, that they shall tremble and be agitated in a dreadful and shocking manner, as if a worm were gnawing the heart of a man, or a fire were consuming it, and yet thus consumed, he did not die' was not generally accepted.[59] The Scriptural evidence too strongly suggested a real distinction between the 'fire' and the 'worm'. Tobias Swinden pointed out that to deny the distinction would entail a nonsense. Mark 9.43-4, 'it is better for thee to enter into life maimed, than having two hands to go into hell, into the fire that never shall be quenched: Where their worm dieth not, and the fire is not quenched', would mean 'It is better to be maimed than to go into hell, into vexation of mind that shall never cease, where their vexation of mind never ceaseth, and the vexation of mind never ceaseth...'[60]

There was, then, a general consensus that the damned would suffer both mental and physical torments. In the words of Richard Younge in 1658,

As the *eyes* shall be tormented with *ugly* and *fearfull sights*, of *ghastly spirits*; the *ears* with *hideous screeching*, and *crying out, howling* and *yelling* like *Dragons*; the *tongue* with *drought* and *thirst*, craving with the *rich glutton in hell*, but so much *water*, as *Lazarus* might bear on the tip of his finger to cool their tongues; and yet this is justly denied them. And for the *minde*, that is filled with *horror* and *ghastly terrors*, etc ... We cannot hold our *finger* for one minute in *scalding lead*; but there both *body* and *soul* shall *fry in everlasting flames*, and be continually tormented, by *infernall fiends*.[61]

The issue of how the damned were to suffer torments in their disembodied state prior to the resurrection of the flesh on the last day was a vexed one. The problem was solved within Scholastic Catholicism by imputing a corporeality to the soul by virtue of which physical punishments could be inflicted, as though the soul were corporeal. This rationale was utilised by the Catholic Nicholas Caussin in 1650. 'The soul separated from the body', he wrote, 'hath not a natural antipathy and disagreement from fire, but what this imperious element cannot have remaining within the limits of nature, it obtaineth by a particular ordinance and disposition of God ... to serve him, ... as an eternal messenger of his anger against a damned soul.'[62]

In late seventeenth-century Protestantism, neo-Platonic theories of the vehicles of the soul provided the same theoretical ground. For those who accepted the notion of the vehicles of the soul, physical torments could be inflicted upon the aerial bodies of the wicked. Thus, for Henry More, the torments of the conscience would bring the aery body into 'intolerable distempers, worse then death itself'.[63] But the aerial body would also be liable to physical torments from demons – 'those grim and remorseless *Officers of Justice*, who are as devoid of all sense of what is good as those that they shall punish'.[64] According to Ralph Cudworth, if the souls of wicked men were not embodied after death, they would have 'no manner of punishment inflicted on them, save only that of remorse of conscience, and future expectation'.[65] Unlike the Catholic Thomas White, who on the grounds of the impossibility of a *post-mortem* embodied state denied the possibility of physical punishments, Cudworth proposed the embodiment of souls immediately after death because of the desirability (to him) that the wicked should physically suffer.

But few Protestants were committed either to God's imputing a corporeality to the soul in the intermediate state to facilitate its physical torment, or to the neo-Platonic account of the vehicles of the soul. Rather, the general consensus was that, between death and the last judgement, the soul would suffer only the torments of loss, but after the last judgement, then reunited with its body, the whole person would suffer both the punishments of sense and the punishments of loss. Archibald Campbell explained the situation particularly clearly:

That they [the wicked] are punished *Privatively* even before their *Resurrection*, and have, what may be called a *Hell* within them, I make no doubt... Thus what torments they feel in their dark *Abyss*, before their *Resurrection* and *Judgement*, arise from the sense they have of their bad situation... but yet the *real Torments* which are proper to *Gehenna*, they do not actually feel until *that day*, that they are to be thrown into the Lake of *Fire and Brimstone*, irretrievably, and by an irreversible *Decree*, when they shall find and feel, not only a *Hell* within them, but also that they are in a *Hell* without them, in which they are to be *Tormented* throughout all the Ages of Ages...[66]

The placing of the punishment of the soul and the punishment of the body in a chronological sequence punctuated by the last judgement also enabled English Protestants to make more sense of their claims that, while there would be both rewards and punishments in the intermediate state, these would be added to after the final judgement. That is to say, the traditional distinction between *poena damni* and *poena sensus*, one used in Catholicism for both the intermediate state of the soul *and* the punishments of body and soul after the last judgement, functioned in Protestantism in service of *its* eschatology. It was difficult in Catholicism effectively to demonstrate how the state of the person after the final judgement could be worse than its prior state, since both mental and physical torments operated on both sides of this divide. To some extent, therefore, the last judgement was redundant, at least in terms of increased happiness or misery. But the Protestant inclination to limit mental torments to the incorporeal soul and physical torments to the resurrected body did imply that, even if one's ultimate destiny was fixed at death, the final judgement would significantly alter one's happiness or unhappiness. Thus, for example, *The Athenian Gazette* saw souls and bodies located in a physical hell after the day of judgement, although prior to it, souls were nowhere. The punishments were accordingly different:

We believe the greatest Torments of wicked Men before the Day of Judgment, and those bad enough, will be their own *Consciences*, and that *Company* they are *condemn'd to*: Which Torments will be both *augmented* instead of their *ceasing*, at the *Day of Judgment*, the first by having all their faults again represented to them and all the World, the second by being Eternally confined by an irreversible doom to those *Infernal Prisons* prepared for the Devil and his Angels. And for the contrary Reasons the *Joy* of the *Saints* must needs be at the same time highly augmented.[67]

CO-PARTNERS IN SIN

The punishment of the body was an essential part of the divine political economy. It was upon the bodies of the damned that their sins were visibly displayed, that the justice of God was manifest. To William Gearing, God's justice required 'that the same Body which hath been instrumental in the actions of righteousness, or unrighteousness, should be rewarded or punished'.[68] The body was, to the Calvinist Daniel Burgess, no mere adjunct to the soul but an essential part of the identity of the person. Thus punishment had to be meted out to the body as well as to the soul. 'Where were *God's Justice*', he inquired, 'if the threaten'd and well-deserved Punishments of Rebellion were executed only upon the *Souls* Rebelling. The *Bodies*, as if Guiltless escaping them; and feeling no more then the *light Afflictions which are but for a Moment*. Altho' they were the Soul's continual Consorts, from their Mother's Belly to the Grave's.'[69]

Because the body was an essential part of the individual, it was seen as a partner in sin, and therefore equally deserving of punishment. And because it was equally deserving of punishment, the resurrection of the body on the last day was a requirement of justice. In his *Death the Sweetest Sleep* in 1681, the nonconformist minister Thomas Lye found it to be 'most just that those *Bodies*, which have been the Souls *Co-partners* in doing good, or evil, should therefore *participate* in the reward and punishment: which cannot be done without a Resurrection'.[70] John Pearson, the Bishop of Chester, in his most well known work, *An Exposition of the Creed*, asserted the necessity of the resurrection of the body for the equitable distribution of reward and punishment.[71] Richard Younge spoke of the body after death, cast into the earth, 'expecting a *fearful resurrection*, when it shall be reunited to thy *soul*; that as they *sinned together*, so they may be everlastingly *tormented together*, ... '[72] John Bunyan used the same image of co-partners in sin to justify the physical torments of the damned.[73]

There were some who argued that only the soul was responsible for sin, and that consequently there was no necessity for the same body to arise on the last day. As we shall see further in the next chapter, those who were committed to the vehicles of the soul, placed little emphasis on the resurrection of the body of flesh, and thus were more inclined to see personal identity as only related to the soul. Henry More, for example, argued that not only was it not a matter of justice that the same physical body should be resurrected, but that it would be the greatest injustice, 'For so shall the Body of an old man be punished for the sins of that Body he had when he was young.'[74] And committed as he was to the notion of the same soul being progressively embodied with different kinds of vehicles, he located personal identity in the sameness of the soul: 'But it being most certain there is no *stable Personality* of a man but what is in his Soul, (for if the Body be Essential to this *numerical Identity*, a grown man has not the same individuation he had when he was Christned;) it is manifest, that if there be the *same Soul*, there is exactly the *same Person*; and that the change of the Body causes no more real difference of Personality then the change of cloaths.'[75] A similar point was made by Humphry Hody, chaplain to Archbishop Tillotson. He maintained that only the soul had sinned, and the notion that the same body that sinned ought to be punished was a nonsensical one: 'all the *Matter* which constituted the Body when the several sins were committed must be rais'd again...', and what monsters we then would be, he exclaimed.[76]

Be the logic of Hody's argument as it may, this was a case where for many the necessity to punish the body in the name of justice took priority. As the anonymous author of *The Resurrection founded on Justice* put it in his reply to Hody, 'The Body and the Soul are here joyned together as *sharers* in all the Concerns and Actions of this Life, which is a state of *Probation*, and therefore they are to stand or fall together in the next, which is a state of *Remuneration*.'[77] In a sermon preached on Easter Monday, 1719, Winch Holdsworth also saw the resurrection of the body as a requirement of divine justice. 'It seems highly congruous', he declared, 'to the *Justice* of God that *those very* bodies, which were *Partners with* and *Instruments to* the *Souls* of Men in the *Good* or *Evil* Actions they did in this Life, sh'd in the other be *Partners with* and *Instruments to* the *Happiness* or *Misery* due to their Sins or Vertues.'[78]

ABOMINABLE FANTASIES

The sufferings of the damned in hell were also augmented by their vision of the happiness of the blessed in heaven. The Biblical justification was the story of Dives the rich man and Lazarus the beggar. The rich man in hell lifted up 'his eyes, being in torments, and seeth Abraham afar off, and Lazarus in his bosom' (Luke 16.23). On the basis of this text, John Bunyan saw the torments of hell increased by the sight of friends, neighbours, acquaintances, even one's father, mother, wife, husband, children, brothers and sisters, enjoying bliss. And on the basis of Luke 13.28–9, he rejoiced that 'There shall come from the East and from the West, that is, those that thou didst never see in all thy life before, and they shall sit down with thy friends, and thy neighbours, thy wife and thy children in the kingdom of heaven, and thou for thy sins and disobedience shalt be shut out, nay, thrust out. O wonderfull torment!'[79] Joseph Stevens made it a central feature of his book, *The Whole Parable of Dives and Lazarus, Explain'd and Apply'd*, in 1697.[80]

In the contrasting symmetries of heaven and hell, just as the sufferings of the damned were increased by the vision of the joys of the blessed, so also the joys of the righteous were heightened by the vision across the great divide of the torments of the wicked. This 'abominable fancy', as F. W. Farrar called it, was a reversal of the story of Dives and Lazarus.[81] But it had its supporters in Augustine and Tertullian, in Thomas Aquinas and Peter of Lombardy. As John Dunton summed it up in 1698, 'every individual Person in Heaven and Hell, shall hear and see all that passes in either State, these to a more exquisite aggravation of their Tortures, by the loss of what the other enjoy, and those to a greater increase of their Bliss, in escaping what the other suffer'.[82] To Richard Baxter, the Scriptures seemed to confirm that, 'as the damned souls shall, from hell, see the saints' happiness, to increase their own torments, so shall the blessed, from heaven, behold the wicked's misery to the increase of their own joy ...'[83]

Somewhat surprisingly for a universalist, the Platonist Peter Sterry declared that death and damnation were part of God's laughter. In relishing the plight of the wicked, Sterry suggested, the blessed shared in the laughter of God.[84] In 1674, in his *Christian Ethicks*, Thomas Traherne found the happiness of the blessed to consist in part in the suffering of the damned: 'if our Righteous Souls be vexed, as Lots

Soul in Sodom was... they shall be recreated and revived with the sight of GODS most Righteous Judgments... by which he rectifies the malignity of the Wicked'.[85] Henry More saw eternal punishment meted out to obdurate sinners as naturally contributing to 'the establishment of the Righteous in their Celestial Happiness'.[86] To the nonconformist John Shower in 1700, the vision of the wicked in hell would add to the felicity of the righteous.[87] The Anglican William Dawes in 1709 also saw it as making the blessed more aware of their happiness; but he also made the somewhat unusual suggestion that the sight of the damned would be the most powerful motive among the saved 'to avoid everything that might endanger their happiness'.[88] The Catholic Francis Blyth in 1740 maintained that the happiness resulting from the vision of the damned spirited the blessed up 'to that exstatic acknowledgement of GOD's goodness.'[89] To the American Calvinist Jonathan Edwards, the sight of the sufferings of the damned would lead to praise and glory of God: 'How joyfully will they sing to God and the Lamb, when they behold this!' even when those among the damned included those 'who were near and dear to them in this world'.[90]

D. P. Walker has made the point that the 'abominable fancy' was virtually obsolete by the end of the seventeenth century. Certainly, from that time it was no longer part of the mainstream tradition. In the later part of that century, and in the first half of the following, references to it were uncommon. Perhaps, just as interesting is the fact that criticisms of it are similarly relatively rare. To be sure, with William King in 1702, for example, there is the suggestion that the blessed might feel pity for the damned, although this would be overcome by their satisfaction at their deliverance:

And though in one respect a view of the misery which the damned undergo might seem to detract from the happiness of the blessed, through pity and commiseration: yet there is another, a nearer, and much more affecting consideration, viz. that all this is the misery which they themselves were often exposed to, and were in imminent danger of incurring; in this view, why may not the sense of their own escape so far overcome the sense of another's ruin, as to extinguish the pain that usually attends the idea of it, and even render it productive of some real happiness?[91]

In 1736, Marie Huber, who was in any case opposed to the doctrine of eternal torments, suggested that the divine goodness entailed not only the ultimate salvation of the wicked but of devils also. 'I am one of those', she wrote, 'who would not be affrighted at finding Devils in Heaven; or, to speak seriously, I am one of those who could not think themselves perfectly happy, did they know any Beings must be eternally miserable.'[92] Similarly opposed to eternal torments, Thomas Burnet expressed his irritation at Tertullian:

> Consider a little, if you please, unmerciful Doctor, what a theatre of Providence this is: by far the greatest part of the human race burning in the flames for ever and ever. Oh what a spectacle on the stage, worthy of an audience of God and angels! And then to delight the ear, while this unhappy crowd fills heaven and earth with wailing and howling, you have a truly divine harmony.[93]

But in spite of the voices both for and against these contrasting symmetries of the saved and the damned, it was an image which does seem quietly to have been slipping out of the mentality of the early modern mind. And by the middle of the nineteenth century, it has virtually disappeared from English Protestantism. The reasons for its doing so are not so clear. Walker suggests that it reflected the beginnings of a change in attitudes to the suffering of others, combined with a tendency to minimise or reject the concept of retributive justice.[94] This suggestion is reinforced by consideration of secular theories of punishment. In his important book, *The Spectacle of Suffering*, Pieter Spierenburg argues that from the end of the seventeenth until the middle of the nineteenth century, an originally positive attitude towards the suffering of others was slowly replaced by a rising sensitivity. As the consequence of an increasing inter-human identification, 'The death and suffering of fellow human beings were increasingly experienced as painful, just because other people were increasingly perceived as fellow human beings.'[95] And this change of sensitivity, he argues, was crucial in the demise of the public spectacle of suffering. By the end of the eighteenth century, the physical pain of the condemned was mirrored in the psychological pain of the spectators. Thus, as this changing sensibility removed the sufferings of the judicially guilty from the sight of the innocent, so, it can reasonably be argued, it removed the sufferings of the divinely guilty from the gaze of the saved.

In his *Discipline and Punish*, Michel Foucault analyses the rise of the modern penitentiary system, and the period of physical punishments which preceded it. He finds two main differences between these two penal systems. The two main features of the earlier system absent to a large extent from the later were the public spectacle of suffering, and the deliberate and conscious infliction of physical punishment. From the middle of the eighteenth century, he argues, there was a displacement in the object of the punitive operation: the punishment of the body was replaced by the judgement of the soul. Thus in the modern judicial system, judgement is not focused only upon the crime, but also upon the criminal – his psychological state, the genetic and environmental causes of his actions, his possible rehabilitation, and so on. No longer to be publicly and physically punished, the criminal is removed from the community, separated from it, isolated from it, not for punishment of the body but for punishment of the soul.

This shift from the punishment of the body to the punishment of the soul from the middle of the eighteenth century was reflected too in the torments of hell. During the same period, there is a diminution in the theological acceptability of the punishment of the senses. Indeed, by the middle of the nineteenth century, the notion of *poena sensus* was under serious attack. Much more acceptable was the belief that the damned would suffer only from the loss of heaven and therefore the exclusion of fellowship with God. To the liberal F. D. Maurice, for example, the thought of the loss of God was sufficiently daunting: 'the thought of His ceasing to punish them, of His letting them alone, of His leaving them to themselves, is the real unutterable horror'.[96] Thus, under the pressure of a changing European sensibility to punishments inflicted upon the body, the prisoners of hell were there to be incarcerated no longer *for* punishment but *as* punishment; but whether these prisoners were to be incarcerated eternally or whether they were eventually to be released after a suitable period of rehabilitation and reformation is a question we shall need yet to return to.

HEAVENLY JOYS

Although there was a contrast of symmetries between the torments of hell and the joys of heaven, the nature of the latter was far less commented upon than that of the former. This is explained by the conviction that an emphasis on the horrors of hell was more conducive to leading a godly life than dwelling on its rewards. To William Bates, 'Carnal Men are more disposed to be wrought upon, by representing the Torments of Hell, than the Joys of Heaven.'[97] As Chateaubriand later summed it up,

Heaven, where boundless felicity reigns, is too far above the human condition for the soul to be strongly affected by the bliss of the elect: one can interest oneself but little in beings who are perfectly happy. This is why poets have succeeded better in the description of hells: at least humanity is there, and the torments of the guilty remind us of the miseries of our life.[98]

As the torments of the damned would include the eternal absence of God, so the happiness of the blessed would consist in living eternally in the presence of God. The Beatific Vision was central in Thomas Browne's image of eternal life. According to him, after God had destroyed the whole world, all that would remain would be an empty space filled with the presence of God. God alone was the place in which the blessed would reside: 'when this sensible world shall bee destroyed, all shall then be as it is now there, an Empyreall Heaven ... to aske where Heaven is, is to demand where the presence of God is, or where wee have the glory of that happy vision'.[99] This theocentric image of the heavenly life reached its classic Puritan statement in Richard Baxter's *Saints' Everlasting Rest*. For Baxter, the focus of heaven was only God:

As all good whatsoever is comprised in God, and all in the creatures are but drops of this ocean; so all the glory of the blessed is comprised in their enjoyment of God: and if there be any mediate joys there, they are but drops from this. If men and angels should study to speak the blessedness of that estate in one word, what can they say beyond this, That it is the nearest enjoyment of God?[100]

So too for William Bates, it was the enjoyment of the divine presence which was 'the supreme felicity of the Saints'.[101]

Though, for Baxter, all joy in heaven would be derived from God's joy, he, like a number of his contemporaries, did distinguish between the primary glory of the vision of God and a secondary glory which consisted of fellowship with the other Saints and angels. Baxter looked forward to the day when he would sit down with Enoch, Noah, Abraham, Isaac, Jacob, Moses, and David; to the time when he would eternally dwell with Peter and Paul, Augustine and Jerome, and with worthies of the Reformation – Luther, Calvin, Zwingli, Beza, Bullinger, indeed with 'all the saints of all ages, whose faces in the flesh we never saw, whom we shall there both know and comfortably enjoy'.[102] Baxter's heaven is, in the final analysis, a heavenly society. He was deeply committed to the belief that our present knowledge would be increased, and therefore that we would once again know our friends in heaven: 'we shall not know each other after the flesh; nor by stature, voice, colour, complexion, visage, or outward shape;... nor by terms of affinity and consanguinity, nor benefits nor such relations; nor by youth or age; nor, I think, by sex: but by the image of Christ, and spiritual relation, and former faithfulness in improving our talents, beyond doubt, we shall know and be known'.[103]

Many of these themes in Baxter recurred throughout the writings of the period. Andrew Marvell, Milton's assistant and Cromwell's court poet, toadyingly placed the Lord Protector alongside Moses, Joshua, and David.[104] To the Anglican Richard Gearing in 1673, the blessed would behold the glory of God, and would behold the face of Christ as do friends now behold each other's faces. But they would also see, not only the faces of all the saved, but also those of the Patriarchs, the Saints, the Prophets, Apostles and Martyrs.[105] And they would also re-acquaint themselves with old friends. If the soul can carry with it a sociable inclination, Gearing surmised, 'then may it for the use and exercise of this desire be admitted to the knowledg of other Souls, and of those especially with whom it had sojourned on earth, that like fellow-travellers... they may thenceforth interchangeably communicate their joys, springing from their present rest and peace'.[106] Henry More wrote beautifully of the love among the aerial citizens reflecting the divine love:

> Now the blest meetings thou arriv'st unto
> Of th' airy *Genii*, where soft winds do blow,
> Where Friendship, Love, & gentle sweet Desire
> Fill their thrice-welcom Guests with joys entire,
> Ever supply'd from that immortal spring
> Whose streams pure Nectar from great Jove doe bring:
> Whence kind converse and amorous eloquence
> Warm their chast minds into the highest sense
> Of Heav'nly Love, whose myst'ries they declare
> 'Midst the fresh breathings of the peaceful Aire.[107]

The issue of friends in heaven was extensively dealt with in 1698 by John Dunton. Written on the death of his wife, *An Essay Proving We shall Know our Friends in Heaven* claimed to be the first book totally devoted to this subject.[108] It was the hope of being reunited with his deceased wife that motivated Dunton's essay. And to this end, he assembled a number of sources where the expectation of meeting husbands, wives, and children was mooted.

For Dunton, life in heaven would be a continuation of the social relations present in this life. Society, he argued, was not comfortable without familiar acquaintance, and heaven would be no different. 'Be assured', he wrote, that familiar acquaintance 'will not be wanting in the Height and Perfection of all Glory, Bliss and Joy. Nay, our Minds being abundantly and beatifically illuminated with all Wisdom and Knowledge, we shall be enabled to know, not only those of former Acquaintance, but also Strangers, and such as we never knew before.'[109] Moreover, he argued, in order to retain our personal identity, our memories of our former lives must remain, and therefore we must have recollections of others.

Dunton was familiar with Baxter's *Saints' Everlasting Rest*. In contrast to Baxter, he maintained that we would know each other by face, stature, voice, and difference of sex. Indeed, on the issue of whether sexual identity would be retained in heaven, he specifically argued against Baxter. Thus, while he maintained that the corporal relation between husbands and wives would cease, the heavenly body would conform to the disposition of the soul which was eternally either male or female: 'the Soul...of the one is Resolute and Constant, that of the other Light, Wavering and Changeable... The Soul of one takes a pride in being Grave and speaking little; the other talks much, and cannot forbear *twatling upon every thing*.'[110]

A similar stereotype of women had appeared in 1691 in volume 3 of *The Athenian Gazette* which Dunton edited, although the discussion of sexual identity in heaven was different. In answer to a reader's question, 'Are there sexes in heaven?', the columnist argued that in a state of perfection and bliss, anything imperfect and accidental would be removed, and consequently sexuality should be. No doubt for his predominantly male readership, he couldn't resist the following: 'We won't add for another Reason what, as we remember, one of the Fathers has said – That *were there any Women in Heaven, the Angels cou'd not stand long*, but wou'd certainly be seduced from their Innocency, and Fall as *Adam* did.'[111] A similar denial of heavenly sexuality was given in volume 5 to the question, 'Is the soul of women inferior, and if so eternally?' There was no essential superiority of men to women in this life, the writer suggested, and therefore would not be eternally. Any superiority in this life was merely an accidental difference arising from differences in the body, and these differences would not be present in resurrected bodies.

Still, in spite of his misogynist leanings, that Dunton was distraught by the death of his wife, and deeply comforted by the thought of their eventual reunion is clear. 'Her Death', he wrote, 'has made me so very melancholy, that I had pin'd away in a few days, had not the hopes of finding her again in Heaven, given me *some Relief*.'[112] The same sentiments were reflected in Elizabeth Singer Rowe's *Friendship in Death*, first published in 1728, with a further fourteen editions between 1733 and 1816. In these twenty letters from the dead to the living, the reader was assured that human love was an essential part of life in the beautiful celestial realm. The spirit of this work is amply conveyed by the letter of Altamont, who had died grieving for his wife Almeria:

The first gentle Spirit that welcom'd me to these new Regions was the lovely *Almeria*; but how Dazling! how divinely Fair! Extasy was in her Eyes, and inexpressible Pleasure in every Smile! her Mein and Aspect more soft and propitious than ever was feign'd by Poets of their Goddess of Beauty and Love... With an inimitable Grace she received me into her aetherial Chariot, which was sparkling Saphire studded with Gold: It roll'd with a spontaneous Motion along the Heavenly Plains, and stop'd at the Morning Star, our destin'd habitation. But how shall I describe this fair, this fragrant, this enchanting Land of Love! The delectable Vales and flow'ry Lawns, the Myrtle Shades and rosy Bowers, the bright Cascades and chrystal Rivulets rolling over orient Pearls and Sands of Gold: Here they spread their silent Waves into broad transparent Lakes, smooth as the Face of Heaven; and there they break with rapid Force through arching Rocks of Diamond and Purple Amethist.[113]

It is a reasonable conjecture that the images of the reunion in heaven of husbands, wives and friends were the result of changing patterns of human relationships. In particular, the desire to be reunited with spouses reflects the growth in the companionate marriage, one in which each partner contributed to the spiritual, emotional, and intellectual well-being of the other. This developed as a norm among pious, often nonconformist, middle-class families in the late seventeenth century, in part at least as the result of seventeenth-century preaching on the desirability of companionship in marriage. There developed as a consequence a greater emphasis on equality and caring within marriage. Richard Baxter and his wife, for example, married each other for their personal qualities. After the death of his wife in 1681, Baxter wrote her biography in which he noted that 'these near nineteen years I know not that we ever had any breach in the point of love, or point of interest'.[114] Thus, although the heavenly reunion of spouses was not to become a commonplace in the Christian idea of heaven until the middle of the nineteenth century, it is to be expected that those couples who had become close intimates in their marriage relationships in the seventeenth and eighteenth centuries should desire a continuation of their love and affection into eternity.

HEAVENLY BODIES

As individuals, the community of saints was to enjoy all physical and mental perfections. To the Calvinist Richard Younge, to whom this world was hell for the godly, its meagre pleasures were as nothing compared with the glories yet to be revealed:

there is no joy here comparable to that in *Heaven*: all *our mirth* here to that is but *pensiveness*: all *our pleasure* here to that but *heaviness*: all *our sweetness* here to that is but *bitterness*: Even *Solomon in all his glory and royalty*, to that, *was but as a spark in the chimny, to the Sun in the firmament. Absoloms beauty*, to that, *is but deformity. Sampsons strength*, to that, *is but infirmity. Methuselahs age*, to theirs, is but *minority* and mortality. *Hazaals speed*, and swiftness, *but a snayles* pace to their celerity. Yea how little, how nothing, are the poor and temporary enjoyments of this life, to those we shall enjoy in the next?[115]

Similarly, the Anglican William Sherlock saw this life as merely a state of trial and probation for the next, one that, he emphasised to his readers, would not be a 'Mahumetane Paradise' of gross corporeal pleasures. Rather, it would be a place of spiritual delights with spiritual bodies 'which will infinitely more contribute to the divine pleasures of the Mind, than these earthly bodies do to our sensual pleasures'.[116]

The spiritual pleasures of the Christian heaven were often in contrast to the corporeal pleasures of the Muslim paradise. The overall image of paradise in the Quran is that of an eternal life that satisfies all human needs and involves human relationships, a life which is sometimes described in terms of 'wide-eyed houris', at others in terms of family relationships.[117] But the Western construction of the image of an Islamic paradise intended to satisfy male sensuality served to highlight its own spiritualised heaven. According to Thomas Herbert, for example, 'Paradise is a place of as much delight as *Mahomets* carnal apprehension was able to imagine, or his fancy contrive.'[118]

Henry Blunt suggested that Muhammad, knowing he had to deal with a rude and sensual people, 'made not his Paradise to consist in

Visions and *Hallelujahs*, but in delicious *fare, pleasant Gardens*, and *Wenches* with great eyes...'[119] According to Humphrey Prideaux, Muhammad's paradise was carefully framed to suit the Arabian penchant for sensual pleasure.[120]

Henry Stubbe was both a mortalist who denied heaven and hell and committed to a deistic civil religion which would have reduced Judaism, Christianity, and Islam to an agreed doctrinal minimum. Consequently, he was the seventeenth century's most sympathetic defender of Islam, and one of the few to deny the contrast between the Christian and Muslim visions of heaven. He censured those who interpreted Christian imagery as spiritual truth but would not allow the same interpretation of analogous Islamic descriptions of paradise. 'For my part', he declared, 'I cannot distinguish betwixt the Paradise of the Jews and Christians, and that which Mahomet promiseth to his followers, and do think that our Notions of the Torments of the Wicked in a lake of fire and brimstone somewhere underground, hath as much folly and absurdity in it as any fable of Mahometans.'[121] But Stubbe was very much a voice crying in the wilderness, and the image of a spiritual Christian paradise in contrast to a sensual Islamic one was to continue until the end of the nineteenth century.[122]

That the bodies of those in the afterlife were fashioned after the virtues and vices of the souls who inhabited them was a common theme: lucid and refulgent, glorious, spiritual, heavenly, transparent, and angelic for the good; gross, dark, foetid, diseased, and demonic for the wicked. This was a common image among the Platonists. Thus, for example, Henry More saw aerial vehicles as manifesting visibly the nature of the soul: 'For if Vertue and Vice can be ever seen with outward eyes, it must be in these aerial Vehicles, which yield so to the Will and Idea of good and pure affections, that the Soule in a manner becomes perfectly transparent through them, discovering her lovely beauty in all the efflorescencies thereof, to the ineffable enravishment of the beholder.'[123] For the Anglican William Gearing in 1673, the many corporeal imperfections in earthly bodies would be removed from heavenly bodies to make them like Christ's, glorious, 'a shining beauty'. The soul, he maintained, full of the light of glory, would be diffused throughout the whole body.[124] Christians would be brought to immortality, declared Thomas Burnet, not in the coarse clothing of our current carcases, but in heavenly bodies 'in the brightness of aetherial Regions...'[125] *The Athenian Gazette* described our resurrection bodies as 'shining and bright'.[126] The contrast between lightness and darkness, blackness and whiteness, heaven and hell, was expressed bizarrely in the same journal in answer to the question whether negroes would arise so on the last day:

> Black is of the colour of Night, frightful, dark and horrid; but White of the Day and Light, refreshing and lovely. Taking then this blackness of the Negro to be an accidental Imperfection ... we conclude thence, that he shall not arise with that Complexion, but leave it behind him in the darkness of the Grave, exchanging it for a brighter and a better at his return agen into the World.[127]

The form of the heavenly body was also a matter of discussion. For Henry More, heavenly bodies would appear in the ordinary form of Angels, 'such a countenance, and so cloathed, as they'.[128] And the angelic form was essentially like the human. Although for More, there would be no lust, nor difference of sex between aerial beings, there would be some discrimination of beauty into male and female. Thomas Burnet agreed that heavenly bodies would be like those of angels, lucid and aethereal, and consisting of celestial matter 'as pure and thin, as the finest Air or Aether... '[129] But unlike More, who believed that souls would have hearing, sight, touch, smell and taste, Burnet's heavenly bodies would have neither palate, throat, bowels, nor sexual parts etc.; in fact, bodies which while recognisably angelic were not obviously human.

Unlike the bodies of the damned, immobilised in their infernal prisons, heavenly bodies would be perfect in their speed and agility. The bodies of the saints in heaven, declared William Gearing, 'shall be able to move from place to place with incredible swiftness... '[130] Our present bodies are now dull and sluggish, John Shower remarked in 1693. But our heavenly bodies, he said, 'shall be nimble and active, like the Body of Christ that, at his Ascension into Heaven, being done in one day, moved many thousands of Miles in an hour; the distance between the highest Heavens and this Earth, being computed to be some hundred millions of Miles'.[131]

The bodies of the blessed would also be of a perfect age, that of Christ's during his ministry on earth. Those who had died in infancy or were severely deformed would be made perfect in heaven. Thus, for example, John Dunton maintained that all divines were generally agreed that 'Infants and Deformed Persons shall be Perfect in Heaven, and rise about the Age of *Thirty*, or our *Saviours* Age at his

Resurrection, which was Thirty-Three.'[132] And this was the same answer given, undoubtedly by Dunton, to the question how the aged, infants, and the deformed were to rise on the last day in the third volume of *The Athenian Gazette*.[133] In spite of our ideally aged bodies, we would none the less recognise each other, but whether by '*glorified Eyes* or *Immediate* Revelation cannot be determined'.[134]

The respondent to the same issue in the first volume of *The Athenian Gazette* thought it improper to say any age, but was certain that, at the very least, we would be endowed with much more physical perfection.[135] William Gearing was similarly unwilling to specify an age for the heavenly body, but he was convinced of its physical perfection: 'The Infant and the Dwarf shall be made a proper man! when the limbs exhaled with famine, shall be replenished with as much miracle as faith! When the Child that left its own Soul before it left the Womb, shall in an instant, without growth be as big as the Mother!'[136] In Rowe's *Letters from the Dead*, the deceased two-year-old child found itself immediately after death 'an active and reasonable Being'.[137]

An unusual problem was offered in the case of the Siamese twins, Lazarus Coloreda and his brother John Baptista who grew from his navel. They had considerable success in exhibition tours around England between 1637 and 1642, and were celebrated in a broadside ballad from the same period, and in a pamphlet on another famous monster of the period, the 'hog-faced woman' from Holland.[138] They were still in the public mind fifty years later as a question on their fate on the day of resurrection to *The Athenian Gazette* reveals. The answer was a careful one:

> we find no lineaments of a Rational soul in *Baptista*, nor so much of the Animal as Brutes have; his Brother shall rise without him at the Day of Judgment, for there will be no Monsters at the Resurrection ... but if he has a Rational Soul ... then he will be ranked among Children, Fools and Ideots at the last Day; but will rise separate with a perfect Body, not with another Body, but the same specifick Body, adapted and fitly organised for a future State.[139]

THE SYMMETRY OF CONTRASTS

In both heaven and hell, the senses of the saved and the damned were intensified: in the case of the latter, to make the punishments of the senses more horrific; in the case of the former, to increase the happiness of the blessed. William Gearing emphasised the symmetry of contrasts: 'if the Damned in Hell shall be so grievously tormented in their senses then shall the senses of the glorified Saints be exceedingly refreshed; for God is not more severe in punishing, then bountiful in rewarding'.[140] Thus, he went on, in the bright light of heaven, the saints would see from one end of it to the other. The ears would eternally hear the 'ravishing Musick sounding forth from the heavenly Quire'.[141] The sense of touch would receive its delights both from the heavenly air, 'and the soft touch of heavenly Bodies...'[142] In the absence of hunger and thirst, he, like others, found little need for the sense of taste.[143] But Gearing thought it not absurd to think that glorified bodies should have some 'delicious and pleasant moisture resting upon the palate, or place of taste, that so by such a means that sensible part may have her full content'.[144] And he was certain that the sense of smell would be refreshed with 'most sweet and pleasant flavours'.[145] For surely, he reasoned, if the damned in hell are punished in these senses, why should not the Saints receive delight and refreshment from them? And as the damned hurled abuse one to another, so the saved would communicate their joys, ever springing from their rest and peace.

In their work *Heaven: A History*, Colleen McDannell and Bernhard Lang make much of the transition from a theocentric view of heaven, centred on the eternal praise and glory of God, to the modern view of heaven initiated, they suggest, by the writings of Emanuel Swedenborg in the second half of the eighteenth century. The modern view of heaven is characterised by four features: first, only a thin veil divides heaven from earth and heavenly life begins immediately after death; second, rather than heaven being seen as a structural opposite to life on earth, heaven is seen as a continuation and fulfilment of material existence; third, although heaven remains a place of rest, the saints are increasingly active in heaven, experiencing spiritual progress; finally, a focus on human love expressed in communal and familial concerns replaces the primacy of the divine love experienced in the form of the beatific vision.[146]

I have suggested in previous chapters that in the period we are considering there were already developments in the notion of heaven as a place in which spiritual progress could be made. And, in this chapter, I have noted a number of occasions on which there is a focus on social life in heaven, and particularly familial concerns. But the first two features of the modern heaven noted by McDannell and Lang were conspicuously absent from the early modern heaven.

Between earth and heaven in the pre-modern period, a great gulf was fixed; the heavenly life stood in marked contrast to the earthly. The sufferings of this world were swallowed up in eternal felicity, the joys of this world infinitely intensified. So, also, the infernal regions appeared in stark relief against the earthly realm. The happiness of this world was not to be found in the dark prisons of hell; and the sufferings of the present life were as 'flea-bites' compared to the horrors there to be eternally endured. This world was half-way between the two kingdoms of good and evil, of light and dark, of total happiness and complete misery – with fortune for some, a preliminary to the delights of heaven, with misfortune for most, a rehearsal for the torments of hell. As Piero Camporesi remarks, this world is a mixed realm, 'a place of aspirations, tensions, the medium space between the highest and the lowest, between the splendours of light, the consolations of peace, the delights of sweetness, of joy, of melody, of whiteness and sweet-smelling odours, and the iniquities of the lowest stratum, the obscenities of the nether-regions; it participates, in a strange and opposing mixture, in the conditions of its two powerful neighbours'.[147]

But the middle Kingdom would eventually disappear. On the last day, the judgement would be made by God. And when this life was done with, and this world passed away, there would remain only a state of total blessedness and a state of interminable misery in the stark symmetry of contrasts between heaven and hell.

CHAPTER 4

The last day

UN-PLATONIC FIRES

This night as I was in my sleep, I Dreamed, and behold the Heavens grew exceeding black; also it thundered and lightned in most fearful wise, that it put me into an Agony. So I looked up in my Dream, and saw the Clouds rack at an unusual rate; upon which I heard a great sound of a Trumpet, and saw also a Man sit upon a Cloud, attended with the thousands of Heaven; they were all in flaming fire, also the Heavens was on a burning flame. I heard then a voice, saying, *Arise ye Dead, and come to Judgement*; and with that, the Rockes rent, the Graves opened, & the Dead that were there-in, came forth; some of them were exceeding glad, and looked upward; and some sought to hide themselves under the Mountains: Then I saw the Man that sat upon the Cloud, open the Book; and bid the World draw near. Yet there was by reason of a Fiery flame that issued out and came from before him, a convenient distance betwixt him and them, as betwixt the Judge and the Prisoners at the Bar. I heard it also proclaimed to them that attended on the Man that sat on the Cloud; *Gather together the Tares, the Chaff, and Stubble, and cast them into the burning Lake*; and with that the Bottomless pit opened, just whereabout I stood; out of the mouth of which there came in an abundant manner Smoak, and Coals of fire, with hideous noises. It was also said to the same persons; *Gather my Wheat into my Garner*. And with that I saw many catch't up and carried away into the Clouds...[1]

In the last four decades of the seventeenth century and the first half of the eighteenth century, the last day became an object, not merely of theological speculation as to its unfolding, nor merely of millenarian expectation as to its time, but also of scientific reflection as to how it would occur. The last day became part of the new science. God remained the primary cause of the end of the world. But the new science opened up fresh vistas for intellectual conjecture on its secondary causes, it engendered novel attempts to place the last day within the parameters of cosmological theorising, and it provided new settings for the ultimate destinies of both the damned and the saved.

The neo-Platonist Henry More was not one of those who expected the last day in the immediate future. To be sure, apocalyptic concerns were at the forefront of his writings from 1660 until his death in 1687. But More's apocalyptic writings deliberately reversed millenarian strategies of interpreting the books of Daniel and Revelation as signalling the imminent return of Christ to earth to rule for a thousand years. Rather, More interpreted the prophecies to mean that the final day of judgement was postponed until at least a thousand years into the future. More's world was one which sought social stability in monarchy and episcopacy, not one which existed in the shadow of the Apocalypse.[2]

More rejected the notion of Christ's rule on earth for a thousand years prior to judgement. This was, he declared, 'a very rash and groundless and unsafe conceit, fit for nothing but heat and tumult both of phansie and action'.[3] But he was convinced that Christ's one-thousand-year rule in heaven, if not on earth, was shortly to begin. At that time, the martyrs would be raised in celestial bodies and ascend to the celestial realms.[4] Simultaneously, Satan would be bound for a thousand years,[5] and the devils and wicked persecutors of the saints of God would be cast down into hell within the fiery core of the earth and imprisoned there until 'the *Claviger* of the *Abyss* with his Ministers brings them out again after the thousand years... '[6]

At the end of the millennial period, Christ would come to earth in judgement with his angels. Then, 'he shall consummate the Happiness of all Believers with everlasting glory, and so restore the Creation to a perfect recovery into what they had fallen from, and punish the obstinate with eternal Fire'.[7] On that last day, the good would ascend into heaven as did Christ on his day of ascension: 'in that day shall all the Faithful renew their strength, and shall mount up with wings as Eagles, and be carried far above the reach of this dismal Fate; that is, they shall ascend up in those *Heavenly Chariots* or *Ethereal Vehicles*... and so enter into Immortality and Eternal rest'.[8] That Christ should come visibly in judgement, and that the good should visibly ascend into heaven was necessary, argued More, to convince the wicked and the atheists that the conflagration to come was not merely an unfortunate natural occurrence. Thus, the good 'should visibly ascend into *Christ's* throne, that is, into heaven, in the open view of them that should be left here on the Earth and in the inferiour Regions of the Air, sentenced to that everlasting fire prepared for the Devil and his Angels'.[9]

More presented a number of images of the conflagration of the world. Christ would initiate the conflagration by an act of his imagination and will. But the process of the world's destruction would be by natural causes. Thus, for example, in 1660 in his *An Explanation of the Grand Mystery of Godliness*, he wrote,

The mere *Fiat* therefore of his Imagination and Will acting upon the *Spirit of Nature*... cannot but prove sufficient, if he so please, to undoe that universal coalition of particles out of which arises the *Compages* and consistence of every earthly Substance, and to turn them into such a flame as some would have the whole earth anciently to have been...[10]

The cosmology of Descartes lurked not far beneath the surfaces of these imaginings. For while More's Spirit of Nature was always intended to undermine the mechanical philosophy of Descartes, it was none the less Descartes who, in his *The Principles of Philosophy* in 1644, had postulated that the earth, far from being merely a Copernican planet, was in fact an abortive sun, with a central fire of the same nature as that in stars. And it was Descartes who had argued that the earth had originated from this central fiery core.[11]

Another echo of Descartes occurred in the same work. Descartes had suggested that planets, after having captured their satellites, moved downwards towards the sun, eventually entering permanent orbits according to their solidity.[12] More, for his part, maintained that the earth was becoming more dry, and less able to retain its moisture. The conflagration would therefore begin when the earth, presumably as a result of its decreasing solidity, moved toward the sun 'So that at last, what by its over-drieness and what by its approaching so near to the fountain of Heat, not only Forrests and Woods, which has happned already, but the subterraneous Mines of Sulphur and other combustible Matter will catch fire, and set the *whole Earth* in a manner on burning.'[13]

This was an opinion which More himself was later to reject. In 1682 in his annotations on Joseph Glanvill's *Lux Orientalis*, he took issue with Glanvill's suggestion that, on the last day, the earth would become a fiery comet and fly off into space. Rather, he argued, on

Cartesian principles, the earth was more likely to be swallowed down into the sun. But he thought that this, too, was finally unlikely. Rather, after the last day, the earth would remain, as a planetary sun, in orbit around the fixed sun at the centre. Moreover, he was inclined, like Glanvill, to the view that the central fire would remain uninvolved in the conflagration.[14]

For More, the immediate causes of the conflagration were a combination of intra- and extra-terrestrial factors: of eruptions of volcanic (Vesuvius, Aetna, Helga, Hecla) and other subterranean fires; of comets, lightning, and falling stars. On that day, declared More, Christ shall cause

> such an universal Thunder and Lightning, that it shall rattle over all the quarters of the Earth, rain down burning Comets and falling Starres, and discharge such claps of unextinguishable fire, that it will do sure execution wherever it falls; so that the ground being excessively heated, those subterraneous Mines of combustible Matter will also take fire: which inflaming the inward exhalations of the Earth, will cause a terrible murmur under ground, so that the Earth will seem to thunder against the tearing and ratling of the Heavens, and all will be filled with sad remugient echoes; Earthquakes and Eruptions of Fire there will be everywhere, and whole Cities and Countries swallowed down by the vast gapings and· wide divulsions of the ground ... this fiery vengeance shall be so thirsty, that it shall drink deep of the very Sea; nor shall the water quench her devouring appetite, but excite it.[15]

The moon and the stars would withdraw their shining, the sun would be turned into blood; nothing but dark clouds charged with thunder and lightning, crackling volcanoes, smoking mountains, tortuous streams of fire from burning forests and woods, the bellowings of the troubled seas, the horror, the stench, the confusion, the 'Lowd Shreeks and howlings of affrighted Men and Beasts, grim and grisly Apparitions, deep and dreadful Groans of tormented Ghosts ... '[16]

Thus, the wicked and the devils would be punished in the fires of God's judgement. But whether they were to be so tormented eternally is a little more opaque. In his Preface to Jeremiah White's *The Restoration of All Things* in 1712, Richard Roach listed More as one of the modern believers in universal salvation, on the basis of More's *Divine Dialogues*, particularly the vision of Bathynous. 'The vision of Bathynous's Silver and Golden Keys, the Keys of Providence', wrote Roach, 'speaks very favourably of this, yea covertly and at a distance

1 The soul held down by pleasure and pain seeks the aethereal realm whence it came. Frontispiece of *Two Choice and Useful Treatises* (London, 1682).

2 The witch of Endor conjures the spirit of Samuel. Frontispiece of the German translation of Joseph Glanvill's *Saducismus Triumphatus*.

3 Spirits and witches in their aethereal and aerial vehicles. Frontispiece of Joseph Glanvill's *Saducismus Triumphatus*.

Man wholly Mortal;
OR,
A TREATISE
WHEREIN

'Tis proved, both Theologically and Philosophically, That as *whole Man sinned,* so *whole Man died;* contrary to that common distinction of *Soul and Body. And that* the *present* going of the Soul into *Heaven or Hell* is a meer *Fiction:* And that at the *Resurrection* is the beginning of our *Immortality;* and then actual *Condemnation* and *Salvation,* and not before.

With Doubts and Objections answered and resolved, both by *Scripture* and *Reason,* discovering the multitude of *Blasphemies* and *Absurdities* that arise from the fancy of the *Soul.*

Also, divers other Mysteries; as of *Heaven, Hell,* the extent of the *Resurrection,* the *New-Creation, &c.* opened, and presented to the Trial of better Judgments.

By R. O.
The second Edition, by the Author corrected & enlarged.

That which befalleth the Sons of Men, befalleth Beasts; even one thing befalleth them all: as the one dieth, so dieth the other; yea, they have all one breath: so that Man hath no pre-eminence above a Beast: for all is vanity. Eccl. 3. 19.

Printed at London, Anno 1675.

4 Title page of the second edition of Richard Overton's *Man Wholly Mortal.*

AN ARGUMENT

Proving,

That *according to the Covenant of Eternal Life revealed in the Scriptures,* Man may be translated from hence into that Eternal Life, without passing through Death, altho the Humane Nature of CHRIST himself could not be thus translated till he had passed through Death.

―――*Nec vanis credite verbis;*
Aspicite en! faciatq; fidem Conspectus.

Anno Dom. 1700.

5 Title page of John Asgill's argument against the necessity of death.

6 The traditional image of the harrowing of hell: 'The Harrowing of Hell' by Jerome Cock.

7 The state of the individual fixed at death for eternity. Illustration to Christopher Sutton, *Disce Mori, learn to dye* (London, 1662).

8 Frontispiece to the eleventh edition of Richard Baxter's *The Saints' Everlasting Rest* (London, 1677).

9 The punishments of the damned, by Luca Signorelli. Fresco in Orvieto Cathedral.

10 William Hogarth's 1762 engraving 'Credulity, Superstition and Fanaticism' satirises the rapidly disappearing world of the devil, witches, ghosts, and spirits. Romaine's 'globe of hell' is juxtaposed to Joseph Glanvill's 'On Witches'.

11 The glories yet to be revealed to us. Title page to Henry Montagu, Earl of Manchester, *Manchester al mondo. Contemplatio Mortis, & Immortalitatis*, 6th impression (London, 1655).

12 The Last Judgement, from the *Small Passion*. Woodcut by Albrecht Dürer.

13 The seven phases in the sacred history of the earth. Frontispiece of Thomas Burnet, *The Sacred Theory of the Earth*, 3rd edn (London, 1697).

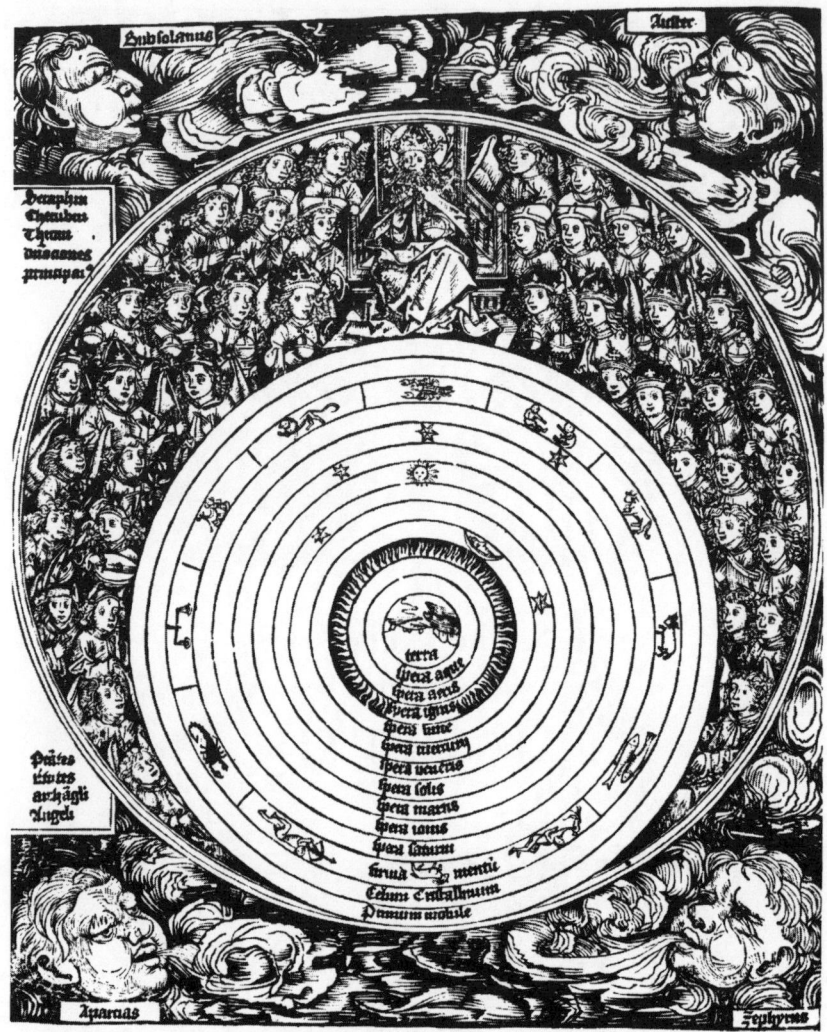

14 The medieval cosmos from Schedel's *Nuremberg Chronicle*, 1493. The earth, at the centre of the universe, was the most removed from the Empyrean, the abode of God and the saints. In the earth-centred universe, hell was located beneath the earth.

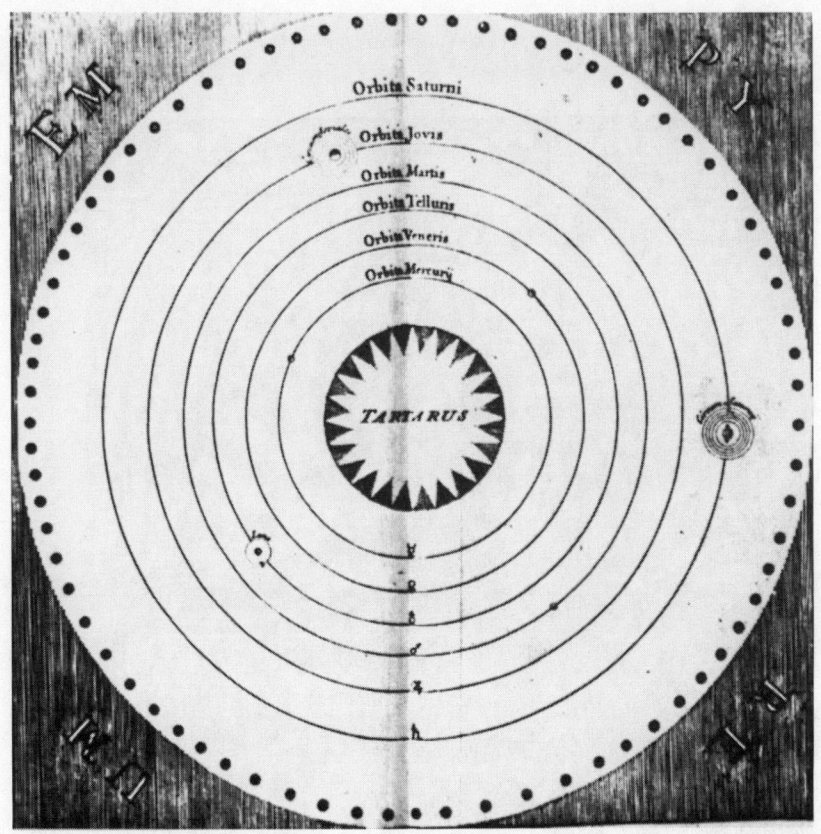

15 In the sun-centred universe of Tobias Swinden, hell was located in the place most distant from the Empyrium, the sun. Illustration to Tobias Swinden, *An Enquiry into the Nature and Place of Hell*.

16 The resurrection of the body prior to the Last Judgement. Giorgio Ghisi, sixteenth century.

involves it; not only in his direct maintaining the Doctrine of Praeexistence which goes hand in hand with it; but laying down the more general Principles from whence it flows.'[17] In the total context of the *Divine Dialogues*, however, it is difficult to interpret More as a universalist. On the contrary, although in this work he never argued for the eternity of hell's torments, he nevertheless did assert the compatibility of God's vindictive justice with his goodness in a discussion of the appropriateness of eternal torments.

More was certainly interested in the question of the value of eternal torments as a deterrent in 1642. In his Preface to *Psychathanasia*, he asked, 'What greater incitement to virtue and justice then eternall happinesse? what greater terrour from wickednesse, then a full perswasion of after-judgement and continual torture of spirit?'[18] His wariness about the issue was still apparent in 1682 in his remarks upon Edward Warren's *No Praeexistence*, 'some being ready to conclude from their *Eternity*, that Religion itself is a mere *Scarecrow* that frights us with such an incredible *Mormo*; others to indulge in their Pleasures, because the Commination is not frightful enough to deter them from extravagant Enjoyments, if Hell Torments be not eternal'.[19] On the other hand, he argued, it would be frivolous to decide the problem 'as the complesent Parson did about the May-pole: they of his Parish that were for a May-pole, let them have a May-pole; but they that were not for a May-pole, let them have no May-pole'.[20] Thus, he argued for eternal torments on the assumption of the compatibility of divine vindictive justice and goodness. And he challenged anyone to

> demonstrate that a Soul may not behave herself so perversely, obstinately, and despightfully against the Spirit of Grace, that she may deserve to be made an everlasting Hackstock of the Divine *Nemesis*, even for ever and ever. And if she deserve it, it is but just that she have it; and if it be just, it is likewise good.[21]

On the other hand, in a number of places, More undoubtedly softened his position on eternal torments. He argued, for example, that the Biblical evidence was not decisive. The crucial text was Matthew 25.46: 'And these shall go away into everlasting punishment: but the righteous into life eternal.' Edward Warren, like most proponents of eternal torments, argued that 'everlasting' had the same signification whether predicated of 'life' or of 'punishment'.[22] In contrast, More argued that it could mean either that which is of a long continuance or properly everlasting, and that while it undoubtedly had the sense of 'everlasting' when predicated of 'life', it had more properly the meaning of only 'long-lastingness' when predicated of 'punishment'.[23] And he went on to foreshadow Archbishop Tillotson's argument that, even if it did mean 'everlasting' when predicated of 'punishment', God was not obliged to carry out punishment into eternity. God owed the righteous eternal life, but the wicked owe God, who can remit their debt:

> Because God in his Comminations to the Wicked is only a *Creditor*, and has still a right and power to remit either part or the whole Debt; but to the Righteous, by vertue of his *Promise*, he becomes a *Debtor* and cannot recede, but must punctually keep his word.[24]

More had wrestled with the fate of the wicked and devils in his *The Immortality of the Soul* in 1659. There he outlined five possible opinions on the fate of wicked souls after the conflagration: that the heat and fire would destroy bodies and souls; that after a long period of punishment, God would annihilate souls; that souls would eventually become senseless; that souls would continue eternally in a tormented sleep; and that, after punishment, souls would sleep until the earth was refurbished and then be clothed again in terrestrial vehicles for another chance at salvation. The first four of these he rejected out of hand, but although he looked upon all of these opinions more as 'some Night-landskap to feed our amused Melancholy, then a clear and distinct draught of comprehensible truth to inform our Judgement',[25] he was less firm in his rejection of the last. And while More nowhere endorsed such a view, his suggestion in his *Annotations* that the earth would not be totally destroyed as a result of the erupting of the central fire, nor by being sucked down into the sun or becoming a fiery comet, but would remain in its orbit around the sun, left open the possibility that the conflagration would end, and that the world would restore itself as a habitable abode in which the wicked would have a renewed hope of salvation.

Like More, Rust's *A Letter of Resolution Concerning Origen* saw the last day as arising primarily from natural causes. The conflagratory fires would well up from sources deep in the earth. Into the ensuing 'farre-spreading Lake of slow-consuming fire and sulphureous stench the unreclamable Devils and obstinately-wicked men shall be by the righteous hand of God precipitated'.[26]

But the wicked would neither be eternally punished nor annihilated. Rather, however wicked these souls had become, they would not be beyond redemption. The goodness of God demanded their eventual restoration, and the punishments of the wicked in the flames of the last day were intended to bring the wicked to repentance:

> And certainly a searching ceaseless pain spreading through Soul and body will so abate and consume all that Joy they formerly took in their brutish rebellion, that any offer of release will be welcome to them now the tumult and hurry of their former lusts and eager affections is slaked ... ; and their close-adhering pain which sticks to them and scorches them worse then *Hercules* his *shirt*, should methinks necessarily force them to take up strong and peremptory resolutions and indignation against those courses whose fruits they now feel so direful to them.[27]

More's fifth position outlined above is an Origenistic one, and it was endorsed by Rust. For, after the bodies of the wicked have been destroyed by the fire, the souls of the wicked, in a disembodied state, would lapse into a state of silence and inactivity, eventually to receive another chance on a reconstituted earth. The reconstitution of the earth would not happen supernaturally but naturally. When the heat abated, the evaporated waters below the aethereal realm would fall down 'in trickling dewie showers' and, mixing with the ashes of the earth, would make it fruitful and vegetative once again.

The souls of brutes would once again be united with matter. All this, Rust declared, 'would almost perswade one that *Man* ought also to appear on the Earth, to be the Father of this great family, the lord, governour, patron and defender of all the creatures therein'.[28] And, he went on to suggest, if one such restoration were possible, one could also accept an 'infinite repetition of *conflagrations* and *re-productions*' so that all, even the most persistently sinful, would ultimately be saved.[29]

A similar scenario was offered by Joseph Glanvill. After death, the wicked were confined in darkness, stench, and horror in cavities within the body of the earth. For him, the Biblical descriptions of a deep pit, a prison, a place of darkness and fire were to be taken literally and not figuratively. Unrepentant by their natures, the wicked progressively continued downwards, '*fixt* and *rooted* in their *sensual* and *rebellious propensions*',[30] until they reached the most intolerable degree of misery.

Glanvill followed the Cartesian doctrine of the central fire. The conflagration would occur when this central fire would increase in vigour, would melt the shell surrounding it, and would spread to the whole interior of the earth. The wicked would then receive the full punishment for their iniquities, 'these fierce and merciless flames sticking close to, yea, piercing through and through their bodies, which can remove no where to avoid this *fiery* over-spreading vengeance'.[31]

Eventually, the fire would burn through to the surface of the earth. At that time, just before the conflagration took hold, Christ would come in the clouds. The sight of Christ and his legions of angels would excite and awaken the spirits of the righteous, whose bodies, melting into the purest flame, would 'ascend in those *fiery Chariots* with our Glorious *Redeemer*, and his illustrious and blessed Attendants to the Coelestial habitations'.[32] The wicked on earth would remain behind in the flames.

But this was not to be the eternal fate of the wicked, at least, said Glanvill, if we consulted philosophy and the Eastern Cabbala. For, they were to remain under the eye and tender care of God's almighty goodness. The flames would eventually separate body and spirit, and without a vehicle, the soul would lapse into senselessness and inactivity. Eventually, only the central orb of fire would remain which would then fly away 'out of this *vortex*, and become a *wandring Comet*, till it settle in some other [vortex]'.[33] Alternatively, if the central fire were to remain uninvolved in the Conflagration, the earth would retain its present place among the planets.

In either case, the smoke and vapour would eventually descend in showers, mingle with the ashes, and reconstitute the earth into 'a Garden of delight and pleasure'.[34] The wicked, then roused from their slumbers, would be joined again to bodies of purified air, and placed in such conditions whereby

> they may amend what was formerly amiss in them, and pursue any *good Resolutions* that they took while under the lash of the fiery tortures; Which those that do, when their good *inclinations* are perfected, and the *Divine Life* again enkindled, they shall in due time re-ascend the *Thrones* they so unhappily fell from, and be circled about with unexpressible felicity.[35]

Myriads of others, who were waiting in the wings (so to say) for terrestrial bodies when the last day came, would then assume terrestrial bodies. Glanvill refused to take refuge in the divine miraculous construction of these bodies. Rather, he thought it probable that 'there may be some pure efflorescences of *balmy* matter ... that may be proper *vehicles* of *life*, into which souls may descend without further *preparation*'.³⁶ All of this implied a further turn of the cosmic wheel, and the possibility of another conflagration, not by water nor by fire but 'by the *Extinction* of the *Sun*'.³⁷ Glanvill nowhere suggested universal salvation, but his cosmology and eschatology, like that of Henry More and George Rust, was undoubtedly congenial to it.

HELL ON EARTH

Thomas Burnet's *The Sacred Theory of the Earth* was one of the first attempts to devise a natural cosmogony and a natural history of the earth to supplement the Biblical version of the earth's natural history. Published in two parts – the Latin part 1 of 1681 translated into English in 1684, the Latin part 2 of 1689 translated into English in 1690 – the work began with an account of the earth's origin, formation and present condition, and ended with a description of the last day and the new heaven and the new earth which would be built on the ruins of the old. Burnet had gone up to Clare College, Cambridge, in 1651, but later (with Ralph Cudworth) he transferred to Christ's. Throughout the 1660s, he remained closely associated with Cudworth and with Henry More. While undoubtedly influenced by Platonist eschatological concerns, he nevertheless eschewed metaphysical speculation to concentrate on the application of the new science to the interpretation of the Scriptures.

M. C. Jacob and W. A. Lockwood have demonstrated that the Latin version of part 2 was deeply influenced by Anglican political millenarianism, itself a product of the social and political instability of England in the period shortly before the Glorious Revolution of 1688.³⁸ In that version, it can be seen that Burnet expected the conflagration of the world to occur about two hundred years thence. However, in the English version of 1691, overtly millenarian statements were excluded, for the Revolution had overcome the threats to the constitutional and ecclesiastical structure presented by James II. Thus, the English version of 1691 appears more as a sequel to the natural history of the first part than its Latin predecessor, and consequently much more as an early scientific explanation of the last day. Indeed, in this version, Burnet was deliberately vague about how it could be determined when the Conflagration would occur. But, that it would be by natural causes under the superintendence of Providence – 'a *mixt Fatality*, a Divine Judgment supported by natural causes',³⁹ he had no doubt.

Like More, Glanvill, and Rust, Burnet saw the Conflagration occurring only to this earth. The celestial regions inhabited by the angels and the stars would be exempt from it. Burnet had two reasons for not accepting that the conflagration would be caused by the sun approaching closer to the earth. First, he argued, were the sun getting closer, the days and years would be getting shorter, and this was manifestly not the case. But second, this would rule out the possibility of the creation of a new heaven and a new earth after the conflagration, as Scripture suggested: 'if the sun should come so near us as to make the *heavens pass away with a noise, and melt the Elements with fervent heat*, and destroy the form and all the works of the Earth, what hopes would there be of a Renovation while the Sun continued in this posture? He would more and more consume and prey upon the Carcase of the Earth, and convert it at length either into a heap of ashes, or a lump of vitrified metal.'[40]

Burnet also accepted Descartes' theory of the fire at the core of the earth. But he rejected it as a cause of the conflagration, in part because its surrounding shell was impenetrable, in part because, even if it were to break through, it would not be sufficient to cause the universal conflagration represented in Scripture, and in part because, were the central fire exhausted and the exterior regions sucked into those empty central spaces, the earth would lose its poise, be flung into another part of the universe, and be incapable of restoration.

The conflagration would be caused, argued Burnet, by a combination of factors – the flaring up of volcanoes, the fuels beneath the earth (sulphur, bitumen, inflammable salts, coal), and meteoric fires from heaven. Because the conflagration was to be both a natural event and a work of divine justice, it was possible to predict where it would begin. The natural requirements for a region's inflammability were 'the sulphureousness of its Soil, and its fiery Mountains and Caverns';[41] divine justice suggested that the home of Anti-Christ, the mystical Babylon, should be the first 'Sacrifice to this Fiery Vengeance';[42] both of these conditions were fulfilled by Rome.

To all intents and purposes, Burnet removed the special providence of God from the Conflagration. Only when all the natural circumstances conspired towards it would Christ come again, 'a Glory surpassing the Sun in its greatest radiancy ... '[43] to take vengeance upon his enemies. The world would turn to fire: 'We think it a great matter to see a single person burnt alive: here are Millions, shrieking in the flames at once. 'Tis frightful to us to look upon a great City in flames; and to see the misery and distraction of the people: here is an Universal Fire through all the Cities of the Earth, and an universal Massacre of their inhabitants.'[44] The conflagration was identified with hell:

> For, Fire and darkness are the two chief things by which that state, or that place used to be describ'd: and they are both here mingled together: with all other ingredients that make that Tophet that is prepar'd of old. Here are Lakes of fire and brimstone: Rivers of melted glowing matter: Ten thousand Volcanos vomiting flames all at once. Thick darkness, and Pillars of smoke twisted about with wreaths of flame, like fiery Snakes. Mountains of Earth thrown up into the Air, and the Heavens dropping down in lumps of fire. These things will all be literally true, concerning that day, and that state of the Earth. And if we suppose *Beelzebub*, and his Apostate crew, in the midst of this fiery furnace: (and I know not where they can be else). It will be hard to find any part of the Universe, or any state of things, that answers to so many of the properties and characters of *Hell*, as that which is now before us.[45]

Like Rust and Glanvill, Burnet expected that the world would be reconstituted after the Conflagration. The process of formation of the new would replicate that of the old, a process which Burnet construed on Cartesian lines. The righteous would then be resurrected and live on the earth throughout Christ's one-thousand-year reign. This would be no sensual Mahometan paradise. Rather,

> we have great reason to hope, that the Soul will have a greater dominion over the Resurrection-body, than she hath over this. And you know we suppose that none will truly inherit the Millennium, but those that rise from the Dead. Nor do we admit any propagation there, nor the trouble or weakness of Infants. But that all rise in a perfect age, and never die.[46]

Millenial life would consist of devotion and contemplation, the entertainments of friendship, and the study of natural science. The questions of this life would then be answered: Where or what is the state of hell? Where are the souls of the wicked to eternity? What is the true state of heaven? And even the Origenistic speculation as to how many turns we shall take upon this stage of the earth and how many trials we shall have, before our doom is finally concluded.

Following Revelation 20, Burnet conjectured that, at the end of this millennium, there would be a further resurrection and the last judgement. The saints would then be translated into heaven, and the earth would again be dissolved by fire, to 'be chang'd into the nature of a Sun, or of a fixt Star: and shine like them in the Firmament'.[47]

In *The Sacred Theory of the Earth*, the fate of the wicked, if not of the good, was much more opaque. The wicked who were still alive at the time of the conflagration would be totally destroyed in the fire, the just and infants miraculously saved from it. But the ultimate fate of the wicked raised on the day of judgement at the second resurrection was undetermined.

The final destiny of both the saved and the damned was however made clearer in Burnet's *De Statu Mortuorum & Resurgentium*. There is little doubt that Burnet did not wish his opinions on the final state of the damned to be common knowledge. Burnet himself had only a few copies printed and circulated among a few intimates. Five years after his death, Richard Mead had a small edition printed in 1720 with the admonition that no reader should transcribe it or give it to the Press. General readers would have discovered why from the unauthorised English translation by Matthias Earbery in 1728.

Burnet was committed to the necessity of the doctrine of eternal torments as a deterrent to wickedness. But his own opinion was that the damned in hell would have a chance of reformation. Thus, although he was convinced that 'the Time will come when this Opinion [of eternal torments] will be reckon'd as absurd and odious, as Transubstantiation is now',[48] he nevertheless declared,

> whatever your Opinion is within yourself concerning these Punishments, whether they are eternal or not; yet always with the People, and when you preach to the People, use the receiv'd Doctrine, and the received Words in the Sense, in which the people receive them: For they are apt to run headlong into Vice, and are to be terrify'd from offending by the apprehension of Punishment only.[49]

It was through his commitment to the double doctrine – that the words of Scripture contain both an exoteric and an esoteric meaning – that Burnet hoped to avoid the charge of disingenuousness. For Burnet, the secret, rational esoteric meaning of the Scriptures (and of other Christian doctrines) was hidden beneath their plain and vulgar meaning, the latter appropriate for the uneducated masses, the former for the educated elite.

Burnet denied a physical location to hell before the conflagration. Consequently, the wicked would only suffer the punishments of loss and not the punishments of sense between death and the day of judgement. In this work, hell is again identified with the first Conflagration of the earth, but also with the final judgement. On the last day, the wicked on earth and the wicked already dead (still in their disembodied state) would suffer physical torments, though how disembodied souls were to do so is not made clear. Nor is it made clear what would happen to them during the millennium, nor after the final resurrection when the blessed would be located above the globe of the moon and the atmospheres of the planets, 'in a sublime Station, remote from Earth, and high in the Starry Regions...'[50]

Burnet was convinced that eternal torment was of no service to God or man: no service to God because it endorsed the image of a God of cruelty, injustice, and barbarity; and no good to man because it offered no possibility of repentance. Against the argument that eternal punishment was deserved because the wicked were irredeemable, he argued that if they could not help continuing to sin, they ought not to be eternally punished, but annihilated by God. That is to say, the orthodox static hell morally demanded the annihilation of the wicked. But if the wicked could refrain from sin, he maintained, and were given intermissions of their pain, there must be a chance of repentance, unless their continuing obduracy were caused by God himself. Their sinful disposition

> cannot be so deep rooted but Fire will purge it out: A Remedy as searching as it is powerful and strong... Moreover in another Life, when the Wicked shall see Christ coming in his Glory... there will be no room for their infidelity; the Fomes peccati in this Flesh will be extinguished; Concupiscence will be no more, and the Food for Vices, for unlawful Pleasures ... be taken away; why therefore, and with what Motives can they adhere for ever to their Sins, unless they are hardened by Heaven?[51]

A morally dynamic hell, even if it did not entail the eventual restoration of all, did suggest there was no human or divine necessity for the millions shrieking in the flames to do so for ever, a stance different from the exoteric one Burnet had presented in *The Sacred Theory of the Earth*, which had suggested the destruction of the wicked in the flaming fire of the cosmic conflagration.[52]

FROM THE EARTH TO THE SUN

John Ray was a naturalist, primarily remembered for his two popular works, *The Wisdom of God Manifested in the Works of his Creation* in 1691, and *Miscellaneous Discourses concerning the Dissolution and Changes of the World* in 1692.[53] In this latter work, Ray explored the final dissolution of the world according to the Scriptures and the Fathers, the ancient philosophers, and various possible natural causes of the dissolution of the world.

Convinced on the basis of tradition that the world would end by fire, he rejected its possible destruction by water or by the extinction of the sun. But he was committed to explore the possibility of its demise being the result of the eruption of the central fire. He totally rejected Descartes' account of the origin of the earth, but he found the notion of a central fire within the earth in no way repugnant to Scripture or reason. And on the basis of the natural history of the appearance and disappearance of other stars, he concluded that the eruption of the central fire within the earth was a possible if not probable cause of the final conflagration. But, on grounds similar to Burnet's, he finally rejected this option.[54] He was, however, even less convinced that the conflagration would be caused by the earth's dryness and inflammability, for, like Burnet, he found no natural evidence of a progressive dehydration of the earth.

Uncertain as he was of the exact causes, he was in no doubt that the instrumental causes of the conflagration would be natural, for there were abundant fuels in the air and within the earth. But, unlike Burnet, he was persuaded that the world would continue for two thousand more years, and then that 'the Accension and the sudden and equal Diffusion of this Fire all the World over' must be the work of God, extraordinary and miraculous.[55]

Ray was convinced that the conflagration would reach right up to the visible heavens, for the new astronomy had shown that the heavenly bodies, far from being not subject to change – 'an idle and ill grounded conceit of the *Peripateticks*'[56] – were of the same nature as the earth. Nevertheless, neither the heavenly bodies nor the earth would be annihilated, but refined and purified:

Now if the place of the Blessed be an Empyreal Heaven far above these visible Heavens, ... and the place of the Damned be beneath, about the middle of the Earth ... Then when all the intermediate Bodies shall be annihilated, what a strange Universe shall we have? Consisting of an immense Ring of Matter, save only one small point for an infernal Dungeon. Those that are of this Opinion have too narrow and mean thoughts of the Greatness, I had almost said Immensity of the Universe, the glorious and magnifick products of the Creator's Almighty Power: and are too partial to themselves to think the whole World was created for no other end but to be serviceable to Mankind.[57]

Ray's commitment to the manifest works of God decentred humankind from the universe. He saw no desirability nor necessity for man to repopulate the reconstituted earth. God could be glorified in other ways, he conjectured: 'There may be a new Race of rational Animals brought forth to act their parts upon this Stage, which may give the Creator as much Glory as man ever did or could. And... there are spiritual and intellectual Beings, which may be as busie, and as much delighted in searching out and contemplating the Works of God in this new Earth, and rendring him the Praise of his Wisdom and Power as Man could be.'[58] A new heaven and a new earth could be created from which the blessed in the empyreal regions and the wicked in the infernal regions might be eternally excluded. The whole creation was under God's providential care and man was part of a much larger moral and (as we would now put it) ecological order.

GODS, SUNS, AND COMETS

Copernicus' sun-centred theory of the world arose as a consequence of his astronomical calculations. But his *De Revolutionibus Orbium Coelestium* in 1543 was imbued with a sense of religious awe and wonder. 'In the midst of all', wrote Copernicus, 'resides the sun. For who could place this great light in any better position in this most beautiful temple [of the world] than that from which it may illumine all at once? So that it is called by some the lamp of the world; by others, the mind; by others the ruler. And Trismegistus calls it the visible God.'[59]

For Copernicus, his discovery had the blessing of Hermes Trismegistus, whom he, along with the neo-Platonists of the Renaissance, believed to be an all-wise Egyptian priest, contemporary of Moses and the fount of wisdom upon whom Plato and the Greeks had depended. Copernicus' new world view was presented within the framework of Hermetic neo-Platonism and its mysticism of the sun.

In contrast, to the Copernican Anglican Tobias Swinden in 1714, the Sun was one of the ancient idols to which men gave worship, imposed upon them by the Devil, 'whereby he made them not only to *deny the God* that is *above*, but in Opposition to him to assert and vindicate the Seat of his own Empire below...'[60] On Copernican grounds, Swinden argued that the sun was the dwelling place of Satan, it was hell.

According to Swinden, until his time, everyone had erroneously located hell beneath the earth. But according to his calculations, the sun was the ideal and precise location of hell. It was a real corporeal fire; it was large enough to contain the vast multitudes of the damned; and, most importantly, it was the centre of the universe, and the furthest possible distance from the region of Angels and happy souls:

> the two Extreams or Opponents in the highest degree, are the *Empyreum*, and the body of the *Sun*. The former of these is confessed by Divines ... to be the Region of Angels and happy Souls. And therefore what more rational than to suppose the latter to be the Seat of Devils and miserable Spirits?[61]

In Swinden's cosmogony, God created the universe to demonstrate his power and glory to rebellious angels. The creation of the body of the sun was God's primary act. The Devil and his angels were immediately thrown down into the sun, there ultimately to be joined by the wicked for eternity immediately upon their deaths. After the last judgement wicked souls, reunited with their bodies, would be dispersed thoughout this solar hell. After the final conflagration, all intermediate bodies would be destroyed, including the earth. Only heaven and the sun would remain, the latter appearing as the lesser of the two works which would endure.

In the earth-centred universe, hell was beneath the earth, and heaven above in the regions of the stars. In Swinden's sun-centred universe, heaven remained above, hell was below the earth in the sun. In Copernicus' sun-centred universe, science and religion met in the lamp of the world, the immortal and visible God. In Swinden's Copernican universe, science and religion met in the dark flames of the sun, the immortal and visible hell:

> the burning Nature of the *Sun's* Body, and the magnitude of it are, to me, not only Arguments of its being the Tartarus or Local *Hell* but, for that very Reason a good Proof too, of the Truth of the *Pythagora-Copernican* System, which hath so placed the *Heaven*, the *Earth*, and the *Hell*, as suited with the Nature and Constitution of each one of them ... [62]

Swinden's theory has a certain common-sense appeal about it. But the benevolent and heroic image of the sun was too ingrained in the symbolism of Western thought for it to have had much chance of success.

The attempted rapprochement between science and religion was perhaps nowhere better demonstrated than in the work of the eccentric and enthusiastic William Whiston, Isaac Newton's chosen successor as Lucasian Professor of Mathematics at Cambridge. In 1696, Whiston published his *A New Theory of the Earth, From its Original, to the Consummation of all Things. Wherein the Creation of the World in Six Days, the Universal Deluge, And the General Conflagration, As laid down in the Holy Scriptures, Are shewn to be perfectly agreeable to Reason and Philosophy*. His primary target was Thomas Burnet.

In his own review in 1690 of his *The Sacred Theory of the Earth*, Burnet indicated that the principal objection to his work was that the Cartesian cosmogony he had presented was inconsistent with the Biblical account of a six-day creation. But, he went on to dismiss the Mosaic account as an allegory, and one never 'intended for a true Physical account of the origine of the Earth'.[63] And he invoked the double doctrine to justify this. His account of the origin of the world was reconcilable with the Scriptures since the latter were written in a vulgar style suitable to the capacity of the people.

Already, in January 1681, Newton had written to Burnet expressing his antagonism to Burnet's allegorising of the Creation account and arguing that, although Moses was popularising, it was finally straightforward scientific truth. Moses was a simplifier, not a falsifier.[64] It was this Newtonian principle which Whiston was to follow in the work which he dedicated to 'Summo Viro Isaaco Newton'. The postulates which Whiston set down in this work were quite acceptable to his patron: 'I. The obvious or Literal Sense of Scriptures is the True and Real one, where no evident Reason can be given to the contrary. II. That which is clearly accountable in a natural way, is not without reason to be ascribed to a Miraculous Power. III. What Ancient Tradition asserts of the Constitution of Nature, or of the Origin and Primitive States of the World, is to be allow'd for True, where 'tis fully agreeable to Scripture, Reason, and Philosophy.'[65]

Cometology was the key to Whiston's theory of the earth.[66] As Simon Schaffer has shown, Whiston, like Halley and Newton, transformed astrology into astronomy. Newtonian cometography, he writes, 'changed the practice which should deal with comets from popular divination to theologically oriented natural philosophy, giving comets a profound but scarcely less dramatic function and prophetic meaning'.[67] According to Whiston, the earth was created when its radically elliptical orbit as a comet changed to an almost circular orbit which allowed for its natural development. After the Fall of Adam and Eve, the impact of a comet caused the end of paradise: the shape and orbit of the earth was changed, the axis of the world was tilted, and seasons, winds, and tides were the result. The universal flood to punish all except Noah and his family occurred also as the result of a comet's passing in close proximity to the earth. The vaporous tail of the comet poured rain upon the earth, the crust of the earth broke under the weight of water, and the 'fountains of the great deep' (Genesis 7.18) were released. Whiston later tried to prove that it was Halley's Comet which was the occasion of the deluge at that time.[68]

Comets would also be the cause of the earth's final destruction. The first conflagration would be caused by the passing of a comet in sufficient proximity to the earth to dry up the oceans and to heat the air sufficiently to allow the subterraneous regions of fire to flare up to the surface. Nevertheless, as the heat receded, there would be a renovation of the earth into its paradisal state, 'a kind of Reiteration of the *Mosaick* six days Creation...'[69] The bodies of the Saints and martyrs would then be raised to be reunited with their souls which after death had resided in the air, to spend the millennium on the restored earth.

After the millennium, there would be the second resurrection (of the wicked), the last judgement, and the final consummation of all things. The earth would be hit by a comet, and would move into a different elliptical orbit, becoming once again a comet. A more graphic description of the fate of the earth occurred in Whiston's 1717 work, *Astronomical Principles of Religion, Natural and Reveal'd*. Having detailed many Biblical texts on the nature of hell, ending with Revelation 14.9–11, Whiston concluded,

Now this Description does in every Circumstance, so exactly agree with the Nature of a Comet, ascending from the Hot Regions near the Sun, and going into the Cold Regions beyond *Saturn*, with its long smoking Tail arising up from it... and this in sight of all the Inhabitants of our Air, and of the rest of the System; that I cannot but think the Surface or Atmosphere of such a comet to be that *Place* of *Torment* so terribly described in Scripture, in which the Devil and his Angels, with wicked Men their Companions, when delivered out of their Prison in the Heart of the Earth, shall be cast for their utter *Perdition* or *second Death*; which will be indeed a terrible but a most useful Spectacle to God's rational creatures.[70]

In another work in 1740, their fate would be slightly different, although comparably grim. When the final conflagration began, Whiston declared, the earth would be turned into a comet; the devil, his angels, and the wicked would be 'thrown down into its burning atmosphere, till they are utterly destroyed ... '[71] The good, inhabiting the air in their spiritual bodies, would find the sufferings of the wicked a useful spectacle; it would 'admonish them above all Things to preserve their Innocence and Obedience; and to *fear him who is* thus *able to destroy both Soul and Body in Hell*'.[72]

When he was a student at Cambridge from 1686 to 1691, Whiston composed ten *Meditations*, one of which, directed against atheists, ended with vehement threats of eternal torment.[73] But by 1709, he had come to doubt the eternity of hell's torments. A temporary period of punishment followed by annihilation, he suggested, was sufficient to meet the ends of religion, and was most agreeable to the divine justice and goodness. The punishments were 'eternal', he maintained, only in the sense that they would 'continue the whole Duration of the Wicked, who are the subjects of it'.[74]

Virtually the identical phrase occurred in a short discourse by John Locke, entitled *Resurrectio et quae sequuntur*, first published in 1829. And it is not improbable that Whiston had read this work and that it had played some role in the development of his own account of the fate of the wicked. In this work, Locke sketched the following programme for the last day. There would be two resurrections, the first of the good with spiritual bodies (following 1 Corinthians 15) when Christ came, the second of the wicked with physical bodies shortly before Christ delivered up the Kingdom to his Father. Scripture, declared Locke, plainly showed that the wicked would be cast into hell fire to be tormented, but also that they would not live for ever. Punishment everlasting 'may be said of that which endures only as long as the subject it affects endures'.[75] The 'unquenchable fire' referred literally to the fire of Gehenna outside Jerusalem which burnt constantly to destroy the carcases of beasts and other filth. Yet, it did not follow, argued Locke, 'that the bodies that were burnt in it were never consumed, only that the worms that gnawed and the fire that burnt were constant and never ceased till they were destroyed'.[76]

Although Whiston wrote a small paper against eternal torments in 1717,[77] it was not until 1740 that he published the work *The Eternity of Hell Torments Considered*, in which his full eschatology was revealed. No longer able to maintain his silence, he completely rejected eternal torments along with the doctrine of the Trinity, predestination to damnation and the doctrine of transubstantiation: 'I think the common opinion for the *proper Eternity* of those torments to be no less absurd, nor less reproachful to christianity than the *Athanasian* Doctrine of the Trinity; the *Calvinist* Doctrine of Reprobation; or the *Popish* Doctrine of Transubstantiation ... '[78]

Before the last judgement, the wicked were confined beneath the earth. Halley's and his own researches demonstrated, he claimed, a large cavity between the external and internal parts of the earth which vindicated Scriptural and traditional descriptions of Hades and Gehenna as being beneath the earth.[79] During this period, the wicked would have a chance for repentance. Whiston was sanguine that the far greater part would be brought to some degree of salvation. Indeed, he was even hopeful that Satan and his wicked angels might eventually freely choose to repent, amend themselves and be saved.

But the incorrigibly wicked who had failed freely to repent would be resurrected on the last day, to be tormented for a period of time proportionate to their sins, and then be ultimately annihilated. As with Locke, the wicked would be raised with physical bodies which would be physically punished in the flames. They would also be raised with the same diseases they had at death. Thus the wicked would be 'equally capable of being corroded and devoured by *worms*, and of being burnt and consumed by *fire* as the sinner was when he offended'.[80]

The irony of Whiston's position has not gone unnoticed. As D. P. Walker wryly remarks, 'It is a "barbarous and cruel" opinion to suppose that God torments the damned eternally in punishment for a short life of sin; but it is, presumably, in harmony with His "astonishing Love toward Mankind" to have them burnt and eaten by worms for several ages.'[81] But for Whiston, the 'rules of right and justice in the world' ruled out torments of equal duration for different crimes in the here and now.[82] The earthly judge sentenced the wicked to various tortures, to be followed by death. The divine judge would sentence the wicked to varied punishments, to be followed by the second death, on the last day. 'And shall not the Judge of all the earth do right?' asked Whiston.[83] To Whiston, no doubt, it appeared not only just but merciful.

RESURRECTION AND PERSONS

Thus saith the Lord God unto these bones; Behold, I will cause breath to enter into you, and ye shall live.[84]

From the time of Tertullian, Christian teachers and theologians had held it as a firm article of their faith that, as the physical body of Jesus rose from the dead, so too on the last day, God would raise the physical bodies of the dead, and grant to them the immortality that had been lost by Adam but restored in Christ. The soul would remain between death and the day of judgement in the bosom of Abraham or in Hades, but it would be reunited with its body to be judged for eternal salvation or eternal damnation.[85]

There was a strong commitment in the seventeenth century to the belief that the resurrection body would be the same as that in which our earthly lives were lived. But there was much controversy as to what 'the same body' might mean. Many were convinced that the resurrection body would be identical with the earthly body. Sir Kenelm Digby, for example, simply pointed out that 'if we will be Christians, and rely upon Gods promises, wee must beleeve that we shall rise againe with the same Body, that walked about, did eate, drinke, and live here on earth'.[86] Those who were dead, declared Bishop Pearson, 'shall rise out of their graves to life in the same bodies in which they lived'.[87] Hieronymus Zanchius, the Renaissance Biblical commentator, flatly condemned all those 'who fancied we shall not have the same, but other new bodies'.[88]

Where the resurrection body was declared to be identical with the earthly body, other problems abounded. The divine John Seager in 1650 deemed it essential that resurrection bodies would have to consist of flesh and bones, of eyes, ears, hands, and feet. Yet, he maintained that they would not need to be of the same substance as our present ones.[89] The crucial problem centred on the dispersal of human remains through the world after death, and their subsequent collection. What was to be the fate of those who had been devoured by cannibals, the beasts of the field, the fowls of the air, and the fishes of the sea?

The Anglican Robert Sharrock surmised that 'No *Canniball*, nor beast, nor foul, nor fish ever converted the whole Body of any Man to his own nourishment... '[90] Moreover, he suggested, perhaps the same material particles are not necessary to make up the same man.

And he went on to foreshadow John Locke in his suggestion that the soul was the criterion of our individual identity. Nevertheless, like many others, Sharrock finally resolved the dilemma of how the parts of persons would be reassembled after scattering and decay by leaving it in the hands of God: 'God can easily dispose those parts to their right owners, as a common herdsman, who keeps all the beasts of a Lordship in one herd, can when he pleaseth distinguish them and send them to their particular masters and owners.'[91] Similarly, William Bates believed that under whatever colours and figures the dispersed matter of our bodies should appear, 'God perfectly discerns, and will separate it for its proper use.'[92] It was God's omniscience, declared the nonconformist divine John Shower in 1693, that enabled him to call forth every bodily part at the appointed time for reunion with its soul.[93] From an earlier period, here is the eloquent Dean of St Paul's, John Donne:

Where be all the splinters of that Bone, which a shot hath shivered and scattered in the Ayre? Where be all the Atoms of that flesh, which a *Corrasive* hath eat away, or a *Consumption* hath breath'd, and exhal'd away from our arms, and other Limbs? In what wrinkle, in what furrow, in what bowel of the earth, ly all the graines of the ashes of a body burnt a thousand years since? In what corner, in what ventricle of the sea, lies all the jelly of a Body drowned in the *generall flood*? What cohaerence, what sympathy, what dependence maintaines any relation, any correspondence, between that arm that was lost in Europe, and that legge that was lost in Afrique or Asia, scores of yeers between? One humour of our dead body produces worms, and those worms suck and exhaust all other humour, and then all dies, and molders into dust, and that dust is blowen into the River & that puddled water tumbled into the sea, and that ebs and flows in infinite revolutions, and still, still God knows in what *Cabinet* every *seed-Pearle* lies, in what part of the world every graine of every mans dust lies; and, *sibilat populum suum*, (as his Prophet speaks in another case) he whispers, he hisses, he beckens for the bodies of his Saints, and in the twinckling of an eye, that body that was scattered over all the elements, is sate down at the right hand of God, in a glorious resurrection.[94]

Thomas Browne adopted the same position. 'I believe', he wrote, 'that our estranged and divided ashes shall unite againe; that our separated dust after so many pilgrimages and transformations into the parts of mineralls, Plants, Animals, Elements, shall at the voyce of God returne into their primitive shapes, and joyne againe to make up their primary and predestinated formes'.[95] But his Baconian-style empiricism and his Platonic belief in nature as symbol united in his quest for natural analogies to the resurrection of the body. Mercury dispersed into a thousand parts returns to its numerical self; stalks and leaves return from the ashes of a plant:

What the Art of Man can doe in these inferiour pieces, what blasphemy is it to affirme the finger of God cannot doe in these more perfect and sensible structures? This is that mysticall Philosophy, from whence no true Scholler becomes an Atheist, but from the visible effects of nature, grows up a reall Divine, and beholds not in a dreame, as *Ezekiel*, but in an ocular and visible object the types of his resurrection.[96]

Like Browne, Robert Boyle was convinced that the resurrection of bodies would happen, not in the course of nature, but by the power of God. Nevertheless, in his 1675 work, *Some Physico-Theological Considerations about the Possibility of the Resurrection*, Boyle attempted to illuminate the Biblical understanding of the resurrection by examples drawn from the natural world, to answer what he saw as the principal objection to its possibility:

When a man is once really dead, divers of the parts of the body will, according to the course of nature, resolve themselves into multitudes of steams, that wander to and fro in the air; and the remaining parts, that are either liquid or soft, undergo so great a corruption and change, that it is not possible so many scattered parts should be again brought together, and re-united after the same manner wherein they existed in a human body, whilst it was yett alive. And much more impossible it is to effect this re-union, if the body have been, as it often happens, devoured by wild beasts or fishes; since in this case, though the scattered particles of the cadaver might be recovered as particles of matter, yet having already passed into the substance of other animals, they are quite transmuted, as being informed by the new form of the beast or fish that devoured them, and of which they now make a substantial part. And yet far more impossible will this re-integration be, if we put the case, that the dead body be devoured by Cannibals; for then the same flesh belonging successively to two differing persons, it is impossible that both should have it restored to them at once, or that any footsteps should remain of the relation it had to the first possessor.[97]

The issue for Boyle was essentially one of personal identity. The above objection only held if the identity of the pre-resurrection body with the post-resurrection depended upon the restoration of all the parts. He mounted a number of arguments against this. Thus, for example, he resorted to an argument first used by Origen.[98] But it was also one which had received general acceptance as the result of the work of Sanctorius whom Boyle cited as having proved the Galenic assumption that a great part of what people eat and drink was discharged by insensible transpiration.[99] Thus, even in this life, Boyle maintained, numerical identity is not dependent on an identity of parts, for the human body is in a state of perpetual flux; apart from skulls and bones, 'in no very great compass of time, a great part of the substance of a human body must be changed ... '[100] Moreover, he suggested, the objection only held if parts were irretrievable. In contrast, he argued, even where the parts of one body were joined with those of another, they may retain their own nature. And, since there were chemical means by which bodies could be recovered from their various guises, 'why should it be impossible, that a most intelligent agent, whose omnipotence extends to all that is not truly contradictory to the nature of things, or to his own, should be able so to order and to watch the particles of a human body, ... that stripping them of their disguises, or extricating them from other parts of matter, to which they may happen to be conjoined, he may re-unite them betwixt themselves, and, if need be, with particles of matter fit to be contexed with them, and thereby restore or reproduce a body ... '[101]

But Boyle himself was not committed to an account of personal identity which entailed a numerical identity of parts. For Boyle, personal identity was retained if a portion of the matter of the former body constituted the resurrection body. This was the understanding of personal identity, he believed, embedded in the Scriptures: 'it is not unconsonant to the expressions of scripture, to say, that a portion of the matter of a dead body, being united with a far greater portion of matter furnished from without by God himself, and completed into a human body, may be reputed the same man, that was dead before'.[102] And drawing on the vision of Ezekiel and his own chemical experiments on the stable and long-lasting texture of bones, he surmised that skeletal remains would ensure the identity of the post- and pre-resurrection bodies, God adding such other parts as he saw fit to restore the body.

Like Browne, Boyle found natural analogies to the re-formation of bodies from mere portions of them. Thus, for example, he reported on two gentlemen of his acquaintance who, from the ashes of a plant, had produced another, suggestive of a 'plastick power' within the plant which enabled it to reproduce itself. And he cited the case of the Polonian physician, Kircherus, who claimed to have reproduced in well-closed vials the 'perfect ideas of plants destroyed by the fire'.[103] Boyle was well aware that, if the soul were a sufficient criterion of personal identity, the problem of the resurrection of the body would be much ameliorated. For, the same person would then be resurrected irrespective of which portions of matter the soul was united with. But he saw, I think, the harder path as the more desirable one. For it was of a piece with the power that the Divine would exert upon the risen bodies of the saints in transforming them from resurrected earthly bodies into the likeness of Christ's glorious body.

The most substantial late seventeenth-century defence of the doctrine that pre- and post-resurrection bodies would be exactly identical in parts was that of Humphrey Hody, chaplain to Archbishop Tillotson. He assembled a collage of Biblical quotations to this effect. Moreover, he argued, Scripture entailed that our resurrection bodies would be like that of Christ's resurrection body – identical with his earthly one. And he went on to make the not unreasonable point that, unless the Biblical texts had not intended to assert that the identical body would be raised, they would not have used the word 'resurrection' to describe such an event.[104] Like many others, he maintained the desirability of punishing the same body which had committed the sins.

Most of his ingenuity, however, was reserved for defending his account of the nature of the resurrection body by appeal to empirical and scientific evidence. Thus, for example, against the classical 'cannibal' objection, he relied upon the power of God to ensure that the particles of one man's body should never so become the particles of another's as to render the resurrection of either an impossibility. And, like Boyle, he invoked the metabolic studies of Sanctorius, to the effect that the body retains only a small part of that which it takes in by way of nourishment. Thus, should one man devour another, 'it appears from *Sanctorius's* Observation that not above the 50th part of the Flesh of the Person Devour'd would become the Flesh of him that ate it. And besides the other 49 parts of the Flesh, there would remain all the *Bones* untouched, which make up a great (the most substantial) part of the Body.'[105] It was after all necessary only that the most important parts of the body be raised – bones, skin, nerves, tendons, ligaments, substance of vessels. Recognising that even one-fiftieth not being raised was sufficient to open his account to criticism, he added an unusual proviso. If God has decreed that all parts should be raised up, he suggested, 'God will take care that no one shall die whilst His Body contains any Particles that belong to another.'[106] But even he thought his readers need not go this far. It was sufficient, if on the day of resurrection, God raise only the necessary parts of the body as it was on its dying day.

He also dealt with the objection that, on the last day, there would not be sufficient matter on the whole surface of the earth to make up the necessary number of bodies for all those who will have lived and died by that time. A complicated set of arithmetical calculations was offered to avoid this claim. Thus, for example, on the ratio of the estimated square feet in England to an estimated number of persons in 10,000 years, he declared that the latter were only one-seventeenth of the former. And taking into account the ratio of the weight of men (with appropriate adjustments for women and children) to the weight of a solid cubic foot of common earth, he concluded,

> it will plainly appear that the weight of a *Humane* Body, taking one with another, is not so great as the weight of a *Solid* Foot of common Earth. It is manifest therefore, that in less than the *Seventeenth* Part of *England*, if you go but *One Foot* deep, there is as much Substance as would make up all the *Humane* Bodies that ever were, are, and will be, tho' the World should last in all 10,000 years.[107]

Hody believed that resurrection bodies would be incorruptible, powerful, spiritual, celestial, glorious, without wrinkle or blemish, beautiful, and comely. Indeed, they would be like Adam's, although not needing food and drink. They would be physically perfect. But gravity created a problem. Because they would have physical weight, they would be unable to be sustained in aethereal heavens. On the one hand, he suggested, their physical weight would not be a problem in such regions. There was no such thing as gravity in regions purely aethereal, since they were 'above the *Reach* and *Activity* of particular *Orbs*'.[108] The more natural solution to the question of the gravitational weight of resurrected bodies was the one Hody preferred: 'Perhaps after all, our *Heaven* will be nothing but a *Heaven upon Earth*, or some glorious solid *Orb* created on purpose for us in those immense Regions which we call Heaven.'[109]

SPIRITUAL BODIES

> It is sown a natural body; it is raised a spiritual body. There is a natural body, and there is a spiritual body.[110]

The notion of the resurrection of the physical body was deeply rooted in the Christian tradition. So it is not surprising that, in the latter part of the seventeenth century in the context of the new science, attempts should have been made to show that, if the resurrection were ultimately a supernatural divine act, there were analogies to it discernible in the natural world. Just as the new science opened up new visions of the last day, so also it led to new reflections on the process of resurrection on the assumption of a necessary continuity of substance between the pre- and post-resurrection bodies.

However, the fifteenth chapter of Paul's first letter to the Corinthians offered alternative understandings of the relationship between the pre- and post-resurrection bodies. In spite of the strong commitment to the resurrection of the same physical body from the time of the early church onwards, in this chapter Paul strongly suggested that the same ego makes use consecutively of two very different kinds of bodies – a natural and a spiritual. For Paul, on the day of resurrection, both those who are living and those who are dead must receive a new kind of body – an incorruptible spiritual body rather than a corruptible natural body.

It was this understanding of the resurrection body as being qualitatively different from that of the earthly body which was utilised by late seventeenth-century Platonists both to bolster their understandings of the vehicles of the soul, and to avoid what they saw as the philosophical and theological difficulties inherent in the traditional doctrine of the resurrection of the same body. Standing, as they often did, midway between Christian orthodoxy and the new science, they offered an account of the resurrection of the body, which was (in their terms) a rational one.

Origen was a key source of inspiration for the interpretation of 1 Corinthians 15 in terms of the neo-Platonic theory of the soul's vehicles. Thus, for example, George Rust in his *A Letter of Resolution Concerning Origen* appealed to 1 Corinthians 15 as Scriptural evidence for the identity of the resurrection body and the aethereal vehicle of the soul. Indeed, he went so far as to claim that Origen's doctrine was identical with that of Paul.

For Rust, the Origenistic account solved the dilemma of bodies rotted in the grave, dispersed through the universe, or evaporated into the air. Moreover, he was unwilling to invoke the power of God as the cause of the restoration of the physical body. This would be to say, wrote Rust, 'that *miracles* are very cheep with him'.[111] It was not only, he declared, unnecessary that we should have the same individual bodies, but unnecessary that they should even be of the same sort. Both Scripture and philosophy concurred that our resurrected bodies shall be appropriate to an aethereal realm:

> as Scripture calls those bodies we hope for in the Resurrection of the just *celestial* and *spiritual* and termes the place of our abode at that blessed time the kingdome of *heaven* and the inheritance in *light*; so Philosophy and Astronomy can demonstrate that the matter of that happy place is mere *light* & liquid *spirit* or *Aether*.[112]

In the context of the neo-Platonic account of the vehicles of the soul, it is clear that the imagery of the resurrection of the body, of the opening of the graves, of the reunion of the soul with its former earthly partner is just that – imagery. For, as it was in its pre-existent life, so also in its existence immediately after death, the soul remained in an embodied aerial or aethereal form. Thus, on the day of judgement, those already dead living in aerial bodies, and those still living on earth, judged for salvation, would ascend to the aethereal realm where they would remain in aethereal bodies for eternity. The wicked who remained on the earth and in aerial bodies in the air would receive punishment. But there could be no resurrection of former bodies.

Thus, for Henry More, for example, the resurrection of the body was merely figurative, and he cited 1 Corinthians 15 in support. Men's rising out of their graves, he declared, signified no more than 'That the same men that die and are buried, shall as truly appear in their own persons at the day of judgement, as if those bodies that were interred should be presently actuated by their souls again and should start out of their graves…'[113] For More, the final reward of a heavenly or aethereal body would be of the highest significance in completing the happiness of the faithful, whether we suppose them to have lived since death in aerial bodies or in no bodies at all. And he thought it quite improbable that, at least for those who were '*Copernicans* or *Cartesians*, and hold the *Heavens* all of them of a fluid, subtile, substance', a heavy, terrestrial body of flesh and bones should live 'in so subtile and piercing an Element'.[114]

Ralph Cudworth also held that the notion of the resurrection of the flesh was a figurative one. Paul's claim that flesh and blood would not inherit the kingdom of heaven[115] entailed for Cudworth that the resurrection body would not be 'this gross body of ours only varnished and gilded over on the outside of it, it remaining still nasty, sluttish and ruinous within, and having all the same seeds of corruption and mortality in its nature which it had before'.[116] For Cudworth, the resurrection of the dead was the vesting of the souls of good men, alive since their deaths in aerial bodies, with aethereal bodies.

Cudworth, following Origen and probably Sanctorius, saw the physical body as in a state of perpetual flux. Personal identity, he argued, was not dependent upon the numerical identity of all the parts of matter, 'our bodies flowing like a river, and passing away by insensible transpiration'.[117] Thus, though between infancy and old age many of the parts of the body have been replaced, we remain the same persons. But Cudworth's understanding of the temporal relationship between the vehicles of the soul in its pre-existent state enabled him to assert a bodily continuity. In his account of the vehicles of the soul, he reported that there were two schools of opinion on this relationship: that the aethereal vehicle was lost when the soul descended into the world and had to be recovered (which was More's, Rust's, and Glanvill's understanding); and that the aethereal body, being incorruptible, 'did always inseparably adhere to the soul, in its after-lapses and descents, into an aerial first, and then a terrestrial body ... '[118]

It was this latter position which Cudworth tentatively held in his exposition of the resurrection: 'it is not at all to be doubted', he wrote,

but that Irenaeus, Origen, and those other ancients, who entertained that opinion, of souls being clothed after death with a certain thin and subtle body suspected it not in the least to be inconsistent with that of the future resurrection; as it is no way inconsistent for one, who hath only a shirt or waistcoat on, to put on a suit of clothes, or exterior upper-garment. Which will also seem the less strange, if it be considered, that even here in this life, our body is, as it were, twofold, exterior and interior; we having, besides the grossly tangible bulk of our outward body, another interior spirituous body, the soul's immediate instrument, both of sense and motion; which latter is not put into the grave with the other, nor imprisoned under the cold sods.[119]

Cudworth's contemporaries were undoubtedly correct when they accused him of having denied the doctrine of the resurrection of the flesh.[120] Even a staunch supporter like Thomas Wise believed that Cudworth had made an error in following Origen, and could only defend Cudworth by finding him guilty of the same inconsistency as Origen.[121] But what is interesting is that, unlike More, Cudworth was able to defend a doctrine of bodily continuity between the pre- and post-resurrection bodies – not a bodily continuity dependent on the physical body, but a bodily continuity of the aethereal body. Thus he was able to suggest that it was in the aethereal vehicle and its union with the soul from the time of creation into eternity that the identity of persons was to be found.

For More, as for Cudworth, there was the problem of bodily continuity between the terrestrial body and the bodies (aerial and aethereal) with which the soul would be clothed after death and on the day of resurrection. In his concept of the journey of the soul, he had envisaged souls, originally in aethereal vehicles, descending through aerial to terrestrial vehicles, eventually to return to their aethereal vehicles and to ascend to the aethereal realm on the last day. That is to say, souls since their creation had been in a series of successively different bodies.

It was quite impossible, therefore, for him to assert any bodily continuity between the various terrestrial, aethereal, and aerial vehicles which had clothed the soul in its journey. He was forced into a psychological expedient. Even though there was no physical continuity between the vehicles, on the last day, he declared, 'we shall feel ourselves to be the self-same Bodies, and seem as much to others to have so, as ever we felt ourselves to have the self-same Body, or appeared to others to have so in this life'.[122] In essence, More was implying that personal identity resided not in the body but in the soul. As More put it, 'it is manifest that if there be the *same Soul*, there is exactly the *same Person*; and that the change of the Body causes no more real difference of Personality then the change of cloaths'.[123]

PERSONAL IDENTITY AND THE SOUL

In the context of his discussion of the resurrection, Henry More had anticipated the theory of personal identity which John Locke was to offer in 1690 in his *An Essay Concerning Humane Understanding*. Committed, like More, to the notion of bodies as being in a state of perpetual flux, Locke argued that, with living creatures, their identity depended on the common life that ran through the varying parcels of matter which went to make them up. Thus, in the case of humans, the identity of the person consisted 'in nothing but a participation of the same continued Life, by constantly fleeing Particles, in succession vitally united to the same organized Body'.[124] According to Locke, then, the 'life' of persons was self-consciousness. In other words, personal identity depended only on self-consciousness, irrespective of whether that self-consciousness was joined to one or a succession of several substances.

In the light of this, he argued, we can conceive that, on the day of resurrection, the same person would be rewarded or punished, made happy or miserable irrespective of the substance with which they would be united on that day: 'The Sentence shall be justified by the consciousness all Persons shall have, that they *themselves* in what Bodies soever they appear or what Substances soever that consciousness adheres to, are the *same* that committed those Actions, and deserve that punishment for them.'[125]

As we have seen, in his own private thoughts about the last day, Locke believed that the righteous would be invested in spiritual bodies for eternal happiness, the wicked in physical bodies for punishment and annihilation. But the clear, and very public, implication of Locke's theory of personal identity in the *Essay* was that, since personal identity was invested only in self-consciousness, and since therefore it was the soul that was alone responsible for righteousness or wickedness, the resurrection of the flesh was not necessary. Although Locke was later to argue that, in spite of the fact that he believed it was not necessary, God could raise the physical bodies of the dead with the very same particles of matter, the die, so to say, was cast.[126] For his opponents wanted to argue that, not only was it theologically possible, but also philosophically essential that the physical bodies of the dead should be raised.

The opening shots were fired in 1697 by Edward Stillingfleet, Bishop of Worcester.[127] Stillingfleet's aim was to demonstrate that Locke's understanding of personal identity destroyed faith in the resurrection of the dead, and this in spite of Locke's claim that reason could not shake the foundations of faith. Stillingfleet argued that Scripture showed that it was 'necessary for the same substance which was united to the Body to be raised up at the Last Day',[128] and to this end he assembled and commented upon a catena of Scriptural passages from the New Testament.

Stillingfleet did not want to defend the necessity of the resurrection of the same individual particles at the point of death, for 'there must be a great Alteration in them in a lingring Disease, as if a Fat Man falls into a Consumption'.[129] Nor did he wish to defend the resurrection of those particles in existence at the various times at which sins were committed, for 'then a long Sinner must have a vast Body, considering the continual spending of Particles by Perspiration...'[130]

But he was convinced that there needed to be some material continuity between the pre- and post-resurrection bodies. Thus, he recognised that the dispute between him and Locke was not a matter of arguing that personal identity depended upon the *same* material substance. Their dispute, he maintained, was whether personal identity 'doth not depend upon a *Vital Union* between the Soul and Body and the Life which is consequent upon it; and therefore in the *Resurrection* the same Material Substance must be reunited; or else it cannot be called a *Resurrection*, but a Renovation'.[131] But unfortunately, he did not argue for the position that personal identity was a matter, not of self-consciousness, but of a vital unity of body, soul, and life. And he made no attempt to explain what he meant by 'the same material substance'.

It was this weakness in Stillingfleet's case that Locke was to attack. In the main, Locke attempted to reduce Stillingfleet's arguments to absurdity. Thus, for example, of Stillingfleet's claim that the particles at the moment of death were unsuitable for Resurrection, Locke remarked, '''tis likely your Lordship thinks these Particles of a decrepit, wasted, withered Body would be too few or unfit to make such a plump, strong, vigorous, well-siz'd Body, as it has pleased your Lordship to proportion out in your Thoughts to Men at the Resurrection ... '[132] and therefore some matter must be added. On the other hand, to avoid making the body too large, suggested Locke, Stillingfleet was committed to leaving out most of the particles of the body to avoid making it 'more vast than your Lordship thinks will be fit ... '[133] But his main attack was directed at Stillingfleet's admission that the same person could exist in this life under several changes of matter. If this were the case, argued Locke, then the same body is not necessary to the same person, and therefore, on Stillingfleet's own principles, there would be no reason why, on the day of resurrection, the same person could not be clothed with any substance appropriate.

The issue of personal identity and its relation to body and soul (mind) was not to be solved by Locke and Stillingfleet, any more than it was advanced in the second quarter of the eighteenth century when the debate initiated by Locke resurfaced.[134] This was not the consequence of any lack of philosophical sophistication in the arguments, either of those who identified personal identity with self-consciousness, or of those who saw personal identity in the unity of bodies and souls. The issues about personal identity which were then debated in the context of discussions about the resurrection of the body have changed little today,[135] although the context in which the debate takes place now is radically different. And if issues concerning bodily identity are no longer exemplified within the framework of the question of the nature of the resurrection body on the last day, this is at least in part because, to non-Christians and to Christians alike, the resurrection of the physical body appears improbable. The Platonist conviction that the resurrection of the body is a sublime allegory is dominant.

CHAPTER 5

Eternal torments

ETERNAL OR TEMPORARY?

For if a man were to have all his sins laid to his charge, and communion with the devils, and as much wrath as the great God of heaven can inflict upon them, I say, if it were but for a time, even ten thousand years, if then it might have an end, there would be ground of comfort, and hopes of deliverance; but here is thy misery, this is thy state for ever, here thou must be for ever ... When thou hast been in hell for as many thousand years as there are stars in the firmament or drops in the sea, or sands on the sea shore, yet thou hast to lie there for ever. O this one word ever, how will it torment thy soul![1]

More than the torments of hell themselves, it was the emphasis on the eternity of them that was intended to provoke horror, effect repentance, and act as an incentive to a good and holy life. Unlike punishments on this side of the grave, the awesome ceremonies of hell went on for ever. 'The great aggravation of this misery', declared Richard Baxter, 'will be its eternity.'[2] To the Anglican divine Matthew Horbery, it seemed that it was 'the Eternity of the Punishment, which gives its chief Weight and Edge, and makes it pierce deepest into the Hearts of Sinners'.[3]

In post-Restoration England all were agreed that *post-mortem* punishments would be meted out to the wicked. The excesses of those radical sectarians who had denied heaven and hell had seen to that. The traditional Christian belief that both after death and after the last judgement the righteous would be rewarded and the wicked punished was strongly reasserted. All were agreed too that there would be gradations of punishment in hell, commensurate with the degrees of sinfulness to be found among those there despatched by the Divine Judge on the last day.

But over the question of the eternity of hell's torments, there was more debate. To be sure, most were committed to arguing that the punishments of the damned in hell would be eternal. Publicly to support the doctrine of the eternal punishment of the wicked was socially, politically, and theologically correct. But from the time of the Restoration, there was a small number by whom it was privately disbelieved, publicly although discreetly questioned, or anonymously challenged, in the name of the conviction that all would ultimately be saved, or the belief that the wicked would be annihilated after a period of punishment appropriate to their wickedness. By the middle of the eighteenth century, it was being publicly rejected, though rarely.

REASON AND SCRIPTURE

On rare occasions, the argument in favour of eternal torments was a natural one: that all men everywhere at all times had so believed. The Anglican Thomas Lewis, for example, responding to the second 1720 edition of Samuel Richardson's annihilationist denial of the eternity of hell's torments, began his defence of eternal punishments with the declaration that it was an innate belief that even the most barbarous accepted. Whoever searches, he declared, into the records of the past will find 'that no one Principle has been more Universally Received than the Doctrine of Hell and of Eternal Punishments in a future State'.[4] Similarly, the Anglican William Dawes argued for the certainty of eternal torments from what he called the 'principles of Nature and Reason'. The Jews, the Phoenicians, the Egyptians, the Greeks, the Latins, the ancient Indians, Gauls, Britons, and Muslims all believed explicitly or implicitly in hell's torments: 'we shall be hard put to it', he wrote, 'to give any one instance of a Man who has been so far able to shake off his Notions and Fears of Hell, that they sh'd never after, when he has been in his sober senses, in a cool, natural, thinking Condition haunt and perplex him'.[5]

It was Scripture, however, which remained the focus of discussions both for and against the eternity of hell. The citation of texts dominated discussions. The Catholic Francis Blyth, for example, was incensed by Whiston's use of the Biblical texts to further his annihilationist cause. To him, Whiston's work was jumbled, trivial, puffed with affectation of learning, an 'ill-picked heap of incongruous texts' tacked together with 'childish remarks and pueril conjectures

... '[6] After a selection of his own Biblical texts, he concluded, 'So express are the Holy Scriptures, both Old and New! Nothing then but wilful obstinacy and infidelity can make those who admit their authority, call the *Eternity* of *Hell-Torments* in question.'[7] William Dodwell similarly attacked Whiston. Reason, he maintained, cannot prove the eternity of hell's torments, though there is nothing horrid or absurd in it. But in Scripture, he argued, eternal torment 'is taught in the plainest and most express terms'.[8]

Dodwell's position was a powerful one. The New Testament evidence for eternal punishment is strong if not decisive. There were several important texts continually cited for the eternity of hell. Most crucial were Matthew 25.46 and 25.41: 'And these shall go away into everlasting punishment: but the righteous into life eternal'; and 'Depart from me, ye cursed, into everlasting fire, prepared for the devil and his angels.' Further support was at hand in Revelation 20.10 in the form of the lake of fire and brimstone in which the devil would be tormented 'unto the ages of ages'.

The symmetry of eternal life and eternal punishment in Matthew 25.46 was central. Matthew Horbery asked the obvious question of the term 'everlasting': 'When apply'd to God, they confessedly denote a proper Eternity: when apply'd to the Happiness of the Saints in Heaven, they have hitherto universally been thought to denote the same ... What Reason is there why they should not denote the same, when apply'd to the punishments of the wicked?'[9] Similarly, an anonymous response to Whiston in 1742 inquired, 'if it [the Scripture] applies the same Adjective ... both to the Glory of the Righteous ... and to the future ordained Punishments of all impenitent Sinners; does not this oblige us to conceive of the *Latter* as equally durable with the *Former*, and both as running parallel with God's own Eternity '*a parte post*'?'[10] The universalist Franciscus van Helmont tried the opposite tack. Of 'everlasting' in Matthew 25.46, he inquired, 'is there any necessity in the World that ... they must be taken in the same sence?'[11]

One response to these questions was to argue, quite correctly, that the term 'everlasting' was used elsewhere in the biblical texts merely to signify 'of a long duration', and that therefore it could do so when applied to punishment. Henry More provided the most eloquent argument to this effect. In response to Edward Warren's suggestion in his *No Praeexistence* that 'everlasting' must mean the same when applied to life as to punishment,[12] More wrote,

For it being undeniably true that αἰώνιος [eternal] signifies as well that which is onely of a *long continuance*, as what is *properly everlasting*; and it being altogether rational, that when words have more significations than one, that signification is to be applied that is most agreeable to the subject it is predicated of, and αἰώνιος [eternal] in that higher sense of property [sic] and *absolutely everlasting*, not being applicable to κόλασις [punishment] ... it is plain that though αἰώνιος [eternal] in Ζωὴ αἰώνιος [life eternal] signifie properly everlasting, that there is no necessity that it should signifie so in κόλασις αἰώνιος [punishment eternal], but have that other signification of *long continuance*, though not of everlastingness ... [13]

Even More, on balance a supporter of eternal torment, does not appear to have been persuaded by his own argument.

A more promising approach was taken by those who argued for the annihilation of the wicked. As we have seen, Thomas Hobbes distinguished between the everlasting fire and the second death of those who were condemned to it. The Baptist Samuel Richardson argued that the 'everlasting fire' referred to the never extinguished fire of the Valley of Hinnom, which would burn as long as there were combustible matter to be consumed by it. But it did not follow that 'that which is cast into it is everlasting; the wicked are compared to Chaffe and Stubble, fire is not long in consuming them ... '[14] Both John Locke and William Whiston were to make the identical point. Logically, it was grasping at straws. As the Anglican divine John Brandon sardonically put it, on these grounds, every fire is everlasting, as is every beard, 'for it is capable of growing whiles the nourishing matter lasteth *i.e.* whiles there is any considerable moisture remaining in his *Pericranium*'.[15]

Annihilationists and universalists also appealed to Scriptural texts in favour of their respective positions. The diversity of opinions on the afterlife within both the Old and New Testaments ensured that Scriptural support could be found, not only for annihilation or universalism, but also for proponents of mortalism or the intermediate state, for advocates of millennialism or purgatory.

Another alternative was to argue for reason against Scripture. Thomas Burnet, for example, argued that, because everything relating to eternal torments on either side was ambiguous, everyone ought to be at liberty to follow his conscience, embrace that opinion most agreeable to sound reason, and reinterpret Scripture accordingly. Thus, he suggested, if we judge eternal torments not to be in accordance with the divine wisdom and justice, then we must either give up the literal interpretation of Scripture or invoke the double doctrine, that is, 'we must distinguish between the literal and the reasonable Hypothesis, the vulgar and the secret one, lest, by a temerarious and unskilful Interpretation, we entertain Thoughts unworthy of the divine Nature'.[16]

Isaac Barrow, a preacher and Isaac Newton's predecessor in the Lucasian Chair of Mathematics at Cambridge, harboured annihilationist sympathies. For him, eternal punishments reflected 'a severity of justice far above all example of repeated cruelty in the worst of men'.[17] Barrow, aware of the ambiguities within the Scriptural evidence, established three principles to resolve the scriptural conflicts: first, that the most literal sense of Scripture has preference over any figurative or mystical sense; second, that Scriptural texts that are few in number and allegorical are to be reconciled to those that are greater in number and clear in meaning; but, third, that when the literal sense is disagreeable to piety or the nature of God, a mystical or spiritual sense is to be preferred.

On all three principles, he argued, annihilation of the wicked was the correct Biblical interpretation, for the literal sense favoured it, the texts for eternal punishment were less in number and less clear in meaning, and annihilation was more in keeping with the mercy of God. The 'everlasting punishment' of Matthew 25.46 was reinterpreted as 'everlasting death', for if it were agreed that death was a punishment, then 'everlasting death or everlasting destruction may be truly called everlasting punishment'.[18] The 'everlasting fire' of Matthew 25.41 was interpreted metaphorically as always opposed to 'everlasting life' and thus signifying everlasting destruction.[19] Reason and Scripture jointly supported the destruction of the damned.

The Swiss protestant theologian Marie Huber was a Platonist in form and a universalist in content. Although she cited a number of texts in favour of the non-eternity of hell and the ultimate restoration of all, crucially, she laid down the principle that the texts are not to be interpreted so as to count against the 'undoubted and fundamental Truths' of reason, specifically that the justice and goodness of God are inseparable.[20] Thus, she was convinced that, in the afterlife, the wicked would recognise evil for what it really was and, far from hating the deity and accusing him of injustice for their punishments, would do homage to his infinite goodness and justice. Reason teaches us, she argued, that *Good* having a *divine Principle*, ought to be stronger than *Evil*, which is essentially nothing but Disorder and Depravation; that *Evil* putting man into a State of Violence, that State cannot continue for ever; that this State of Violence supposes its contrary in Man, struggling against it ... that God being the God of Order, and the undoubted Sovereign of the Universe, can never consent that Disorder and Confusion should prevail there for ever.[21]

For Huber then, in the afterlife, the divine love would enable us, over time, to see ourselves truly, to repent of our past wickedness, and to perfect ourselves morally, eventually to achieve that peace and freedom which would vindicate God's saving purpose.

WRATH, MERCY, AND JUSTICE

It would be simplistic to suggest that the debate over eternal torments simply reflected a dispute between reason and Scripture. 'Reason over Scripture' was a manifesto for those who perceived themselves progressive and enlightened in contrast to the hide-bound traditionalism of the supporters of the eternal punishment of the wicked. 'Reason' implied, not so much the power of the human mind to arrive independently at truth, but a commitment to avoid intolerance, extremism, and bigotry. Advocates and opponents of eternal torments alike provided rational arguments which of necessity orbited within a 'Biblical space'. But the meaning of the Bible was itself determined within a context of debates centred on the nature of God, on the polarities between his attributes of justice and mercy, and the implication of these for the ultimate destiny of those in hell. Thus, for example, Anthony Collins delighted in arguing that the Bible was the foundation for differences of Christian opinion. The debate upon eternal punishment was, he caustically suggested, 'a Specimen of the Diversity of Opinions of the Priests of the Church of *England*, all pretended to be deduc'd from the Scriptures'.[22]

The concept of the wrath of God provided some with sufficient reason for eternal torments. Thomas Goodwin wrote his *A Discourse of the Punishment of Sin in Hell* in 1680 to demonstrate the wrath of God to be the immediate cause of punishment in hell. And he argued that only eternal torments could satisfy the injury done to God by the wicked: 'Sin in thee and the Injury of it to God is an eternal Stain, which Hell Fire cannot eat out, or satisfy God, but in an Eternity of time'.[23] Eternal punishment, he declared, is 'an Act of Avenging Wrath'.[24] Not only physical torment but mental torments were necessitated since it was a property of vengeance that the wicked should be sensible of their misery. But Goodwin's vengeful God was no merely arbitrary cruel tyrant but one whose justice could only be expressed in the eternal torments of the damned.

For Goodwin, and for many others, vengeance and retributive justice were intimately entwined. The doctrine of eternal torments retained a medieval element of the law of vengeance combined with an early modern concern for retributive justice. To John Brandon, for example, the greatest part of mankind were ungodly, sensual, disobedient, and therefore richly deserving of eternal punishment, just as criminals were punished on this side of the grave. 'It is no disparagement to the goodness of a King or Judge', he wrote, 'to condemn common Robbers or Murderers, nor to condemn many of them: Yea, Justice requires him so to do, and their Multitude can be no reason at all to excuse them in their wickedness.'[25] The wicked were traitors to the divine Kingdom. Is it not just, inquired William Bates in 1691, that 'Treason against the *Great and Immortal King* should be revenged with Everlasting Death?'[26] To William Dawes, the annihilation of the wicked infringed the natural law of the immortality of the soul. Could there be any reason, he demanded, 'for supposing, that God will over-rule and change the natural course and order of things, only to save from just punishment such Wretches, such Ingrates, such Rebels, such Traytors, as these?'[27] Jonathan Edwards' logic was impeccably retributive. Since God infinitely hates sin, 'it is suitable that he should execute an infinite punishment upon it; and so the perfections of God require that he should punish sin with an infinite, or which is the same thing, with an eternal punishment'.[28]

It was difficult to integrate the concept of divine retributive justice with God's goodness and mercy. Thomas Hobbes found it difficult to believe

that God who is the Father of Mercies, that doth in Heaven and Earth all that hee will; that hath the hearts of all men in his disposing; that worketh in men both to doe, and to will; and without whose free gift a man hath neither inclination to good, nor repentance of evil, should punish mens transgressions without any end of time, and with all the extremity of torture, that men can imagine, and more.[29]

Similarly, for Samuel Clarke, the real difficulty over the question of eternal torments lay in 'how it is reconcileable with the Goodness of

God, to put *any Persons* at all upon a necessity of making such an Option, wherein if they chuse amiss, the Misery they incur must be irrecoverable'.[30]

Others saw the God of eternal punishments as Satanic, vicious and cruel. Matthew Tindal, for example, in his *Christianity as Old as Creation*, lamented those who 'impute such Actions to him [God], as make him resemble the worst of Beings, and so run into downright Demonism'.[31] The Presbyterian annihilationist Samuel Bourn believed that the God of eternal retributive punishment was a projection of the worst of human values, and an encouragement to social intolerance. Those who believe in such a God, he declared, 'have become more arbitrary, bigotted, fierce, unmerciful, and more addicted to hate and persecute their fellow-creatures.'[32]

Those who argued for eternal torments were forced to reinterpret the goodness and mercy of God accordingly. With the Catholic Francis Blyth, for example, it is hard to distinguish his rhetorical assertion of the mercy of God from what is in effect a denial of it. The justice of God, he argued, demands the eternal torment of the wicked, and, 'they cannot be eternal, unless GOD is as merciful as he is just in inflicting them.'[33] For Blyth, the mercy of God can only be understood from the primacy of his retributive justice: 'It is unmerciful, you say, for GOD to give sinners their desert; is it mercy then for worms, for wretches, for wicked sinners, to rob GOD of his due? And must GOD be made more merciful than becomes him as GOD to be, merely to prove him less just than he really is and must be?'[34] Similarly, William Dodwell reasoned that the mercy of God had not to do with an indiscriminate communicating of felicity to all, but had to be guided by 'Equity, Honour and his own Divine Glory'.[35] Jonathan Edwards was consistently forthright. 'It would be a great defect, and not a perfection in the Sovereign and Supreme Judge of the World, to be merciful in such a sense that he could not bear to have penal justice executed.'[36]

The implication of the dominance of God's justice over his mercy could be mitigated by arguing that the penalties for sins were something which followed naturally and inevitably upon the sinner, self-inflicted wounds rather than externally imposed tortures. Joseph Addison, for example, saw the wicked as destined to become their own tormenters: 'Those evil Spirits, who by long Custom, have contracted in the Body Habits of Lust and sensuality, Malice and

Revenge, an Aversion to everything that is good, just or laudable, are naturally seasoned and prepared for Pain and Misery.'[37] Addison went on to praise John Scott who, in his *The Christian Life*, had psychologised heaven and hell as symptoms of order and disorder within individuals. For Scott, 'There is as inseparable a Connection between *Grace* and *Glory*, *Sin* and *Hell*, as there is between *Fire* and *Heat*, *Frost* and *Cold*, or any other necessary *Cause* and its *Effect*.'[38] Matthew Horbery maintained that the punishments of the wicked were not inflicted by God but, because they were the 'natural and necessary Consequence and Result of things', they could not be cruel and barbarous.[39] But arguments of this sort did not solve the issue of God's lack of mercy. As D. P. Walker has pointed out, although a God who allows punishments to happen is less cruel than one who actively imposes them, 'there is little if any moral difference between allowing the occurrence of a disaster together with the resultant suffering, which you could prevent, and actively causing the disaster and the suffering'.[40]

The most obvious justification of retributive justice was to see it, whether in the human or the divine sphere, as the result of the misuse of an absolutely free human will. Thus, the wicked, because they alone were responsible for their choices, were deserving of punishment. This was implicit in William Bates' asking 'if Sin with an eternal Hell in its Retinue be chosen and embraced, is it not equal that the Rational Creature should inherit his own choice?'[41] The argument was further developed by Matthew Horbery in his response to William Whiston. To Whiston, the doctrine of the love of God was absolutely inconsistent with those 'common but barbarous and savage opinions' of eternal torments

> as if much the greater part of mankind are under a state of reprobation, unalterable reprobation, and must inevitably be damned: and that such their damnation is to be *coeternal* with the duration of their Creator himself; and that the torments, the exquisite torments of the most numerous and most miserable creatures, are determined without the least pity, or relenting, or bowels of compassion in their Creator, to be in everlasting fire, and in the flames of Hell; without abatement, or remission for endless ages of ages. And all this for the sins of this short life; fallen into generally by the secret snares of the Devil, and other violent temptations; which they commonly could not either prevent, or avoid; and this without any other advantage to themselves, or to others, or to God himself, than as instances ... of the absolute and supreme power and dominion of the cruel and inexorable author of their being ...[42]

Horbery, by contrast, argued that men freely could have avoided sin, that the Devil only aggravated already corrupt hearts, or that since many persons are formed incurably evil, the ratio of length of life to length of punishment was irrelevant. Moreover, he maintained, God's goodness was demonstrated in his gift of free will: 'Must God then to prevent his accidental Consequence, or Abuse, of Liberty, create no free Beings at all?'[43] Similarly, Francis Blyth saw God's goodness as vindicated because the having of free will is a higher good. God's goodness resides in his having 'created man to be eternally happy in his own right, and to avoid eternal *misery* if he so pleases, and created him in a state, and with means [free-will], suited to that purpose'.[44] Since the wicked could have done otherwise, God is both just and merciful, he argued, 'in rewarding the wicked with those infinite punishments which they inflexibly chuse, earn, and prefer to infinite felicity'.[45] And for Blyth, as we have seen, God's mercy is further demonstrated in his allowing to the saved the sight of the damned to increase their felicity.

While the free-will defence of God's goodness may be philosophically defensible, it is difficult to see how God's mercy is demonstrated in inflicting retributive punishments on evil-doers, especially if the wicked cannot change, are divinely prevented from so doing, or can only change for the worse. The goodness of God was more appropriately vindicated by the extension of free will beyond the grave in a morally dynamic state, where there were the possibilities of individual repentance, of moral and religious development, and of divine forgiveness and the gift of salvation;[46] that is to say, where the divine goodness was interpreted in a framework of curative or reformative justice.

Francis van Helmont, Lady Conway, Henry Hallywell, and Archibald Campbell suggested the ultimate restoration of all through an understanding of God's justice as essentially reformative. Thomas Burnet and William Whiston saw God's justice as reformative, at least until the final day of judgement, when the divine goodness would be shown in the destruction of the incurably wicked rather than their eternal punishment. To Burnet, for example, the orthodox hell did not reflect the Christian God:

We conceive the God of the Christians to be the wisest of Beings; that he is neither cruel nor unjust to the Race of Men; that there is nothing barbarous or dismal in his Worship; that he has neither instituted, nor suffered any Thing that is barbarous, any Thing that is inhuman ... Besides, Jesus the

Head and the Captain of the Christian Dispensation ... is the greatest Lover of human Kind; and suffered his own Blood to be shed to redeem us from Evil and Misery.[47]

And it served no purpose to man 'if there is no Room for Repentance, and he who is *Tormented* can never grow better ... Let this Punishment be severe, let it be bitter, nay let it be lasting, but let it at length have an End ... '[48]

INFINITE OFFENCE

A common argument for the necessity of eternal or infinite punishment was the status of him against whom sin had been committed. As John Ray put it simply in 1692, 'God is an infinite person, and Sin being an injury and affront to him, as being a violation of his Law an infinite punishment must be due to it.'[49] The Catholic Nicholas Caussin in 1650 had linked it with a similar principle in secular justice. 'It is one thing', he declared, 'to offend a peasant, another thing a Merchant, another thing a Judge, another a King ... Nay, were all the greatness, grace, and majesty of a hundred thousand worlds poured and quintessenced in one body, what would it be in comparison of God but one grain of sand?'[50] William Bates saw sin against God as contempt of God's majesty, the most unnatural rebellion against God, and treason against the great and immortal king. Thus, he argued, ''Tis a rule in all Courts of Judicature, that the degrees of an Offence arise according to the degrees of Dignity of the Person offended: Now the Majesty of God is truly infinite against whom Sin is committed; and consequently the Guilt of Sin exceeds our boundless Thoughts.'[51]

This was not a rule in the seventeenth-century English system of criminal justice, although it can be argued that, in effect, this was how the system worked. In Douglas Hay's view, for example, an arbitrary system was clothed in the vesture of impartial legality exercising its prerogatives of justice, mercy, and terror to maintain the social relations between the elite and the common people.[52] And one might add that the preaching of the terror of hell's torments in the context of the justice and mercy of God was intended to do the same. However that may be, the rhetoric was clearly intended to place all sin on a level with crime, and infinitely more serious than that most wicked of crimes, treason against the king. To the theocratic Jonathan Edwards, 'sin' and 'crime' were interchangeable. It was common sense, he argued, that 'sins committed against anyone' were heinous in proportion to the dignity of the one offended. Thus, 'sin against God, being a violation of infinite obligations, must be a crime infinitely heinous, and so deserving of infinite punishment'.[53]

Critics found the argument inept for a number of reasons. Franciscus van Helmont, for example, pointed out that, on the principle of the infinite difference between the sinner and God, then the least sin merited the same degree of punishment as the greatest, and this, he implied, was contrary to justice.[54] The same point was made by Thomas Burnet. If it was not the nature of the sin, but the nature of him against whom sin was committed which was crucial, then all punishments ought to be infinitely awful, 'for the Reason which you give is full as strong for the Greatness of the Punishments, as for their Duration'.[55] And this, he argued, was clearly unjust. David Hume put the converse point succinctly: 'Punishment, according to *our* conception, should bear some proportion to the offence. Why then eternal punishment for the temporary offences of so frail a creature as man?'[56]

This was a telling argument, difficult to refute within the context of the late seventeenth and early eighteenth centuries. The principle that punishments should be more proportionate to crime was, from the time of the Restoration, progressively incorporated into the English penal code. As J. M. Beattie has pointed out, the dominance of capital punishment, at the time of the Restoration, for the vast majority of those offences tried at the assizes 'was clearly being felt then as a serious problem, and a central theme in the administration of the criminal law in the last decades of the seventeenth century and into the eighteenth is the variety of attempts made to broaden the penal options open to the courts'.[57]

Moreover, that the punishments of hell were proportionate to sins committed was, as we have seen, part of both the Catholic and Protestant theological tradition. Archbishop Tillotson, for example, admitted that fault was heightened by the dignity of the person offended, but not to an infinite degree. For then all sins would be equal, in which case, 'there can be no reason for the degrees of punishment in another World'.[58] That all punishments from God as well as all sins should be equal was, he concluded, palpably absurd.

UNFULFILLED THREATENINGS?

Tillotson himself was accused of denying the eternity of hell's torments. He addressed himself to this issue in a sermon entitled 'Of the Eternity of Hell-Torments' which he preached before the Queen at Whitehall on 7 March 1690, several months before he became Archbishop of Canterbury. It was an exaggeration to claim that Tillotson denied eternal punishments, although he was accused of this on numerous occasions during the next half-century, not least because he was seen as giving comfort to Queen Mary for the consequences of her usurpation of her father's throne. But his Latitudinarian tolerance promoted a God who was not *obliged* eternally to torment the wicked. Anthony Collins, not without a hint of irony, approved: 'What a charming Idea does he give us of the *Deity*. It is alone sufficient, without any further Argument, to make the *Atheist* wish there were a deity.'[59] The non-juring Bishop of Thetford deplored it. When it was first published, he wrote, 'the Atheists, and Deists, and Socinians of the Town, carried it about them to show it in all Places, glorifying everywhere in the Doctrines of it, and extolling the Author for Man who durst speak Truth, and set Mankind free from the Slavish Notion of Eternal Torments'.[60]

For Tillotson, the question of eternal torments was not one of retributive justice, but one which had to do with deterrence. Punishments ought to be meted out, he argued, not from the quality and degree of the offence, nor from the duration and continuation of it, but only so as to 'secure the observation of the Law, and deterr Men from the breach of it'.[61] It was not a matter of justice after the offence, but of wisdom and prudence in the law-giver. Thus, to secure his law from violation, 'he [God] may before-hand threaten what penalties he thinks fit and necessary to deter Men from the Transgression of it'.[62]

Tillotson was in no doubt that the Scriptures, especially Matthew 25.46, clearly threatened eternal punishments. But, he suggested, although God was obliged to fulfil his promises of rewards, he was under no moral obligation to carry out his threats: 'He that threatens keeps the right of punishing in his own hand, and is not oblig'd to execute what he hath threatned any further than the reasons and ends of Government do require.'[63] That he explicitly rejected the annihilation of the wicked strongly implied that, were God not to carry out his threats, there would be room for repentance in the next world, and all would still have a chance for salvation. Nevertheless, at the same time, he urged that it remained prudent to continue to act as if the doctrine of eternal punishments were true. And he would not endorse the preaching of the possibility that God may not carry out his threats: 'it would be a very impious design to go about to teach or perswade any thing to the contrary, and a betraying Men into that misery which had it been firmly believed might have been avoided'.[64]

In effect, Tillotson was extending to divine justice a principle which had become fundamental in English criminal law by the late seventeenth century, and common after the development of transportation in 1718, that of royal pardon from capital punishments.[65] Defending Tillotson in 1727, Jean Le Clerc made the point explicitly:

> As among Men, Criminals are publickly condem'd to the Death they have deserv'd, tho' there is an Order for their Pardon, which they are not to be made acquainted with till the Moment they expect to die. It might after the same manner happen ... that God would condemn to pains unlimited, as to their duration, such Men as his Mercy would afterwards release at different Times, after they had suffer'd as his Justice would require.[66]

Few were sympathetic to Tillotson's plea for mitigation. One anonymous critic maintained that if the Bible threatened eternal torments, God had a right to inflict it, and no one was at liberty to say otherwise.[67] The Anglican divine Richard Venn argued that God was obliged to execute his threats. If his goodness allowed him to threaten eternal torments, it could not be inconsistent with his goodness to put those threats into effect.[68] Jonathan Edwards declared that God's truthfulness demanded the execution of his threats: 'Though strictly speaking, God is not properly obliged to the creature to execute, because he has threatened, yet he was obliged not absolutely to threaten, if at the same time he knew that he should not, or would not fulfil, because this would have been inconsistent with his truth.'[69] To Richard Jenks, Tillotson was threatening the security of the state: 'Religion is ... the firmest Foundation for Civil Government; and the Church the best Security for the State; and those who enervate the Sanctions of Divine Laws, are the Instruments of Annarchy and Confusion in the World.'[70]

THE ULTIMATE DETERRENT?

> Heaven and Hell suppose two distinct species of men, the good and the bad: but the greatest part of mankind float betwixt vice and virtue. Were one to go round the world with an intention of giving a good supper to the righteous and a sound drubbing to the wicked, he would frequently be embarrassed in his choice, and would find the merits and demerits of most men and women scarcely amount to the value of either... The chief source of moral ideas is the reflection on the interests of human society. Ought these interests, so short, so frivolous, to be guarded by punishments eternal and infinite? The damnation of one man is an infinitely greater evil in the universe than the subversion of a thousand millions of kingdoms.[71]

Most would vehemently have disagreed with David Hume. The main objective of secular punishment in the late seventeenth century and for most of the eighteenth century was deterrence. Only thus could social stability be maintained. Similarly, without exception, supporters of eternal punishments argued that they were an absolutely central element in the maintenance of individual morality and consequently the security of the state. The necessity of harsh deterrents justified both the disproportion between crime and secular punishment and between sin and eternal punishment. According to Robert Sharrock,

> There is no proportion or Equality in the value between a Mans life, and a mans goods. Yet by our Law, the Man that robs you of your goods forfeits his own life. And there was a necessity of this Law, because some men are so addicted to Robbery and stealing, that a lesse punishment would be no terror to them. And so we may reply, that it is reasonable upon that account as well as diverse others, that the punishment of Hell should be eternall; because a lesse punishment would Scarce suffice to affright wicked men from their sinfull course of life.[72]

Far from its being rational, the dominant image of human nature was that of a frail, feeble and innately sinful creature, dominated by the desire for pleasure and sensual gratification, unable to act from a sense of disinterested virtue. Robert South, for example declared that 'The Mind of Man is naturally licentious, and there is nothing, which it is more averse from, than Duty. Nothing which it more abhors than Restraint. It would if let alone, lash out, and Wantonize in a boundless Enjoyment and Gratification of all its Appetites, and Inclinations.'[73]

To be sure, there was a recognition by some that virtue was its own reward, and that actions motivated solely by hopes of rewards or fear of punishment lacked the rational disinterestedness necessary to morality. But there was often the intimation that this was not sufficient. Samuel Clarke, for example, noted, 'though Virtue is unquestionably *worthy to be chosen for its own sake*, even without any appreciation of Reward; yet it does not follow that it is therefore entirely self-sufficient, and able to support a Man under all kinds of sufferings, and even Death it self, for its sake; without any prospect of future recompense'.[74]

Anthony Ashley Cooper, third Earl of Shaftesbury, was passionately committed to the idea of disinterested virtue, and attacked the value of the notion of hell as a deterrent: 'in some respects, there can be nothing more fatal to virtue than the weak and uncertain belief of future reward and punishment. For the stress being laid wholly here, if this foundation come to fall, there is no further prop or security to men's morals. And thus virtue is supplanted and betrayed.'[75] But even Shaftesbury admitted that, at least for those too feeble or depraved to follow the rational dictates of disinterested virtue, 'the principle of fear of future punishment, and hope of future reward, how mercenary or servile soever it may be accounted, is yet in many circumstances a great advantage, and support to virtue'.[76]

The rhetoric implied a division of society into two groups – the elite and the mob. Shaftesbury's rational gentlemen could follow disinterested virtue, the mob needed hopes of reward and fear of punishment: 'for those who have no better a Reason for being *honest* than the Fear of a *Gibet* or a *Jail*; I shou'd not, I confess, much covet their Company, or Acquaintance'.[77] John Ray was not suggesting that he or other members of the Royal Society were in need of severe sanctions. The bestial mob were more obviously in his mind:

The very thought of an eternal Hell intervening (and it will often intrude itself) strikes a cold damp to his very Heart in the midst of his Jollities, and will much qualifie and allay all his Pleasures and Enjoyments. Rid him of this fear, and he will be apt to despise Hell and all its Torments, be they never so grievous or lasting. Take off this Bridle, and ... he will rush into Sin *as a Horse rusheth into the battel*.[78]

The fear that the denial of eternal torments would lead to moral anarchy was held not only by its supporters but, on occasion, by its doubters also. Tillotson, as we have seen, advised against preaching that God may not fulfil his threats. Thomas Burnet wrote his *De Statu Mortuorum* 'for the perusal of the Learn'd only'. The truth had to be kept from the masses:

> whatever your Opinion is within yourself, and in your own Breast concerning these Punishments, whether they are eternal or not; yet always with the People, and when you preach to the People, use the receiv'd Doctrine, and the received Words in the Sense, in which the People receive them: For they are apt to run headlong into Vice, and are apt to be terrify'd from offending by the Apprehension of Punishment only.[79]

The doctrine of eternal torment was also seen as necessary to good government. Indeed, the consistency with which eternal torment was defended as necessary to the state strongly suggests how fragile many perceived the state to be. John Shower, for example, maintained that civil society can never be supported 'if there be no restraint upon the Lusts and Passions of Men; and these can never be sufficiently restrained, without the Hopes and Fears of another World'.[80] William Dawes preached to King William and Queen Anne that only the belief in eternal punishments kept men in tolerable order and subjection.[81] To the Anglican Thomas Lewis, since eternal torments ensured the ends of government and the public good, God's justice and goodness were vindicated in his inflicting of them.[82]

The principle that secular crime was discouraged by the enormous disparity between the nature of the offence and the severity of the punishment was deep-seated. That sin would be similarly discouraged and public order preserved by the disparity between temporal sins and eternal punishments was seldom challenged. Only a few committed to annihilationism or universalism questioned its deterrent value. The Baptist Samuel Richardson believed that the greatest sinners hoped it would not be their destiny, expected to repent before their deaths, or soon overcame their fears of it. Indeed, he argued, it increased sin by causing fear, leading to hard thoughts of God, provoking to envy and unbelief, causing melancholy, and leading to suicides.[83] Francis van Helmont saw it as causing irreligion since its unreasonableness led to suspicion of other Christian doctrines which were asserted with the same confidence.[84] Marie Huber was convinced that, as a deterrent, it was simply ineffective since 'everyone is persuaded, that he himself is not of the number of the Wicked, whose Portion shall be in the Lake of Fire and Brimstone'.[85] Pierre Cuppé saw the belief in universal restoration as a more effective incentive to a moral and religious life. The assertion of God's universal mercy was 'more powerful to affect the Hearts of the most harden'd, than the terrifying Pictures of the most rigorous Judgements of God'.[86]

Such utilitarian considerations were rare, and were unpersuasive in a social context where disproportion between offence and punishment, whether at the mundane or infernal realms, appeared the only guarantee of social stability. Still, those who were arguing that the disproportion between sin and eternal punishment was not an effective deterrent, that the divine justice was reformative rather than retributive, and that persons could and would repent of their sins if given the opportunity so to do in the infernal prisons, were theologically foreshadowing reforms to the system of secular criminal justice that were progressively to be put into effect after the middle of the eighteenth century.

In 1769, William Blackstone's recognition that severity of punishment was not an effective deterrent to crime would no doubt have been applauded by all those who, in the preceding one hundred years, were disturbed by the disproportion between sin and its eternal punishment. 'Punishments of unreasonable severity', Blackstone concluded, 'especially where indiscriminately afflicted, have less effect in preventing crimes, and amending the manners of a people, than such as are more merciful in general, yet properly intermixed with due distinctions of severity.'[87] From this time, the rhetorical links between secular and eternal punishments were shattered. Arguments that only punishments to all eternity could ensure social stability forfeited their persuasive power. Where abominations on this side of the grave were disappearing on the grounds of justice, eternal abominations on the other side could no longer be cogently defended.

Notes

INTRODUCTION
1 Aldous Huxley, *The Devils of Loudon* (New York, 1952), p. 39.

I THE JOURNEY OF THE SOUL
1 E[dward] W[arren], *No Praeexistence. Or a Brief Dissertation against the Hypothesis of Humane Souls, Living in a State Antecedaneous to This* (London, 1667), Epistle to the Reader. For the attribution of this to Edward Warren, see W. R. Alger, *A Critical History of the Doctrine of a Future Life* (Philadelphia, 1864), p. 705.
2 See Joseph Glanvill, *Lux Orientalis; or an Enquiry into the Opinion of the Eastern Sages concerning the Praeexistence of Souls*... in *Two Choice and Useful Treatises* (London, 1682), Preface.
3 Thomas Birch, *The Works of the Honourable Robert Boyle*, 6 vols. (London, 1744–72), vol. 6, pp. 630–1.
4 D. P. Walker, *The Ancient Theology* (Ithaca, New York, 1972), p. 12.
5 See Henry More, *The Immortality of the Soul, so farre forth as it is demonstrable from the Knowledge of Nature and the Light of Reason* (London, 1659), p. 246.
6 See Glanvill, *Lux Orientalis*, p. 26. See also C. P., *A Dissertation Concerning the Prae-existency of Souls*... (London, 1684). On the attribution of this work to von Rosenroth, see D. P. Walker, *The Decline of Hell: Seventeenth-Century Discussions of Eternal Torment* (London, 1964), p. 127. See also Joseph Glanvill, 'A Letter on Preexistence from Dr. Joseph Glanvill to Richard Baxter', *Bibliotheca Platonica* 1 (1890), 191.
7 G. W. Butterworth (ed.), *Origen: On First Principles* (Gloucester, Massachusetts, 1973), p. 67.
8 See W. H. Fremantle (trans.), *Letters and Select Works of St. Jerome* (New York, 1893), pp. 238–44.
9 See Max Schär, *Das Nachleben des Origenes im Zeitalter des Humanismus* (Basel and Stuttgart, 1979), pp. 23–47.
10 Edgar Wind, 'The Revival of Origen', in Dorothy Milner (ed.), *Studies in Art and Literature for Belle da Costa Greene* (Princeton, 1954), p. 412.
11 See Walker, *The Decline of Hell*, p. 15. On the salvation of Satan, see C. A. Patrides, 'The Salvation of Satan', *Journal of the History of Ideas* 28 (1967), 467–78.

12 More, *The Immortality of the Soul*, p. 246.
13 See Marjorie H. Nicolson, *Conway Letters* ... (New Haven, 1930), p. 192, n. 1; Walker, *The Decline of Hell*, pp. 125–6; Charles F. Mullett, 'A Letter by Joseph Glanvill on the Future State', *The Huntington Library Quarterly* 1 (1937), 447–56.
14 See Nicolson, *Conway Letters*, pp. 196–7.
15 Henry More, *A Collection of Several Philosophical Writings*, 2nd edn (London, 1662), pp. xxi-xxiii.
16 Nicolson, *Conway Letters*, p. 194.
17 *Ibid.*, p. 192.
18 [George Rust], *A Letter of Resolution concerning Origen and the Chief of his Opinions* (London, 1661), p. 31. See also C. P., *A Dissertation*, pp. 21–2, 26–9.
19 Glanvill, *Lux Orientalis*, p. 75.
20 Henry Beveridge (trans.), *Institutes of the Christian Religion by John Calvin*, 2 vols. (London, 1953), vol. 1, pp. 214–15.
21 Glanvill, *Lux Orientalis*, preface.
22 See Katharine Park and Lorraine J. Daston, 'Unnatural Conceptions: The Study of Monsters in Sixteenth and Seventeenth-Century France and England', *Past and Present* 92 (1981), 20–54.
23 [Rust], *A Letter of Resolution concerning Origen*, p. 29.
24 Henry More, *The Immortality of the Soul* in *A Collection of Several Philosophical Writings* (London, 1662), p. 112.
25 See Jacques le Goff, *The Birth of Purgatory* (Chicago, 1984), p. 229.
26 Glanvill, *Lux Orientalis*, p. 52.
27 Alexander Roberts and James Donaldson (eds.), *Ante-Nicene Christian Library*, 25 vols. (Edinburgh, 1867–97), vol. 15, pp. 475–6.
28 See Don C. Allen, *Doubt's Boundless Sea: Skepticism and Faith in the Renaissance* (Baltimore, 1964), p. 160.
29 Geoffrey Keynes (ed.), *The Works of Sir Thomas Browne*, 4 vols. (London, 1964), vol. 1, p. 47.
30 Quoted by Norman T. Burns, *Christian Mortalism from Tyndale to Milton* (Cambridge, Massachusetts, 1972), p. 172.
31 Henry Hills, *A Short Treatise Concerning the Propagation of Souls* (London, 1667), p. 23.
32 [Rust], *A Letter of Resolution concerning Origen*, pp. 28–9. See also Glanvill, *Lux Orientalis*, p. 10.
33 See Keith Thomas, 'The Puritans and Adultery: The Act of 1650 Reconsidered', in Donald Pennington and Keith Thomas (eds.), *Puritans and Revolutionaries* (Oxford, 1978), pp. 257–82.
34 See e.g. Edward Tyson, 'A Relation of two Monstrous Pigs, with the resemblance of Humane Faces, and two young Turkeys joined by the Breast ... ', *Philosophical Transactions of the Royal Society* 21 (1699), 431–5.
35 More, *The Immortality of the Soul*, p. 241. See also Glanvill, *Lux Orientalis*, p. 11; C. P., *A Dissertation*, p. 12.
36 See Glanvill, *Lux Orientalis*, p. 17. See also Thomas Hobbes, *Leviathan*,

(London, 1983), pp. 210–11. On Hobbes on the soul, see David Johnston, *The Rhetoric of Leviathan: Thomas Hobbes and the Politics of Cultural Transformation* (Princeton, 1986).

37 On the relation of More and Descartes, see S. P. Lamprecht, 'The Role of Descartes in Seventeenth-Century England', *Studies in the History of Ideas*, 4 (1935), 181–240; and C. Webster, 'Henry More and Descartes: Some New Sources', *The British Journal for the History of Science* 4 (1968–9), 359–77.
38 More, *The Immortality of the Soul*, p. 141. See also C. P., *A Dissertation*, pp. 11–12; and Glanvill, *Lux Orientalis*, p. 22.
39 Hills, *A Short Treatise*, p. 11.
40 See Shirley A. Roe, *Matter, Life, and Generation: Eighteenth-century embryology and the Haller–Wolff debate* (Cambridge, 1981); and Peter J. Bowler, 'Preformation and Pre-Existence in the Seventeenth Century: a Brief Analysis', *Journal of the History of Biology* 4 (1971), 221–44.
41 [Rust], *A Letter of Resolution concerning Origen*, p. 44. See also Glanvill, *Lux Orientalis*, p. 40; and C. P., *A Dissertation*, ch. 3.
42 See, e.g., F. M. van Helmont, *The Paradoxical Discourses of F. M. van Helmont, concerning the Macrocosm and Microcosm ... Set down in Writing by J. B.* (London, 1685), p. 107.
43 Samuel Parker, *An Account of the Nature and Extent of the Divine Dominion and Goodnesse, especially as they refer to the Origenian Hypothesis Concerning the Pre-existence of Souls* (Oxford, 1666), p. 233.
44 Glanvill, *Lux Orientalis*, pp. 88–9.
45 See Francis R. Johnson, *Astronomical Thought in Renaissance England: A Study of the English Scientific Writings from 1500 to 1645* (New York, 1968).
46 See Henry More, *Psychodia Platonica; or a platonicall song of the soul, consisting of foure severall poems...* (Cambridge, 1642), bk 3, canto 3.
47 Johnson, *Astronomical Thought*, p. 289.
48 On the twofold theology, see Peter Harrison, *'Religion' and the Religions in the English Enlightenment* (Cambridge, 1990), pp. 85–92. On Origen on the twofold theology, see Butterworth (ed.), *Origen*, pp. 278–85.
49 Quoted by Marjorie H. Nicolson, 'Milton and the *Conjectura Cabbalistica*', *Philological Quarterly* 6 (1927), 7. See also Henry More, *Conjectura Cabbalistica*, 2nd edn (London, 1662), p. 53.
50 Nicolson, *Conway Letters*, p. 82.
51 More, *Conjectura Cabbalistica*, pp. 45–6.
52 *Ibid.*, pp. 23–4.
53 *Ibid.*, p. 27.
54 Nicolson, *Conway Letters*, p. 83.
55 See David S. Katz, 'Henry More and the Jews', in Sarah Hutton (ed.), *Henry More (1614–1687): Tercentenary Studies* (Dordrecht, 1990), pp. 174–88.
56 Nicolson, *Conway Letters*, p. 323. On the life of van Helmont see *ibid.*, pp. 309ff. For an excellent account of the relationship between More, Conway and van Helmont see Allison Coudert, 'A Cambridge Plato-

nist's Kabbalist Nightmare', *Journal of the History of Ideas* 36 (1975), 633–52. My only criticism of the latter is that she fails to make sufficiently clear the differences between pre-existence and transmigration.

57 On Lurianic cabbalism see Gershom Scholem, *Major Trends in Jewish Mysticism* (New York, 1961), ch. 7.
58 Van Helmont, *The Paradoxical Discourses*, p. 107.
59 The millennium was fixed by van Helmont for 1777, thus giving the year of creation as 2223 BC.
60 [F. M. van Helmont], *Two Hundred Queries moderately Propounded concerning the Doctrine of the Revolution of Humane Souls*... (London, 1684), p. 61. Although this work was published anonymously, van Helmont admitted to his authorship of it in his *Paradoxical Discourses*. See pp. 138, 159.
61 See *ibid.*, p.159. Van Helmont appears to suggest here a span of $333\frac{1}{3}$ years between death and birth. But the overall chronology is coherent, I think, only if we take the $333\frac{1}{3}$ years to be the period between one birth and the next. See also, N. N., *A Letter to a Gentleman Touching the Treatise Entituled Two Hundred Queries concerning the Doctrine of the Revolution of Humane Souls, and its Conformity to the Truths of Christianity*... (London, 1689), pp. 8, 16. This work is essentially a summary of *Two Hundred Queries*.
62 *Ibid.*, p. 33.
63 See *ibid.*, p. 69.
64 *Ibid.*, p. 93. The identity of these children born during the millennium is not clear. As we shall see, *Seder Olam* attempted to present a more coherent picture of the relationship between those raised, those remaining, and their 'spiritual' progeny.
65 On the eternity of hell's torments, see ch. 5 below.
66 See Nicolson, *Conway Letters*, p. 315.
67 [Van Helmont], *Two Hundred Queries*, pp. 114–15.
68 See Peter Loptson (ed.), *The Principles of the Most Ancient and Modern Philosophy by Anne Conway* (The Hague, 1982), p. 19.
69 See *ibid.*, p. 25; and Nicolson, *Conway Letters*, p. 453, n. 9.
70 See Walker, *The Decline of Hell*, p. 141, n. 2.
71 The Biblical source of the chronology is Psalm 90.4: 'For a thousand years in thy sight are but as yesterday when it is past, and as a watch in the night.'
72 Anon., *Seder Olam: or, The Order, Series, or Successions of all the Ages, Periods, and Times of the Whole World* (London, 1694), p. 24.
73 *Ibid.*, p. 27.
74 *Ibid.*, p. 87.
75 *Ibid.*, p. 59.
76 See *ibid.*, p. 225. These amendments brought *Seder Olam* into agreement with van Helmont and are therefore feasibly attributable to him.
77 *Ibid.*, p. 94.
78 Keynes (ed.), *The Works of Sir Thomas Browne*, vol. 1, p. 48.

79 More, *Conjectura Cabbalistica*, p. 44.
80 Ralph Cudworth, *The True Intellectual System of the Universe...*, 3 vols. (London, 1845), vol. 3, p. 308.
81 John Dunton (ed.), *The Athenian Gazette*, 1691, no. 7.
82 See Butterworth (ed.), *Origen*, p. 74. This only appears in the Greek text. Rufinus' Latin translation completely reverses the Greek.
83 Mullett, 'A Letter', 454. Glanvill was reflecting on Origen, but his suggestions are redolent of Plotinus. Of the descent of the soul, Plotinus said, 'All that is fixed is that each several soul descends to a recipient indicated by affinity of condition; it moves towards the thing which it there resembled, and enters, accordingly into the body of man or animal.' S. Mackenna and B. Page (trans.), *Enneads* (Chicago, 1952), 4. iii. 12. I am grateful to Dr Peter Harrison for this reference.
84 Loptson, *The Principles*, pp. 184–5.
85 *Ibid.*, p. 193.
86 *Ibid.*, p. 192.
87 Two notable exceptions were Peter Sterry and Jeremiah White who managed to combine predestinationist views with neo-Platonic theology. See Walker, *The Decline of Hell*, chapter 7.
88 See Butterworth (ed.), *Origen*, p. 134.
89 Hobbes, *Leviathan*, p. 111.
90 William Molesworth (ed.), *The English Works of Thomas Hobbes*, 11 vols. (New York, 1839–45), vol. 5, pp. 110–12. Quoted by Samuel Mintz, *The Hunting of Leviathan: Seventeenth-century Reactions to the Materialism and Moral Philosophy of Thomas Hobbes* (Cambridge, 1962), p. 115.
91 The rejection of Calvinism was intimately bound up with the progressive triumph of 'Arminianism' in England during the seventeenth century. Originally, the term referred to the Dutch theologian Jacob Arminius, an opponent of Calvinism, and a rigorous supporter of the doctrine of free grace as opposed to predestination. In England, the theological meaning became inextricably entwined with political considerations especially during the 1630s. I cannot resist recounting the epigram of Bishop Morley of Winchester (as reported by Samuel Mintz, *The Hunting of Leviathan*, p.117). In reply to the question, 'What do the Arminians hold?', Morley declared, 'All the best bishoprics and deaneries in England'. On Arminianism in England, see Rosalie L. Colie, *Light and Enlightenment: A Study of the Cambridge Platonists and the Dutch Arminians* (Cambridge, 1957). See also P. White, 'The Rise of Arminianism Reconsidered', *Past and Present* 101 (1983), 34–54; N. Tyacke and P. White, 'Debate: The Rise of Arminianism Reconsidered', *Past and Present* 115 (1987), 201–29; and J. M. Atkins, 'Calvinist Bishops, Church Unity, and the Rise of Arminianism', *Albion* 18 (1986), 411–27.
92 Joseph Mede, *Works in five Bookes*, 4th edn (London, 1677), p. xix. Quoted by Colie, *Light and Enlightenment*, p. 23.
93 *DNB*, vol. 9, p. 918.

Notes to pages 25–30

94 Samuel Hoard, *Gods Love to Man-Kinde. Manifested by Dis-proving his Absolute Decree for their Damnation* (London, 1656), p. 14.
95 Richard Ward, *The Life of the Learned and Pious Dr. Henry More* (London, 1710), pp. 6–7.
96 See George Rust, *A Discourse of Truth*... (London, 1682), p. 175.
97 Joseph Glanvill, Preface to *ibid.* See also Henry More, *An Explanation of the Grand Mystery of Godliness*... (London, 1660), p. 504; Henry More, *Divine Dialogues*... (London, 1668), pp. 361–3; [Henry Hallywell], *Deus Justificatus: Or, The Divine Goodness Vindicated and Cleared, against the Assertors of Absolute and Inconditionate Reprobation*... (London, 1668), p. 4. On the attribution of this work to Hallywell, see Nicolson, *Conway Letters*, p. 293, n. 4.
98 [Hallywell], *Deus Justificatus*, p. 255.
99 Glanvill, *Lux Orientalis*, p. 52. See also More, *The Immortality of the Soul*, pp. 242–3.
100 Parker, *An Account*, p.37.
101 W[arren], *No Praeexistence*, p. 7.
102 *Ibid.*, p. 17.
103 See e.g. Parker, *An Account*, p. 162.
104 See Rust, *A Discourse of Truth*, pp. 189–90; [Hallywell], *Deus Justificatus*, pp. 275–6; and Henry More, *Annotations upon the Two Foregoing Treatises, Lux Orientalis, or, An Enquiry into the Opinion of the Prae-existence of Souls; and the Discourse of Truth*... (London, 1682), p. 43.
105 Loptson, *The Principles*, p. 157.
106 See Parker, *An Account*, p. 162.
107 See More, *Annotations*, p. 45.
108 See W[arren], *No Praeexistence*, p. 20.
109 More, *Annotations*, p. 77.
110 [Hallywell], *Deus Justificatus*, pp. 37–8.
111 See E. R. Dodds (trans.), *Proclus: The Elements of Theology* (Oxford, 1933); and John F. Finamore, *Iamblichus and the Theory of the Vehicle of the Soul* (Chico, California, 1985).
112 Cudworth, *The True Intellectual System*, vol. 3, p. 270. Cudworth recognised too that for some neo-Platonists the aethereal body was lost and needed to be regained. See also Dodds, *Proclus*, pp. 319–20.
113 Glanvill, *Lux Orientalis*, pp. 114–15. See also More, *Annotations*, p. 122.
114 [Rust], *A Letter of Resolution concerning Origen*, p. 54.
115 In *The Immortality of the Soul*, More defined the Spirit of Nature as 'A substance incorporeal but without sense or animadversion, pervading the whole matter of the Universe, and exercising a plastic power therein, according to the sundry predispositions and occasions of the parts it works upon, raising such Phenomena in the world, by directing the parts of the matter and their motion, as cannot be resolved into mere mechanical power' (More, *The Immortality of the Soul*, p. 450). As can be seen from the above passage, the major role of the Spirit of

Nature was to explain those regularities or irregularities in nature incapable of mechanical explanations. See Michael Boylan, 'Henry More's Space and the Spirit of Nature', *Journal of the History of Philosophy* 18 (1980), 395–405.
116 Glanvill, *Lux Orientalis*, p. 98.
117 *Ibid.*, pp. 121–2.
118 See More, *The Immortality of the Soul*, p. 270.
119 *Ibid.*, p. 343. See also Cudworth, *The True Intellectual System*, vol. 3, p. 265.
120 *Ibid.*, pp. 411–12.
121 *Ibid.*, p. 419.
122 Glanvill, *Lux Orientalis*, p. 93.
123 More, *Annotations*, pp. 114–15. See also Richard Baxter, *The Certainty of the World of Spirits. Fully evinced by unquestionable histories of apparitions and witchcrafts, operations, voices, &* ... (London, 1691), pp. 1–6.
124 More, *The Immortality of the Soul*, pp. 439, 441.
125 Glanvill, *Lux Orientalis*, p. 133. See also p. 132.
126 See Chapter 2.
127 One of the substantial criticisms of the pre-existence of souls was our failure in this life to remember details of our pre-existent life. In part, for this reason, More is led to the somewhat desperate expedient of maintaining that in the period of insensibility between the aerial and terrestrial lives, we lose our memory of our former aerial and aethereal experiences.
128 More, *The Immortality of the Soul* in *A Collection of Several Philosophical Writings*, pp. 6–7. See also Henry More, ΑΝΤΙΨΥΧΟΠΑΝΝΥΧΙΑ, *or a Confutation of the Sleep of the Soul after Death* (Cambridge, 1642), p. 3; and Cudworth, *The True Intellectual System*, vol. 3, p. 319.
129 *Ibid.*, p. 3.
130 John Henry, 'A Cambridge Platonist's Materialism: Henry More and the Concept of Soul', *Journal of the Warburg and Courtauld Institutes* 49 (1986), 194.
131 See More, *The Immortality of the Soul*, pp. 342–3.
132 Henry More, *An Antidote against Atheisme, or An Appeal to the Natural Faculties of the Minde of Man, whether there be not a GOD* (London, 1652), p. 164. See also Joseph Glanvill, *A Whip for the Droll, Fiddler to the Atheist: Being Reflections on Drollery and Atheism* (London, 1668), pp. 176–7.
133 Joseph Glanvill, *A Blow at Modern Sadducism in some Philosophical Considerations about Witchcraft* ... (London, 1668), epistle dedicatory.
134 Benjamin Camfield, *A Theological Discourse of Angels and their Ministries. Wherein their existence, nature, number, order and offices are modestly treated of* ... (London, 1678), p. 172.
135 Charles Wolseley, *The Reasonableness of Scripture-Belief* (London, 1672), sigs. A3–4. Quoted by Mintz, *The Hunting of Leviathan*, p. 134.

136 Thomas Bromhall, *A Treatise of Specters. Or, an History of apparitions, oracles, prophecies, and predictions* ... (London, 1658), p. 343.
137 See George Sinclair, *Satans Invisible World Discovered* (Edinburgh, 1685), Preface.
138 Cudworth, *The True Intellectual System*, p. 642.
139 Birch, *The Works*, vol. 6, pp. 57–8.
140 Glanvill, *A Blow at Modern Sadducism*, pp. 115–17.
141 On witchcraft in England, see Keith Thomas, *Religion and the Decline of Magic* (Harmondsworth, 1980), pp. 517–58. Much useful information is still to be gleaned from Wallace Notestein, *A History of Witchcraft in England from 1558 to 1718* (Washington, 1911). On European witchcraft, see, for example, Richard Kieckhefer, *European Witch Trials* (London, 1976); Wayne Shumaker, *The Occult Sciences in the Renaissance* (Berkeley, 1972), ch. 2; and Alan C. Kors and Edward Peters, *Witchcraft in Europe, 1100–1700* (London, 1972). For spirit and witchcraft relations, see, for example, Joseph Glanvill, *Saducismus Triumphatus: or, Full and Plain Evidence concerning Witches and Apparitions* ... , 3rd edn (London, 1689); Meric Casaubon, *A Treatise Proving Spirits, Witches, and Supernatural Operations by Pregnant Instances and Evidence* (London, 1672); Bromhall, *A Treatise of Specters*; J. Aubrey, *Miscellanies* ... (London, 1696); Baxter, *The Certainty of the World of Spirits*; and Sinclair, *Satans Invisible World Discovered*. For 'sceptical' approaches during this period, see, for example, John Webster, *The Displaying of Supposed Witchcraft. Wherein is affirmed that there are many sorts of Deceivers and Impostors, and Divers persons under a passive Delusion of Melancholy and Fancy* (London, 1677); Thomas Ady, *A Candle in the Dark: Shewing the Divine Cause of the distractions of the whole Nation of England and of the Christian World* (London, 1655); Balthazar Bekker, *The World Bewitch'd; An Examination of the Common Opinions Concerning Spirits* ... (London, 1695); anon., *The Doctrine of Devils, Proved to be the grand Apostasy of these later Times* ... (London, 1676). The Dutch translator of this work ascribed it to N. Orchard, a New England preacher.
142 See e.g. Moody E. Prior, 'Joseph Glanvill, Witchcraft, and Seventeenth-Century Science', *Modern Philology* 30 (1932–3), 167–93; and Allison Coudert, 'Henry More and Witchcraft', in Sarah Hutton (ed.), *Henry More (1614–1687): Tercentenary Studies* (Dordrecht, 1990), 115–36.
143 Glanvill, *A Philosophical Endeavour* in *A Blow at Modern Sadducism*, p. 15.
144 On the relation between Glanvill and Webster, see Thomas H. Jobe, 'The Devil in Restoration Science: The Glanvill–Webster Witchcraft Debate', *Isis* 72 (1981), pp. 343–56.
145 Scot, Reginald, *The Discovery of Witchcraft, proving that the Compacts and Contracts of Witches with Devils and all Infernal Spirits or Familiars, are but Erroneous Novelties and Imaginary Conceptions* (London, 1665), p. 28. The appendix, 'A Discourse concerning the Nature and Substance of Devils and Spirits', is separately paginated.

146 Stuart Clark, 'The Scientific Status of Demonology', in Brian Vickers (ed.) *Occult and Scientific Mentalities in the Renaissance* (Cambridge, 1984), p. 368.
147 Interestingly, most European demonologists did not accept that such transformations did physically take place. See Shumaker, *The Occult Sciences*, p. 93.
148 Glanvill, *A Philosophical Endeavour* in *A Blow at Modern Sadducism*, p. 20.

2 FROM THE HOUR OF DEATH TO THE DAY OF JUDGEMENT

1 Edmund Calamy, *Sermon Before the Lords on Christmas Day, 1644*. Quoted by Norman T. Burns, *Christian Mortalism from Tyndale to Milton* (Cambridge, Mass., 1972), p. 73.
2 See George H. Williams, *The Radical Reformation* (London, 1962).
3 *Martin Luthers Werke* (Weimar, 1912–21), vol. 17, p. 235. Quoted by Paul Althaus, *The Theology of Martin Luther* (Philadelphia, 1966), p. 414.
4 John Calvin, *An Excellent Treatise of the Immortalytie of the soule* (London, 1581), Preface.
5 Henry Beveridge (trans.), *Institutes of the Christian Religion by John Calvin*, vol. 2, p. 267. On Calvin's eschatology, see Heinrich Quistorp, *Calvin's Doctrine of the Last Things* (London, 1955).
6 See Heinrich Bullinger, *An Holsome Antidotus of counter-poysen, agaynst the pestylent heresye and secte of the Anabaptistes...* (London, 1548), pp. 215ff.
7 Philip Schaff, *The Creeds of Christendom*, 4th edn, 3 vols. (New York, 1919), vol. 3, p. 842.
8 Mortalism may be found before the Reformation in England, notably among the Lollards. See John A. F. Thomson, *The Later Lollards 1414–1520* (Oxford, 1965), pp. 36, 41, 82, 160–1, 185–6, 248.
9 This article was omitted from the thirty-nine Articles of 1562, much to the joy of many mortalists, who were subsequently able to argue that consequently the Church of England was not opposed to mortalism.
10 Schaff, *The Creeds of Christendom*, vol. 3, pp. 459–60.
11 See D. D. Wallace, 'From Eschatology to Arian Heresy: The Case of Francis Kett', *Harvard Theological Review* 67 (1974), 459–73.
12 John Hull, *Saint Peters Prophesie of these Last Daies. Discovering the Iniquity of the Time, and Atheisme of the Age...* (London, 1610), epistle dedicatory.
13 See Keynes (ed.), *The Works*, vol. 1, p. 16. In fact, Browne had a firm distaste for sectarians and separatists, a result of his preference for order and harmony in matters ecclesiastical. On the other hand, he was also committed to the desirability of freedom of thought for individuals within the fabric of the Church. See *ibid.*, vol. 1, pp. 17–18.
14 *Ibid.*, vol. 1, p. 40.
15 *Ibid.*, vol. 1, p. 60.
16 *Ibid.*, vol. 1, p. 42.
17 *Ibid.*, vol. 1, p. 63. On Browne's Platonism, see Leonard Nathanson, *The Strategy of Truth: A Study of Sir Thomas Browne* (Chicago, 1967).

18 Barry Reay, 'Introduction', in J. F. McGregor and B. Reay (eds.), *Radical Religion in the English Revolution* (Oxford, 1984), p. 13.
19 See e.g. Christopher Hill, *Milton and the English Revolution* (London, 1979), pp. 317ff.; and Thomas Edwards, *Gangraena: Or a Catalogue and Discovery of Many of the Errours, Heresies, Blasphemies and Pernicious Practices of the Sectaries of this time* ... (London, 1646).
20 See Norman Cohn, *The Pursuit of the Millennium* (London, 1970), p. 296.
21 Quoted by *ibid.*, p. 288.
22 Quoted by Reay, 'Introduction', 13.
23 Burns, *Christian Mortalism*, pp. 74–5. The bracketed references are to part and page numbers in *Gangraena*. Annihilationists who preached the extinction of the individual at death need to be distinguished from those who believed that God extinguished the individual after a period of punishment in hell. The latter was not a position held by radicals. See Chapter 5.
24 See Keith Thomas, *Religion and the Decline of Magic* (Harmondsworth, 1980), pp. 561–2.
25 Quoted by Christopher Hill, *The World Turned Upside Down* (Harmondsworth, 1975), p. 173.
26 Lodowick Muggleton, *The Acts of the Witnesses of the Spirit*... (London, 1699), pp. 12–13.
27 John Reeve and Lodowick Muggleton, *Joyful News from Heaven*... (London, 1658), p. 11.
28 Richard Coppin, *Divine Teachings*... (London, 1653), p. 8. See also A. L. Morton, *The World of the Ranters* (London, 1970), p. 73.
29 Joseph Salmon, *Heights in Depths* (London, 1651), pp. 37–8.
30 Quoted by Hill, *The World Turned Upside Down*, p. 228.
31 Coppin, *Divine Teachings*, p. 75.
32 See J. F. McGregor and B. Reay, *Radical Religion in the English Revolution* (Oxford, 1984), p. 204.
33 Quoted by Nigel Smith, *A Collection of Ranter Writings from the Seventeenth Century* (London, 1983), pp. 236, 239.
34 Quoted by Smith, *A Collection of Ranter Writings*, p. 172.
35 *Ibid.*, p. 182.
36 Hobbes, *Leviathan*, p. 211.
37 *Ibid.*, p. 338.
38 *Ibid.*, p. 243.
39 The orthodox and Calvinist position was that the soul was naturally immortal. Nathaniel Henry's suggestion that Hobbes' theory was not mortalist but orthodox and Calvinistic appears a little odd. See Nathaniel M. Henry, 'Milton and Hobbes: Mortalism and the Intermediate State', *Studies in Philology* 48 (1951), 241–4.
40 Basil Willey, *The Seventeenth Century Background* (London, 1953), p. 105.
41 J. G. A. Pocock, 'Time, History and Eschatology in the Thought of Thomas Hobbes', in J. H. Elliott and H. G. Koenigsberger (eds.), *The Diversity of History* (Ithaca, New York, 1949), 186.

42 Hobbes, *Leviathan*, p. 333. See also Johnston, *The Rhetoric of Leviathan*, ch. 7.
43 See *ibid.*, p. 242.
44 *Ibid.*, p. 342.
45 *Ibid.*, p. 343.
46 *Ibid.*, p. 247.
47 *Ibid.*, p. 247.
48 *Ibid.*, p. 342. In his debate with Archbishop Bramhall in which Bramhall suggested that the lives of the wicked after Judgement Day gave little appearance of being punitive, Hobbes suggested that Bramhall knew that his opinion was that after the Resurrection there would be no wicked men at all upon the earth but only the elect. This suggests that the wicked rather than being raised up to be punished and then annihilated would be merely left in their graves. See William Molesworth (ed.), *The English Works of Thomas Hobbes*, 11 vols. (New York, 1839–45), vol. 4, p. 359.
49 [Richard Overton], *Man Wholly Mortal* (London, 1655), pp. 8–9. The work was published anonymously by R. O., but there is little doubt that its author was Richard Overton. See Don M. Wolfe, 'Unsigned Pamphlets of Richard Overton: 1641–1649', *Huntington Library Quarterly* 21 (1957–8), 167–201; and Perez Zagorin, 'The Authorship of *Mans Mortalitie*', *The Library* 5 (1950–1), 179–82. Clement Writer, biblical critic and mortalist, was suspected by his contemporaries of its authorship. See Edwards, *Gangraena*, p. 114.
50 Norman T. Burns makes a strong case for Overton's mortalism being intimately related to his Christian beliefs and not to either an incipient Deism or an irreligious naturalism. See Burns, *Christian Mortalism*, pp. 154ff.
51 Overton, *Man Wholly Mortal*, pp. 33–4.
52 *Ibid.*, pp. 38–9.
53 Alexander Ross, *The Philosophicall Touch-Stone*... (London, 1645), pp. 122–3.
54 *Ibid.*, p. 127.
55 The best discussion of Milton's mortalism remains Burns, *Christian Mortalism*. But see also Henry, 'Milton and Hobbes'; C. A. Patrides, '"Paradise Lost" and the Mortalist Heresy', *Notes and Queries* 102 (1957), 250–1; and George Williamson, 'Milton and the Mortalist Heresy', *Studies in Philology* 32 (1935), 553–79.
56 On the possible direct influence of Overton on Milton, see Burns, *Christian Mortalism*, pp. 169ff.
57 Frank A. Patterson (ed.), *The Works of John Milton*, 18 vols. (New York, 1931–8), vol. 15, pp. 40–1.
58 Hill, *The World Turned Upside Down*, pp. 378–9.
59 Anon., *The Way to Heaven in a String: or, Mr. A---'s Argument Burlesqu'd. A Poem* (n.p., 1701).

60 *The Journals of the House of Commons*, vol. 15 (25/10/1705–1/4/1708), p. 474.
61 The most substantial account of Asgill remains Keningdale Cook, 'John Asgill; and the Cowardliness of Dying', *Fraser's Magazine* 4 (1871), 150–66. On Whiston, see Eamon Duffy, '"Whiston's Affair": the Trials of a Primitive Christian 1709–1714', *Journal of Ecclesiastical History* 27 (1976), 129–50. On Sacheverell, see Geoffrey Holmes, *The Trial of Dr. Sacheverell* (London, 1973).
62 John Asgill, *A Collection of Tracts* (London, 1715), p. 38.
63 John 11. 25–6.
64 Asgill, *A Collection of Tracts*, p. 40.
65 *Ibid.*
66 Daniel Defoe, *An Enquiry into the Case of Mr. Asgil's General Translation* (London, 1704), p. 8.
67 John Asgill, *An Argument* (London, 1700), p. 61.
68 Quoted by Cook, 'John Asgill', 160.
69 Asgill, *An Argument*, p. 11.
70 *Ibid.*, p. 95.
71 *Ibid.*, pp. 81–2.
72 Stephen Crisp, *A Faithful Warning and Exhortation to Friends* (London, 1684), p. 15.
73 Asgill, *An Argument*, p. 82.
74 *Ibid.*, p. 83.
75 *Ibid.*, p. 67.
76 *Ibid.*, p. 93.
77 *Ibid.*, p. 106.
78 See e.g. anon., *The Way to Heaven in a String*; and anon., *An Account of Mr. Asgil's Strange and Wonderful Translation which will happen upon the Twelfth of July next* (London, 1717). William Whiston also was satirised in this article as one who would accompany Asgill on his public translation into heaven from Hampstead Heath. His inclusion in this work may well have been related to the appendix on Christ's ascension in Whiston's 1708 work, *The Accomplishment of Scripture Prophecies*. Here, Whiston proposed the view that Christ had ascended on the evening of his resurrection, and that the appearances of Christ during the forty days after his resurrection were the results of periodic descents from heaven. This would only have involved Christ in a series of fifty-mile journeys, 'since the utmost height of our Air, as far as appears from the best Observations, is but about 45 or 50 Miles from the Earth'. William Whiston, *The Accomplishment of Scripture Prophecies* (Cambridge, 1708), p. 297. The details of Whiston's calculation may be seen in his 'Scheme of the Seven Heavens' contained at the conclusion of his *Memoirs*. Henry More also believed the distance from earth to the aethereal realm to be 50 miles. See *Annotations* (London, 1682), pp. 114–15.
79 Samuel Taylor Coleridge recorded his impressions of Asgill on the front

cover of his own copy of Asgill's *Collection of Tracts* which he had acquired in January 1827. Coleridge believed that Asgill was so much the humorist that Asgill himself no longer knew whether he was in earnest or in jest. Coleridge's copy of Asgill, *A Collection of Tracts*, is held in the British Library. See also Henry N. Coleridge (ed.), *The Literary Remains of Samuel Taylor Coleridge*, 2 vols. (London, 1836), vol. 1, p. 395; and Henry Morley (ed.), *Table Talk of Samuel Taylor Coleridge* (London, 1884), p. 127, n. 35.
80 Defoe, *An Enquiry*, Preface.
81 *Ibid.* Defoe appears to have been fond of Pascal's Wager. In 1704 in *The Storm*, he similarly chided atheists for their irrationality in failing to recognise that, if they were wrong, they had everything to lose, but if right, nothing to gain: 'No gamester will set at such a main; no man will lay such a wager, where he may lose but cannot win.' Quoted by Walter Wilson, *Memoirs of the Life and Times of Daniel de Foe*, 3 vols. (London, 1830), vol. 2, p. 268, n. 37.
82 *Ibid.*, p. 16.
83 *Ibid.*, p. 29.
84 *Ibid.*, p. 31.
85 *Ibid.*, p. 23.
86 See *ibid.*, p. 39.
87 See *The Journals of the House of Commons*, vol. 15 (25/10/1705–1/4/1708), pp. 473–4.
88 See e.g. Robert Southey, *The Doctor*, 7 vols. (London, 1834–47), vol. 6, p. 3; Morley, *Table Talk*, p. 127; *Biographia Britannica*..., 2nd edn, 5 vols. (London, 1778–93), vol. 1, p. 221.
89 Roland Stromberg, *Religious Liberalism in Eighteenth-Century England* (Oxford, 1954), p. 13.
90 The term refers to those who refused to swear allegiance to William and Mary on the grounds that the oaths already made to James II were inviolable. The Archbishop of Canterbury, a number of his fellow bishops, and some 300–400 clergy were suspended and deprived of their offices.
91 On the life of Dodwell see Francis Brokesby, *The Life of Mr. Henry Dodwell*... (London, 1715). Brokesby too was a non-juring companion of Dodwell at Shottesbrooke.
92 See Thomas Babington Macaulay, *The History of England from the Accession of James II*, 6 vols. (London, 1914), vol. 4, pp. 1724–6.
93 *Biographia Britannica* (1778–93), p. 327. Interestingly, the *Dictionary of National Biography* ignores the whole issue.
94 Edmund Chishull, *A Charge of Heresy, Maintained against Mr. Dodwel's late Epistolary Discourse, concerning the Mortality of the Soul* (London, 1706), Preface. The charge of heresy put forward by Chishull aroused the wrath of Dodwell's non-juring companion at Shottesbrooke, Thomas Hearne. He damned Chishull with faint praise as 'a confident, opinionative little writer'.

95 John Turner, *Justice Done to Human Souls*... (London, 1706), pp. 7–8. See also Samuel Clarke, *A Letter to Mr. Dodwell* (London, 1731), p. 2.
96 Henry Dodwell, *A Preliminary Defence of the Epistolary Discourse, concerning the Distinction between Soul and Spirit* (London, 1707), pt 1, p. 97. This work is in two parts, separately paginated, the first directed against Clarke's *A Letter*, and Turner's *Justice Done to Human Souls*, the second against Chishull's *A Charge of Heresy*.
97 See Dodwell, *An Epistolary Discourse, Proving, from the Scriptures and the First Fathers, that the Soul is a Principle Naturally Mortal* (London, 1706), pp. 145–6.
98 Henry Dodwell, *The Scripture Account of the Eternal Rewards or Punishments of all that hear of the Gospel*... (London, 1708), p. 251. This is, as we shall see later, a common motif.
99 *Ibid.*, p. 272.
100 See Chishull, *A Charge of Heresy*, p. 47. The fortieth was the one more relevant: 'XL. *The soulles of them that departe this life doe neither die with the bodies, nor sleep idle.* Thei whiche saie, that the soulles of suche as departe hens doe sleepe, being without al sence, fealing, or perceiuing, vntil the daie of iudgement, or affirme that the soulles die with the bodies, and at the laste daie shal be raised vp with the same, doe vtterlie dissent from the right beliefe declared to vs in holie Scripture.' See Charles Hardwick, *A History of the Articles of Religion*... (London, 1884), p. 348.
101 See Dodwell, *An Epistolary Discourse* (London, 1706), p. xxvi.
102 See Dodwell, *A Preliminary Defence* (London, 1707), pt 2, p. 33.
103 On Henry Layton, see *DNB* vol. 11, pp. 747–8. Interestingly, Francis Blackburne thought Layton's 1703 work, *Arguments and Replie in a Dispute concerning the Nature of the Humane Soul*, to be the work of Dodwell. Francis Blackburne's *An Historical View of the Controversy concerning an Intermediate State and the Separate Existence of the Soul between Death and the General Resurrection*, 2nd edn (London, 1772) remains the most useful contemporary source of the mortalist controversy.
104 For a bibliography of Coward's works, see *DNB*, vol. 4. p. 1299.
105 William Coward, *Second Thoughts Concerning Human Soul*... (London, 1702), pp. 22–3. This work and his *Grand Essay*... (London, 1704) were declared heretical by Parliament in 1704 and ordered to be burnt by the common Hangman. See *The Journals of the House of Commons*, vol. 14 (1703–4), p. 380. Coward was probably influenced by John Locke's notion that a power of thinking might be super-added to matter. Clearly, Locke's notion was at the centre of Samuel Clarke's *A Letter to Mr. Dodwell* and the Deist Anthony Collins' *A Letter to the Learned Mr Henry Dodwell*. These works, a reply to Collins by Clarke, and a further response by Collins are all contained in Samuel Clarke, *A Letter to Mr. Dodwell* (London, 1731). The original debate between Collins and Clarke occurred between 1706 and 1708.
106 There is some confusion in Dodwell as to whether those who were ignorant of the Gospel would even be raised. He was accused of denying

the general resurrection. See e.g. Thomas Milles, *The Natural Immortality of the Soul asserted, and Proved from the Scriptures and First Fathers* (Oxford, 1707), p. 24; and Turner, *Justice Done to Human Souls*, p. 46. Although Dodwell did argue that it was not heretical to deny the resurrection of all, his overall view seems to have been that the ignorant would be raised, but only in the latter part of the day when judgement for heaven and hell would be completed.

107 Dodwell, *An Epistolary Discourse*, p. 43. Dodwell appears uncertain whether unbaptised infants immediately died, or were preserved in an intermediate state until the day of resurrection at which time they were annihilated, or were baptised in the intermediate state.

108 John Norris, *A Letter to Mr. Dodwell, Concerning the Immortality of the Soul of Man...* (London, 1709) p. 47.

109 *Ibid.*, pp. 61–2.

110 Clarke, *A Letter*, p. 18. See also Daniel Whitby, *Reflections on Some Assertions and Opinions of Mr. Dodwell...* (London, 1707), p.62. On occasion, Dodwell did suggest that both Jews and Gentiles would be saved by the Mosaic and Natural Law, although this cannot be said to dominate his thought. See e.g. Dodwell, *An Epistolary Discourse*, p. 211.

111 *Ibid.*, p. 11.

112 Dodwell, *An Epistolary Discourse* (London, 1706), p. 19.

113 See Clarke, *A Letter*, p. 19.

114 Milles, *The Natural Immortality of the Soul*, p. 26.

115 Whitby, *Reflections*, p. 75.

116 *Stromateis*, 6. 6. Quoted by Ralph V. Turner, 'descendit ad inferos. Medieval Views on Christ's Descent into Hell', *Journal of the History of Ideas* 27 (1966), 174. On Origen on the harrowing of hell, see e.g. Henry Chadwick (trans.), *Origen: Contra Celsum* (Cambridge, 1953), 11. 43, pp. 99–100.

117 See especially, *Theologische Realenzyklopädie* (Berlin, 1986), vol. 15, pp. 455–461. See also, Turner, 'descendit ad inferos', 173–94; Dewey D. Wallace, 'Puritan and Anglican. The Interpretation of Christ's Descent into Hell in Elizabethan Theology,' *Archiv für Reformationsgeschichte* 69 (1978), 248–87. On the medieval literature on visions of hell, see D. D. R. Owen, *The Vision of Hell* (New York, 1971); and Jacques le Goff, 'The Learned and Popular Dimensions of Journeys in the Otherworld in the Middle Ages', in S. L. Kaplan (ed.), *Understanding Popular Culture* (Berlin, 1984), pp. 19–37.

118 See Dodwell, *An Epistolary Discourse* (London, 1706), p. 175.

119 See Whitby, *Reflections*, p. 85.

120 See Turner, *A Letter*, pp. 18–19.

121 Dodwell, *A Preliminary Defence*, pt 2, pp. 31–2.

122 *Ibid.*, p. 32.

123 Whitby, *Reflections*, p. 137. See also Clarke, *A Letter*, pp. 4, 62.

124 Clarke, *A Letter*, p. 68. This is perhaps to read too much into Clarke's

comments at this point. But we do know that William Whiston reported that Clarke and Isaac Newton did not accept eternal torments. Indeed, wrote Whiston, 'Dr. *Clarke* thought that "few or no thinking Men were really of different sentiments in that Matter".' William Whiston, *Historical Memoirs of the Life and Writings of Dr. Samuel Clarke*, 3rd edn (London, 1748), p. 75. See also Walker, *The Decline of Hell*, pp. 95–6.
125 See Dodwell, *A Preliminary Defence*, pt 1, pp. 85–6.
126 Turner, *Justice Done to Human Souls*, pp. 118–19. See also Chishull, *A Charge of Heresy*, pp. 6–7; and *Biographia Britannica*, vol. 1, p. 324.
127 Chishull, *A Charge of Heresy*, p. 3. See also, Clarke, *A Letter*, pp. 47–8; Milles, *The Natural Immortality of the Soul*, p. 2; Norris, *A Letter to Mr. Dodwell*, p. 51; Turner, *Justice Done to Human Souls*, p. 14; Whitby, *Reflections*, p. 19.
128 See Dodwell, *A Preliminary Defence*, pt 1, p. 14.
129 On morals and manners during the English Enlightenment, see John Redwood, *Reason, Ridicule and Religion: The Age of Enlightenment in England, 1660–1750* (London, 1976), ch.8.
130 Quoted by Gordon Rupp, *Religion in England, 1688–1791* (Oxford, 1986), p. 295.
131 See Hobbes, *Leviathan*, pp. 337–8.
132 [Joachim Stegmann], *Brevis Disquisitio: or, a Brief Enquiry touching a Better Way ... To Refute Papists, and Reduce Protestants to Certainty and Unity in Religion* (London, 1633), p. 27.
133 Henry More, *A Modest Enquiry into the Mystery of Iniquity ...* (London, 1664), p. 86.
134 Le Goff, *The Birth of Purgatory*, p. 233.
135 Nicholas Caussin, *The Holy Court in Five Tomes* (London, 1650), p. 431.
136 Le Goff, *The Birth of Purgatory*, p. 292.
137 As we shall see later, however, the resurrection of the body on the last day would increase both happiness and misery.
138 William Strong, *The Worm that Dyeth Not, or, Hell Torments in the Certainty and Eternity of Them* (London, 1672), pp. 283–4. This work was published after Strong's death in 1654.
139 William Sherlock, *A Practical Discourse Concerning Death*, 9th edn (London, 1696), p. 266. See also, T. C., *An Impartial Examination and Refutation of the Erroneous Tenents of Thomas Moor; in his dangerous Writings, intituled, Clavis Aurea, etc.* (London, 1698), p. 11.
140 Richard Jenks, *The Eternity of Hell Torments Asserted and Vindicated ...* (London, 1707), p. 10.
141 Tobias Swinden, *An Enquiry into the Nature and Place of Hell*, 2nd edn (London, 1727), p. 288.
142 Matthew Horbery, *An Enquiry into the Scripture-Doctrine Concerning the duration of Future Punishment ...* (London, 1744), p. 211.
143 W[arren], *No Praeexistence*, p. 44.

144 William Dawes, *Sermons Preach'd Upon Several Occasions before King William, and Queen Anne* (London, 1707), p. 72.
145 William Lupton, *The Eternity of Future Punishment Proved and Vindicated* (Oxford, 1708), p. 6.
146 Ignored by Protestant theologians because they were Catholics. Still, although Digby's attempt to combine Aristotelianism with the new mechanical philosophy was ultimately ill-fated, he did enjoy a considerable reputation among those engaged in establishing the mechanical philosophy – Hobbes, Descartes, Boyle, and so on. See Robert H. Kargon, *Atomism in England from Hariot to Newton* (Oxford, 1966).
147 The first edition was published in Paris in 1644; the first English edition followed a year later.
148 This was translated into English in 1659 under the title *The Middle State of Souls from the hour of death to the Day of Judgement*. On Digby and his relation to White see John Henry, 'Atomism and Eschatology: Catholicism and Natural Philosophy in the Interregnum', *The British Journal for the History of Science* 15 (1982), 211–39. I am particularly indebted to his discussion.
149 Kenelm Digby, *Observations upon Religio Medici* (London, 1643), p. 12.
150 Kenelm Digby, *Two Treatises: in the one of which, the nature of bodies; in the other, the nature of mans soule, is looked into* (London, 1645), p. 117.
151 *Ibid.*, p. 117.
152 *Ibid.*, p. 118.
153 Henry, 'Atomism and Eschatology', 225.
154 As we shall see later, in the next chapter, White rejects the notion of *poena sensus*, retaining only the *poena damni*.
155 Thomas White, *The Middle State of Souls. From the hour of death to the Day of Judgment* (London, 1659), pp. 5–6.
156 *Ibid.*, pp. 71–2.
157 Quoted by Piero Camporesi, *The Fear of Hell: Images of Damnation and Salvation in Early Modern Europe* (Cambridge, 1990), p. 49.
158 White, *The Middle State of Souls*, p. 3.
159 *DNB*, vol. 13, p. 1097.
160 London, 1680.
161 John Shower, *Heaven and Hell; or the Unchangeable State of Happiness or Misery for all Mankind in another World* (London, 1700), p. 103.
162 Swinden, *An Enquiry*, p. 76.
163 See *ibid.*, p. 87.
164 See Christopher Love, *Hell's Terror: Or, A Treatise of the Torments of the Damned, as a Preservative against Security* (London, 1653), sermon 5. By the time, this was published, Love would have had several years personally to verify his account. He was executed for treason in 1651.
165 This work was translated from a French manuscript of 1740, preceding by 25 years its eventual publication in French, and Cuppé's death

shortly afterwards in 1744. See E. R. Briggs, 'Pierre Cuppé's debts to England and Holland', *Studies on Voltaire and the Eighteenth Century* 6 (1958), 37–66.
166 [Pierre Cuppe'], *Heaven Open to all Men*... (London, 1743), pp. 6–7.
167 Matthew Horbery, *An Enquiry*, p. 207.
168 Max Weber, *The Protestant Ethic and the Spirit of Capitalism* (London, 1930), p. 97.
169 Anne Conway, *The Principles of the most Ancient and Modern Philosophy*... (London, 1692), p. 76.
170 [Peter Sterry], *The Rise, Race, and Royalty of the Kingdom of God in the Soul of Man* (London, 1683), p. 385.
171 See *ibid.*, p. 438.
172 Peter Sterry, MS 291, Emmanuel College Library, Cambridge, p. 96. On the Sterry manuscripts at Emmanuel College, see V. De Sola Pinto, 'Peter Sterry and his Unpublished Writings', *Review of English Studies* 6 (1930), 385–407. On Sterry, see also V. de Sola Pinto, *Peter Sterry: Platonist and Puritan 1613–1672* (Cambridge, 1934); and Walker, *The Decline of Hell*, pp. 104–21.
173 Sterry, *The Rise, Race, and Royalty of the Kingdom of God*, p. 52.
174 Sterry, MS 291, p. 100.
175 The work was published anonymously. However, in a letter to Lady Conway in March 1668, Henry More wrote of a book, a copy of which he had been unable to acquire, which 'asserts a capacity after this life of improving their time for the attainment of eternall happinesse'. He went on to remark that its authorship had been attributed to himself, Dr Worthington, and Hallywell. Marjorie Nicolson identifies the work as *Deus Justificatus*. However, this work does not contain the theory described by More, whereas *A Private Letter of Satisfaction* does. See Nicolson, *Conway Letters*, pp. 292–3. It was also attributed to Hallywell by Archibald Campbell in his *The Doctrines of a Middle State Between Death and the Resurrection: of Prayers for the Dead: and the Necessity of Purification; plainly proved from the Holy Scriptures*... (London, 1721), p. 63.
176 [Henry Hallywell], *A Private Letter of Satisfaction to a Friend*... (London[?], 1667), p. 28.
177 *Ibid.*, p. 35.
178 *Ibid.*, p. 36.
179 *Ibid.*, pp. 38–9.
180 Archibald Campbell, *The Doctrines of a Middle State*, pp. 111–12.
181 See le Goff, *The Birth of Purgatory*, ch. 2.
182 Campbell, *The Doctrines of a Middle State*, p. xx.
183 *Ibid.*, p. 57.
184 *Ibid.*, p. 139.
185 [Hallywell], *A Private Letter*, p. 70.

186 F. J. Sheed (trans.), *The Confessions of St. Augustine, Books I-X* (New York, 1942), Book IX. xiii, p. 169.
187 William Chase Green (trans.), *Saint Augustine: The City of God against the Pagans* (London, 1958–72), vol. 7, p. 117.
188 Campbell, *The Doctrines of a Middle State*, p. 67.
189 *Ibid.*, p. 70.

3 THE CONTOURS OF HEAVEN AND HELL

1 Shower, *Heaven and Hell*, pp. 17–18.
2 *The true narrative of the execution of John Marketman, chyrurgian, of Westham in the county of Essex, for committing a horrible & bloody murther* (n.d.), pp. 3–4. Quoted by J. A. Sharpe, *Crime in Seventeenth-Century England: A County Study* (Cambridge, 1983), p. 142.
3 Lawrence Stone, *The Family, Sex and Marriage in England 1500–1800* (Harmondsworth, 1979), pp. 62–3.
4 Richard Baxter, *The Saints' Everlasting Rest: or, a Treatise of the Blessed State of the Saints in their Enjoyment of God in Glory ...* (London, 1846), p. 252.
5 *Ibid.*, p. 240.
6 *Ibid.*, p. 244.
7 Love, *Hell's Terror*, p. 41.
8 Thomas Vincent, *Fire and Brimstone From Heaven, From Earth, in Hell ...* (London, 1670), p. 129.
9 Richard Younge, *A Serious and Pathetical Description of Heaven and Hell, According to the Pencil of the Holy Ghost* (London, 1658), p. 22.
10 [Richard Stafford], *A Discourse of the Misery of Hell ...* (London, 1697), p. 2.
11 Love, *Hell's Terror*, pp. 42–3.
12 Quoted by Christopher Hill, *A Tinker and a Poor Man: John Bunyan and his Church 1628–1688* (New York, 1989), p. 184.
13 John Bunyan *A Few Sighs from Hell, or, the Groans of a damned Soul ...* (London, 1658), in Roger Sharrock (ed.), *The Miscellaneous Works of John Bunyan* (Oxford, 1976–), vol. 1, p. 300. See also Love, *Hell's Terror*, p. 44.
14 Love, *Hell's Terror*, p. 43.
15 Robert Sharrock, *De Finibus Virtutis Christianae ...* (Oxford, 1673), p. 41.
16 William Gearing, *A Prospect of Heaven: or, a Treatise of the Happiness of the Saints in Glory ...* (London, 1673), p. 226.
17 Vincent, *Fire and Brimstone*, p. 100.
18 See Michel Foucault, *Discipline and Punish: The Birth of the Prison* (Harmondsworth, 1979), p. 34.
19 Sharrock (ed.), *The Miscellaneous Works*, vol. 1, p. 300.
20 Vincent, *Fire and Brimstone*, p. 100.
21 See Baxter, *The Saints' Everlasting Rest*, p. 246.

22 Sharrock, *De Finibus*, p. 41. See also Love, *Hell's Terror*, p. 45.
23 Gearing, *A Prospect of Heaven*, p. 226.
24 Sharrock (ed.), *The Miscellaneous Works*, pp. 274–5.
25 Love, *Hell's Terror*, p. 47.
26 Dawes, *Sermons*, p. 58.
27 See Baxter, *The Saints' Everlasting Rest*, pp. 253–4.
28 William Bates, *The Four Last Things: viz. Death, Judgment, Heaven, Hell, practically considered and applied, in several discourses*, 2nd edn (London, 1691), p. 6.
29 More, *The Immortality of the Soul*, p. 441.
30 *Ibid.*, p. 434.
31 Love, *Hell's Terror*, pp. 46–7.
32 Bromhall, *A Treatise of Specters*, p. 350.
33 Thomas Goodwin, *A Discourse of the Punishment of Sin in Hell; Demonstrating the Wrath of God to be the immediate Cause thereof* (London, 1680), p. 98.
34 Joseph Trapp, *Thoughts upon the Four Last Things: Death, Judgment, Heaven, Hell* (n.p., 1734–5). Quoted by Hypatia Bradlaugh Bonner, *The Christian Hell from the First to the Twentieth Century* (London, 1913), p. 77.
35 Samuel Richardson, *A Discourse of the Torments of Hell...* (London, 1660), pp. 42–3. See also Campbell, *The Doctrines of a Middle State*, p. 96.
36 John Brandon, Το πυρ το αἰώνιον: *or Everlasting Fire no Fancy. Being an answer to a late pestilent pamphlet entituled 'The Foundations of Hell-Torments shaken and removed'* (London, 1678), p. 33.
37 Vincent, *Fire and Brimstone*, p. 85. See also Dawes, *Sermons*, p. 58; and Thomas Lewis, *The Nature of Hell, the Reality of Hell-Fire, and the Eternity of Hell-Torments, explained and vindicated...* (London, 1720), pp. 14, 24. This last work was a response to the second edition in 1720 of Richardson, *A Discourse*.
38 [Stafford], *A Discourse of the Misery of Hell*, p. 3.
39 Vincent, *Fire and Brimstone*, p. 102.
40 William Beveridge, *Of the Happiness of the Saints*, 3rd edn (London, 1698), p. 4.
41 Goodwin, *A Discourse*, p. 49.
42 Patterson (ed.), *The Works of John Milton*, vol. 2, p. 10.
43 See John M. Steadman, 'Milton and Patristic Tradition: The Quality of Hell-Fire', *Anglia* 76 (1958), 116–28; and Theodor Spencer, 'Chaucer's Hell: A Study in Mediaeval Convention', *Speculum* 2 (1927), 177–200.
44 Sharrock, *De Finibus*, p. 23.
45 *Ibid.*, p. 48. See also, John Denison, *A Three-Fold Resolution, verie necessarie to saluation. Describing Earths Vanitie, Hels Horror, Heauens Felicitie* (London, 1608), pp. 397–8.
46 Vincent, *Fire and Brimstone*, p. 103.
47 See especially Emma Disley, 'Degrees of Glory: Protestant Doctrine and the Concept of Rewards Hereafter', *The Journal of Theological Studies* 42 (1991), 77–105.

48 [Orchard], *The Doctrine of Devils*, p. 119.
49 Bates, *The Four Last Things*, p. 162.
50 William Dodwell, *The Eternity of future Punishment asserted and vindicated. In Answer to Mr. Whiston's late Treatise on that Subject* (Oxford, 1743), p. 80. See also Swinden, *An Enquiry*, p. 324; and Patterson (ed.), *The Works of John Milton*, vol. 16, p. 373.
51 See Disley, 'Degrees of Glory.'
52 Dunton (ed.), *The Athenian Gazette*, 3.8. In the history of the English press, *The Athenian Gazette* was the first paper devoted to the interests of the general public. The questions of the public were here answered by an editorial staff consisting of Dunton, Richard Sault the mathematician, and Samuel Wesley, the father of John Wesley. Thus any person with twopence to spend could send their question through the penny-post, and receive their answer by purchasing *The Athenian Gazette* at a cost of one penny. Its contents therefore are rich, not merely for the answers given, but for the insights into the kinds of question present in the public mind. On the history of this journal, see John Underhill (ed.), '*The Athenian Oracle.*' *A Selection* (London, 1896[?]).
53 Patterson (ed.), *The Works of John Milton*, vol. 16, p. 371. See also Caussin, *The Holy Court in Five Tomes*, p. 427; and Love, *Hell's Terror*, p. 39.
54 See e.g. Camporesi, *The Fear of Hell*, pp. 21–2.
55 See Piero Camporesi, *The Incorruptible Flesh: Bodily Mutation and Mortification in Religion and Folklore* (Cambridge, 1988), ch. 6.
56 William Strong, *The Worm that Dyeth Not*, pp. 8–9.
57 *Ibid.*, p. 10.
58 There was much division over the things to which the images of fire and worms were to be applied in the early church. Augustine, for example, in *The City of God* remarked that 'the unquenchable fire and the ever-living worm are differently explained by different persons. In fact, some refer both to the body, others refer both to the soul; still others refer the fire to the body in the literal sense, and the worm to the soul in the figurative sense, an interpretation which seems more plausible.' William Chase Greene (trans.), *Saint Augustine: The City of God against the Pagans* (London, 1960), vol. 6, p. 393.
59 William Pringle (ed.), *Commentary on the Book of Isaiah by John Calvin* (Grand Rapids, Michigan, 1984), vol. 3, p. 439.
60 Swinden, *An Enquiry*, p. 37. I am indebted to Walker, *The Decline of Hell*, p. 61, for this point.
61 Younge, *A Serious and Pathetical Description*, pp. 4–5.
62 Caussin, *The Holy Court in Five Tomes*, p. 430.
63 More, *The Immortality of the Soul*, p. 439.
64 *Ibid.*, p. 441.
65 Cudworth, *The True Intellectual System of the Universe*, vol. 3, p. 323.
66 Campbell, *The Doctrines of a Middle State*, p. 38. See also Thomas Burnet,

A Treatise Concerning the State of Departed Souls Before, and At, and After the Resurrection... (London, 1733), pp. 340–1.
67 Dunton (ed.), *The Athenian Gazette*, 4.29. See also Younge, *A Serious and Pathetical Description*, p. 9.
68 Gearing, *A Prospect of Heaven*, p. 200.
69 Daniel Burgess, *The Death and Rest, Resurrection and Blessed Portion of the Saints*... (London, 1692), pp. 48–9.
70 Thomas Lye, *Death the Sweetest Sleep* (London, 1681), p. 15.
71 See John Pearson, *An Exposition of the Creed* (London, 1659), pp. 747–8.
72 Younge, *A Serious and Pathetical Description*, p. 9. See also, Goodwin, *A Discourse*, p. 37.
73 See Sharrock (ed.), *The Miscellaneous Works*, vol. 3, p. 243.
74 More, *An Explanation of the Grand Mystery of Godliness*, p. 223.
75 *Ibid.*, p. 223. On this issue he foreshadowed Locke's identification of personal identity with self-consciousness. See Chapter 4.
76 Humphry Hody, *The Resurrection of the (same) Body Asserted*... (London, 1694), p. 211.
77 N. B., *The Resurrection founded on Justice: or, a vindication of this great standing reason assigned by the ancients and moderns* (London, 1700), pp. 12–13.
78 Winch Holdsworth, *A Sermon preach'd before the University of Oxford on Easter-Monday 1719*... (Oxford, 1720), p. 17. See also A. Fleury, *A Short Essay on the General Resurrection*... (Dublin, 1752), p. 152.
79 Sharrock (ed.) *The Miscellaneous Works*, vol. 1, p. 274.
80 See Joseph Stevens, *The Whole Parable of Dives and Lazarus, Explain'd and Apply'd* (London, 1697), pp. 88–9.
81 F. W. Farrar, *Eternal Hope* (London, 1878), p. 66.
82 [John Dunton], *An Essay Proving We shall Know our Friends in Heaven*... (London, 1698), p. 78. See also Sharrock, *De Finibus*, p. 76.
83 Baxter, *The Saints' Everlasting Rest*, p. 67.
84 See [Peter Sterry], *A Discourse of the Freedom of the Will* (London, 1675), pp. 143–5.
85 Quoted by N. I. Matar, 'Heavenly Joy at the Torments of the Damned in Restoration Writings', *Notes and Queries* 33 (1986), 467.
86 More, *Annotations*, p. 76.
87 Shower, *Heaven and Hell*, p. 11.
88 Dawes, *Sermons*, p. 74.
89 Francis Blyth, *Eternal Misery: the necessary Consequence of Infinite Mercy abused* (London, 1740), p. 24.
90 Jonathan Edwards, *The Works of President Edwards* (New York, 1844), vol. 4, pp. 293, 291.
91 Quoted by Walker, *The Decline of Hell*, pp. 31–2.
92 Marie Huber, *The World Unmask'd: or, the Philosopher the greatest Cheat*... (London, 1736), p. 289.
93 Quoted by Walker, *The Decline of Hell*, p. 32. For Tertullian on the 'abominable fancy', see *De Spectaculis*, 30.

94 Walker, *The Decline of Hell*, p. 30.
95 Pieter Spierenburg, *The Spectacle of Suffering: Executions and the evolution of Repression: from a preindustrial metropolis to the European experience* (Cambridge, 1984), p. 185.
96 Quoted by Michael Wheeler, *Death and the Future Life in Victorian Literature and Theology* (Cambridge, 1990), p. 188.
97 Bates, *The Four Last Things*, p. 213.
98 Quoted by D. J. Enright, *The Oxford Book of Death* (Oxford, 1987), p. 179.
99 Keynes (ed.), *The Works of Sir Thomas Browne*, vol. 1, p. 60.
100 Baxter, *The Saints' Everlasting Rest*, p. 18.
101 Bates, *The Four Last Things*, p. 7.
102 Baxter, *The Saints' Everlasting Rest*, p. 70.
103 *Ibid.*, pp. 69–70.
104 See Colleen McDannell and Bernhard Lang, *Heaven: A History* (New Haven, 1988), p. 173.
105 See Gearing, *A Prospect of Heaven*, pp. 228–38.
106 *Ibid.*, p. 292.
107 More, *The Immortality of the Soul*, p. 419.
108 Elizabeth, a daughter of Samuel Annesley the divine, married Dunton in 1682. Her sister married Samuel Wesley, and another sister married Daniel Defoe. Dunton married Sarah Nicholas shortly after the death of Elizabeth. The marriage was never a happy one and the couple eventually separated.
109 [Dunton], *An Essay*, p. 29.
110 *Ibid.*, p. 64.
111 Dunton (ed.), *The Athenian Gazette*, 3.13.
112 [Dunton], *An Essay*, p. 2.
113 Elizabeth Singer Rowe, *Friendship in Death, in Twenty Letters from the Dead to the Living*, 3rd edn (London, 1733), pp. 7–8. On her reputation and her work, see John J. Richetti, *Popular Fiction before Richardson: Narrative Patterns 1700–1739* (Oxford, 1969), pp. 239–61. The structure of Rowe's heaven is very much a precursor of those paradisal realms created for popular consumption in the Victorian period, most notable of which was Elizabeth Stuart Phelps' 1868 novel *The Gates Ajar*. On love in the heavenly realm in the nineteenth century, see McDannell and Lang, *Heaven: A History*, ch. 8.
114 Quoted by Stone, *The Family, Sex and Marriage in England 1500–1800*, p. 235.
115 Younge, *A Serious and Pathetical Description*, p. 15.
116 Sherlock, *A Practical Discourse Concerning Death*, pp. 61–2.
117 See e.g. Quran, 44.54, 52.20, 55.72, 56.22; and cf. 13.23, 40.8.
118 Thomas Herbert, *Some Yeares Travels into Divers parts of Africa and Asia the Great* (London, 1665), p. 346.
119 Henry Blunt, *A Voyage into the Levant...* (London, 1664), pp. 122–3.

120 See Humphrey Prideaux, *The True Nature of Imposture Fully Displayed in the Life of Mahomet*... (London, 1697), p. 25.
121 Henry Stubbe, *An Account of the Rise and Progress of Mahometanism with the Life of Mahomet* (London, 1911), p. 167. On Stubbe's mortalism, see James R. Jacob, *Henry Stubbe, radical Protestantism and the early Enlightenment* (Cambridge, 1983).
122 See Philip C. Almond, *Heretic and Hero: Muhammad and the Victorians* (Wiesbaden, 1989).
123 More, *The Immortality of the Soul*, pp. 411–12.
124 Gearing, *A Prospect of Heaven*, pp. 213, 215.
125 Burnet, *A Treatise Concerning the State of Departed Souls*, p. 182.
126 Dunton (ed.), *The Athenian Gazette*, 1.23.
127 *Ibid.*, 3.29.
128 More, *The Immortality of the Soul*, p. 343.
129 Burnet, *A Treatise Concerning the State of Departed Souls*, p. 209.
130 Gearing, *A Prospect of Heaven*, p. 215.
131 John Shower, *Death a Deliverance; Or, a Funeral Discourse, Preach'd (in Part) on the Decease of Mrs. Mary Doolittle*... (London, 1693), pp. 77–8.
132 [Dunton], *An Essay*, p. 53.
133 Dunton (ed.), *The Athenian Gazette*, 3.23.
134 [Dunton], *An Essay*, p. 54.
135 Dunton (ed.), *The Athenian Gazette*, 1.25.
136 Gearing, *A Prospect of Heaven*, p. 204.
137 Rowe, *Friendship in Death*, p. 9.
138 See Park and Daston, 'Unnatural Conceptions', 21–2; and Hyder E. Rollins, *The Pack of Autolycus* (New York, 1969), pp. 7–9, 10–11.
139 Dunton (ed.), *The Athenian Gazette*, 1.29.
140 Gearing, *A Prospect of Heaven*, p. 226.
141 *Ibid.*, p. 241.
142 *Ibid.*, p. 244.
143 See e.g. Bates, *The Four Last Things*, p. 8.
144 Gearing, *A Prospect of Heaven*, p. 245.
145 *Ibid.*, p. 245.
146 McDannell and Lang, *Heaven: A History*, p. 183.
147 Camporesi, *The Fear of Hell*, p. 2.

4 THE LAST DAY

1 John Bunyan, *The Pilgrim's Progress from This World to That which is to come*... (London, 1678), pt 1, pp. 52–3. See also Younge, *A Serious and Pathetical Description*, p. 9; Vincent, *Fire and Brimstone*, p. 84; Bates, *The Four Last Things*, p. 126.
2 See my 'Henry More and the Apocalypse', *Journal of the History of Ideas* 54 (1993), 189–200.
3 More, *An Explanation of the Grand Mystery of Godliness*, p. 181.

4 See Henry More, *Apocalypsis Apocalypseos; or the Revelation of St. John the Divine unveiled* ... (London, 1680), p. 208; and Henry More, *Paralipomena Prophetica* (London, 1685), p. 153.
5 See More, *Apocalypsis Apocalypseos*, p. 206.
6 More, *Paralipomena Prophetica*, p. 163. See also Henry More, *A Plain and Continued Exposition of the Several Prophecies of the Divine Visions of the Prophet Daniel*... (London, 1681), pp. 44, 226–7; and More, *Apocalypsis Apocalypseos*, p. 209.
7 More, *An Explanation of the Grand Mystery of Godliness*, pp. 215–16.
8 *Ibid.*, p. 41. See also p. 227; and Henry More, *An Exposition of the Seven Epistles to the Seven Churches; together with a Brief Discourse of Idolatry* (London, 1669), pp. 162–3.
9 *Ibid.*, p. 163. See also More, *An Explanation of the Grand Mystery of Godliness*, pp. 41, 217.
10 More, *An Explanation of the Grand Mystery of Godliness*, p. 237.
11 See René Descartes, *Principles of Philosophy* (Dordrecht, Holland, 1983), 3.181.
12 See *ibid.*, 3.140.
13 More, *An Explanation of the Grand Mystery of Godliness*, p. 240.
14 See More, *Annotations*, p. 141.
15 More, *The Grand Mystery of Godliness*, p. 238.
16 *Ibid.*, p. 445.
17 [Jeremiah White], *The Restoration of All Things* (London, 1712), Preface. Among other universalists, Roach cited Gerrard Winstanley, Joseph Alford, Archbishop Tillotson, the author of *A Letter of Resolution concerning Origen*, Peter Sterry, and the author of *Enochian Walks with God*, and *Revelation of the Everlasting Gospel Message*, namely, the leader of the Boehmenist Philadelphian Society Jane Lead. On Mrs Lead, see Walker, *The Decline of Hell*, pp. 218–30.
18 More, *Psychodia Platonica*, preface to *Psychathanasia*.
19 More, *Annotations*, p. 72.
20 *Ibid.*, pp. 72–3.
21 *Ibid.*, pp. 75–6.
22 W[arren], *No Praeexistence*, p. 18. And see Chapter 5.
23 See More, *Annotations*, pp. 73–4.
24 *Ibid.*, p. 75.
25 More, *The Immortality of the Soul*, p. 536.
26 [Rust], *A Letter of Resolution concerning Origen*, p. 74.
27 *Ibid.*, p. 77.
28 *Ibid.*, p. 86.
29 *Ibid.*, p. 87.
30 Glanvill, *Lux Orientalis*, p. 136.
31 *Ibid.*, p. 137.
32 *Ibid.*, p. 140.
33 *Ibid.*, p. 141.

34 *Ibid.*, p. 143.
35 *Ibid.*, p. 144.
36 *Ibid.*, p. 146.
37 *Ibid.*, p. 149.
38 See M. C. Jacob and W. A. Lockwood, 'Political Millenarianism and Burnet's *Sacred Theory*', *Science Studies* 2 (1972), 265–79. See also Margaret C. Jacob, *The Newtonians and the English Revolution, 1689–1720* (Sussex, 1976), ch. 3; and Margaret C. Jacob, 'Millenarianism and Science in the Late Seventeenth Century', *Journal of the History of Ideas* 37 (1976), 335–41.
39 Thomas Burnet, *The Sacred Theory of the Earth* (London, 1965), p. 288.
40 *Ibid.*, p. 268.
41 *Ibid.*, p. 41.
42 *Ibid.*, p. 288.
43 *Ibid.*, p. 301.
44 *Ibid.*, p. 304.
45 *Ibid.*, p. 305.
46 *Ibid.*, p. 372.
47 *Ibid.*, p. 376.
48 Burnet, *A Treatise Concerning the State of Departed Souls*, p. 357.
49 *Ibid.*, p. 366.
50 *Ibid.*, p. 315.
51 Quoted by Walker, *The Decline of Hell*, p. 164.
52 For a direct criticism of Burnet's morally dynamic hell, see Matthew Horbery, *An Enquiry*, pp. 252ff.
53 On Ray and his works, see Charles E. Raven, *John Ray Naturalist: His Life and Works* (Cambridge, 1950); and Neal C. Gillespie, 'Natural History, Natural Theology, and Social Order: John Ray and the "Newtonian Ideology"', *Journal of the History of Biology* 20 (1987), 1–49.
54 See John Ray, *Miscellaneous Discourses concerning the Dissolution and Changes of the World...* (London, 1692), p. 170. Ray was followed in this conjecture by the Anglican cleric and enthusiastic footballer Thomas Robinson. Like Ray, he was persuaded that there was a central fire. He also thought it probable that the conflagration would be caused by the eruption of the central fire, and that the earth would remain a fiery planet with the wicked eternally upon it. He referred the reader to Ray for more information. See Thomas Robinson, *New Observations on the Natural History of this World of Matter and this World of Life...* (London, 1698), p. 177.
55 *Ibid.*, p. 172.
56 *Ibid.*, p. 189.
57 *Ibid.*, pp. 197–8.
58 *Ibid.*, p. 199.
59 Quoted by Frances Yates, *The Sun-Centred World* (London, Open University), audio.

60 Swinden, *An Enquiry* (London, 1727), p. 188.
61 *Ibid.*, p. 145.
62 *Ibid.*, p. 154.
63 Burnet, *The Sacred Theory of the Earth*, p. 407.
64 See Frank Manuel, *Isaac Newton Historian* (Cambridge, Massachusetts, 1963), pp. 139–40. On Newton's religion, see especially Frank Manuel, *The Religion of Isaac Newton* (Oxford, 1974).
65 William Whiston, *A New Theory of the Earth, from its Original to the Consummation of all Things*... (London, 1696), p. 95. On the Newtonianism of Whiston, see especially James E. Force, *William Whiston: Honest Newtonian* (Cambridge, 1985).
66 Whiston has a modern counterpart in Immanuel Velikovsky, the Russian Jewish doctor who wrote the controversial *Worlds in Collision* (Garden City, New York, 1950). In this, he argued that various extraordinary events of the past were to be explained by the close approaches of comets to the earth. Velikovsky was familiar with the work of Whiston though he erroneously cited Whiston's *New Theory of the Earth* as the work in which Whiston had identified Halley's comet of 1680 with the comet of the Biblical Deluge. See *ibid.*, p. 42.
67 Simon Schaffer, 'Newton's Comets and the Transformation of Astrology', in Patrick Curry (ed.), *Astrology, Science and Society: Historical Essays* (Woodbridge, Suffolk, 1987), p. 243.
68 See William Whiston, *The Cause of the Deluge Demonstrated: Wherein it is proved that the famous Comet of AD 1680, came by the Earth at its Deluge*... (London, 1714). Whiston's cometology was not original. Halley himself had proposed, in 1687, that the Deluge might have been caused by the shock of a comet or the like. This was later to cause a complex priority dispute with Whiston. See the fascinating account of cometology by Schaffer, 'Newton's Comets'.
69 Whiston, *A New Theory of the Earth*, p. 375.
70 William Whiston, *Astronomical Principles of Religion, Natural and Reveal'd*, 2nd edn (London, 1717), p. 156.
71 William Whiston, *The Eternity of Hell Torments Considered* (London, 1740), p. 110.
72 William Whiston, *Astronomical Principles of Religion*, p. 156.
73 See William Whiston, *Memoirs of the Life and Writings of Mr. William Whiston*..., 3 pts. (London, 1749), vol. 1, pp. 77–82.
74 William Whiston, *Sermons and Essays*... (London, 1709), p. 220.
75 King, Peter, *The Life of John Locke*, 2 vols. (London, 1830), vol. 1, p. 148.
76 *Ibid.*, vol. 1, p. 149.
77 See Whiston, *Memoirs*, vol. 1, p. 286. This was presumably never published.
78 Whiston, *The Eternity of Hell Torments Considered*, p. 2. Whiston, like Newton and (probably) Samuel Clarke, was an Arian. And he shared with Newton a dislike for Athanasian Trinitarianism. In the last of his

essays in *Sermons and Essays* in 1709, he made his Arianism public. The following year, he was charged by the University of Cambridge with teaching doctrines contrary to established Anglican belief, dismissed from his Chair, and banished from the University. See Duffy, '"Whiston's Affair"', 129–50.
79 See *ibid.*, p. 3. Whiston was, presumably, referring to Edmond Halley, 'An Account of the cause of the Change of the Variation of the Magnetic Needle', *Philosophical Transactions* 16 (1692), 563–78. I am grateful for this reference to Ms Patricia Fara of Imperial College, London.
80 Whiston, *The Eternity of Hell Torments Considered*, p. 109.
81 Walker, *The Decline of Hell*, p. 101.
82 Whiston, *The Eternity of Hell Torments Considered*, pp. 108–9.
83 *Ibid.*, p. 109.
84 Ezekiel 37.5.
85 For two excellent recent overviews of issues pertaining to the resurrection of the body, see Caroline Walker Bynum, 'Material Continuity, Personal Survival, and the Resurrection of the Body: A Scholastic Discussion in its Medieval and Modern Contexts', *History of Religions* 30 (1990), 51–85; and Gedaliahu G. Stroumsa, '*Caro Salutis cardo*: Shaping the Person in Early Christian Thought', *History of Religions* 30 (1990), 25–50.
86 Digby, *Observations*, pp. 78–9.
87 Pearson, *An Exposition of the Creed*, p. 763.
88 Quoted by C. A. Patrides, 'Renaissance and Modern Thought on the Last Things: A Study in Changing Conceptions', *The Harvard Theological Review* 51 (1958), 180.
89 John Seager, *A Discovery of the World to Come according to the Scriptures* (London, 1650) p. 70.
90 Sharrock, *De Finibus*, p. 125.
91 *Ibid.*, p. 125. The appeal to God's power was a common theme among early Christian apologists. Clement of Rome, Justin Martyr, Athenagoras, Irenaeus, and Tertullian defended the resurrection by referring to the divine omnipotence. See Henry Chadwick, 'Origen, Celsus, and the Resurrection of the Body', *Harvard Theological Review* 41 (1948), 84–102.
92 Bates, *The Four Last Things*, p. 49.
93 Shower, *Death a Deliverance*, p. 52.
94 John Donne, *Fifty Sermons* (London, 1649), p. 3.
95 Keynes (ed.), *The Works of Sir Thomas Browne*, vol. 1, p. 58.
96 *Ibid.*, p. 59. See also Robert Russel, *Seven Sermons ...*, 13th edn (London, 1705), p. 171.
97 Birch (ed.), *The Works of the Honourable Robert Boyle*, vol. 4, pp. 195–6.
98 See Chadwick, 'Origen', 86–8.
99 Sanctorius or Santorio Santorio (1561–1636) is noted for his having introduced experimental procedure into the study of metabolism. To test Galen's theory of insensible transpiration, he constructed a large scale upon which, for the next thirty years, he periodically ate, worked

and slept. He reported that the sum total of visible excreta was less than the amount of substance generated. Sanctorius' 1614 work *De Statica Medicina* was translated into English in 1676 by John Davies under the title *Medicina Statica: or, Rules of Health, in Eight Sections of Aphorisms*.
100 Birch (ed.), *The Works*, vol. 4, p. 196.
101 *Ibid.*, vol. 4, p. 201.
102 *Ibid.*, vol. 4, p. 195.
103 *Ibid.*, p. 194. The reference is to Athanasius Kircher (1601–80), who, for his prodigious activity in a variety of fields, is sometimes thought of as the last Renaissance man.
104 See Hody, *The Resurrection*, p. 132.
105 *Ibid.*, p. 187.
106 *Ibid.*, p. 189.
107 *Ibid.*, pp. 194–5.
108 *Ibid.*, p. 205.
109 *Ibid.*, p. 205.
110 1 Corinthians 15.44.
111 [Rust], *A Letter of Resolution concerning Origen*, p. 64.
112 *Ibid.*, p. 67.
113 More, *An Explanation of the Grand Mystery of Godliness*, p. 224.
114 More, *A Modest Enquiry into the Mystery of Iniquity*, pp. 494–5. The reference here was specifically to Christ's resurrection body, which for More was identical to our future aethereal vehicles.
115 1 Corinthians 15.50.
116 Cudworth, *The True Intellectual System of the Universe*, vol. 3, p. 315.
117 *Ibid.*, vol. 3, p. 317.
118 *Ibid.*, vol. 3, p. 270.
119 *Ibid.*, vol. 3, pp. 338–40.
120 A summary of the arguments mounted against Cudworth may be found in Thomas Wise's introduction to his abridgement of Cudworth's *The True Intellectual System of the Universe, A Confutation of the Reason and Philosophy of Atheism* (London, 1706).
121 See *ibid.*, p. 130.
122 More, *A Modest Enquiry into the Mystery of Iniquity*, p. 405.
123 More, *An Explanation of the Grand Mystery of Godliness*, p. 223.
124 John Locke, *An Essay Concerning Humane Understanding* (London, 1690), p. 179.
125 *Ibid.*, p. 188.
126 See John Locke, *Mr. Locke's Reply to the Right Reverend the Lord Bishop of Worcester's Answer to his Second Letter* ... (London, 1699), p. 206.
127 The main focus of Stillingfleet's attacks on Locke's *Essay* was the latter's perceived anti-Trinitarianism. Only in his 1697 *The Bishop of Worcester's Answer to Mr. Locke's Second Letter* did he broach the issue of the resurrection of the dead.
128 *Ibid.*, p. 34.

Notes to pages 141–7

129 *Ibid.*, p. 34.
130 *Ibid.*, p. 35.
131 *Ibid.*, p. 44.
132 Locke, *Mr. Locke's Reply*, p. 176.
133 *Ibid.*, p. 176.
134 It was initiated in 1724 by the dramatist and philosopher, Catharine Cockburn. In 1702, she had written *A Defence of the Essay of Human Understanding* which led Locke, in a letter on 13 December 1702, to describe her as his greatest protectress. In the mid 1720s, she became involved with Winch Holdsworth on the issue of the resurrection of the body, which debate spawned a number of writings. For her life and works, see Thomas Birch (ed.), *The Works of Mrs. Catharine Cockburn...* (London, 1751). For works against Locke's position see Robert D'Oyly, *Four Dissertations...* (London, 1728); Henry Felton, *The Resurrection of the same Numerical Body...* (London, 1725); Fleury, *A Short Essay on the General Resurrection*. Winch Holdsworth in *A Sermon* and *A Defence of the Doctrine of the Resurrection of the Same Body...* (London, 1727) adopted a position opposed to Locke derived from Boyle, who also probably influenced Samuel Johnson, *The Resurrection of the Same Body, as Asserted and Illustrated by St. Paul* (London, 1741).
135 However, there is a greater tendency today to identify the self with the body, a position implicit if seldom expressed by the materialists among the radical sectarians in the seventeenth century.

5 ETERNAL TORMENTS

1 Sharrock (ed.) *The Miscellaneous Works*, vol. 1, pp. 275–6.
2 Baxter, *The Saints' Everlasting Rest*, p. 247.
3 Horbery, *An Enquiry*, p. 305.
4 Lewis, *The Nature of Hell*, p. 1.
5 Dawes, *Sermons*, p. 31.
6 Blyth, *Eternal Misery*, pp. ii–iii.
7 *Ibid.*, p. 33.
8 Dodwell, *The Eternity of future Punishment*, p. 12.
9 Horbery, *An Enquiry*, pp. 33–4.
10 Anon., *The Scripture Account of the Eternity, or Endless Duration, of the Joys of Heaven, and the Torments of Hell, Stated, Explained, and Vindicated* (London, 1742), p. 48. See also Blyth, *Eternal Misery*, p. x; Dawes, *Sermons*, p. 65; Lewis, *The Nature of Hell*, p. 31; Lupton, *The Eternity of Future Punishment*, p. 4; Ray, *Miscellaneous Discourses*, p. 222; Richard Venn, *Tracts and Sermons on Several Occasions* (London, 1740), p. 50.
11 [Van Helmont], *Two Hundred Queries*, p. 113.
12 See W[arren], *No Praeexistence*, p. 18.
13 More, *Annotations*, p. 74. See also, Burnet, *A Treatise Concerning the State of Departed Souls*, p. 355.

14 Richardson, *A Discourse*, p. 20.
15 Brandon, *Everlasting Fire no Fancy*, p. 7.
16 Burnet, *A Treatise Concerning the State of Departed Souls*, p. 357.
17 Isaac Barrow, *Sermons and Fragments attributed to Isaac Barrow D. D....* (London, 1834), p. 210. There is some dispute over the authorship of this particular text. For it has also been found under a different title and ascribed to a John Whitefoot, rector of Heigham near Norwich. See Alexander Napier (ed.), *The Theological Works of Isaac Barrow*, 9 vols. (Cambridge, 1859), vol. 1, pp. xxix–xxx. C. A. Patrides has suggested that, in a series of sermons entitled 'The Doctrine of Universal Redemption asserted and explained', Barrow supported a modified universalism. But the universalism of these sermons is not so much an eschatological universalism, as a soteriological one. That is to say, in latitudinarian vein, the thrust of Barrow's argument is that God in Christ is the saviour of all men not merely of the faithful. But this does not entail that all will be saved. See Patrides, 'The Salvation of Satan', 475, n. 31; and John Tillotson (ed.), *The Works of the Learned Isaac Barrow, D. D.* (London, 1716), vol. 2, Sermons 39–43.
18 *Ibid.*, p. 222.
19 *Ibid.*, p. 220.
20 Huber, *The World Unmask'd*, p. 263.
21 *Ibid.*, pp. 287–8. On discussions of the afterlife in eighteenth-century France, see John McManners, *Death and the Enlightenment: Changing Attitudes to Death among Christians and unbelievers in eighteenth-century France* (Oxford, 1981), chs. 5, 6.
22 Anthony Collins, *A Discourse of Free-Thinking, occasion'd by the rise and growth of a sect call'd Free-Thinkers* (n.p., 1713), p. 68.
23 Goodwin, *A Discourse*, p. 192.
24 *Ibid.*, p. 79.
25 Brandon, *Everlasting Fire no Fancy*, p. 130.
26 Bates, *The Four Last Things*, p. 141.
27 Dawes, *Sermons*, p. 83.
28 Edwards, *The Works*, vol. 4, p. 269.
29 Hobbes, *Leviathan*, p. 342.
30 Clarke, *A Letter*, p. 68.
31 Matthew Tindal, *Christianity as old as the Creation* (London, 1730), p. 78.
32 Samuel Bourn, *A Series of Discourses...*, 2nd edn, 4 vols. (London, 1768), vol. 1, p. 403.
33 Blyth, *Eternal Misery*, p. 21.
34 *Ibid.*, p. 26.
35 Dodwell, *The Eternity of future Punishment*, p. 68.
36 Edwards, *The Works*, vol. 4, p. 267.
37 D. F. Bond (ed.), *The Spectator* (Oxford, 1965), iv.72.
38 John Scott, *The Christian Life*, 2nd edn (London, 1683), Preface.
39 Horbery, *An Enquiry*, p. 174.

40 Walker, *The Decline of Hell*, p. 63.
41 Bates, *The Four Last Things*, p. 141.
42 Whiston, *The Eternity of Hell Torments Considered*, pp. 18–19.
43 Horbery, *An Enquiry*, p. 166.
44 Blyth, *Eternal Misery*, p. 42.
45 *Ibid.*, p. 40.
46 See Chapter 2 above.
47 Burnet, *A Treatise Concerning the State of Departed Souls*, p. 344.
48 *Ibid.*, p. 345.
49 Ray, *Miscellaneous Discourses*, p. 228.
50 Caussin, *The Holy Court in Five Tomes*, p. 432.
51 Bates, *The Four Last Things*, p. 208.
52 See Douglas Hay, et al., *Albion's Fatal Tree: Crime and Society in Eighteenth-Century England* (London, 1975), ch. 1.
53 Edwards, *The Works*, vol. 4, p. 228. See also Venn, *Tracts and Sermons*, p. 67.
54 [Van Helmont], *Two Hundred Queries*, p. 126.
55 Burnet, *A Treatise Concerning the State of Departed Souls*, p. 349. See also Samuel Colliber, *The Christian Religion Founded on Reason: Or Two Essays on Natural and Revealed Religion* (London, 1729), p. 143.
56 Richard Wollheim (ed.), *Hume on Religion* (London, 1963), p. 266.
57 J. M. Beattie, *Crime and the Courts in England 1660–1800* (Princeton, 1986), p. 450. Before the Glorious Revolution of 1688, there were about fifty crimes which were capitally punished. This was increased significantly after 1688. See J. A. Sharpe, *Crime in Seventeenth-Century England* (Cambridge, 1983), p. 142.
58 John Tillotson, *Of the Eternity of Hell-Torments. A Sermon Preach'd before the Queen at White-Hall, March the 7th, 1689–90* (London, 1708), p. 5.
59 Collins, *A Discourse of Free-Thinking*, p. 172.
60 George Hickes, *Some Discourses upon Dr. Burnet and Dr. Tillotson, Occasioned by the Late Funeral Sermon of the Former upon the Later* (London, 1695), p. 45.
61 Tillotson, *Of the Eternity of Hell-Torments*, p. 6.
62 *Ibid.*, pp. 7–8.
63 *Ibid.*, p. 8.
64 *Ibid.*, pp. 11–12.
65 See Beattie, *Crime and the Courts*, pp. 430–6.
66 See Swinden, *An Enquiry*, p. 416.
67 See anon., *The Scripture Account of the Eternity*, p. 67.
68 See Venn, *Tracts and Sermons*, p. 65.
69 Edwards, *The Works*, vol. 4, p. 273.
70 Jenks, *The Eternity of Hell Torments*, p. 14.
71 Wollheim, *Hume on Religion*, pp. 266–7.
72 Sharrock, *De Finibus*, p. 31.
73 Robert South, *Twelve Sermons upon Various Occasions* (London, 1718), p. 210.

74 Samuel Clarke, *A Discourse Concerning the Unchangeable Obligations of Natural Religion...* (London, 1706), p. 116.
75 Shaftesbury, Anthony Ashley, 3rd Earl of, *Characteristics of Men, Manners, Opinions, Times...*, 3 vols. (London, 1900), vol. 1, p. 275. See also Walker, *The Decline of Hell*, ch. 10.
76 *Ibid.*, vol. 1, p. 270.
77 *Ibid.*, vol. 1, p. 125.
78 Ray, *Miscellaneous Discourses*, p. 238. See also anon., *The Scripture Account of the Eternity*, p. 74; [John Hartliffe], *A Discourse against Purgatory* (London, 1685), p. 16; Dawes, *Sermons*, p. 78; Blyth, *Eternal Misery*, pp. 65, 67; Dodwell, *The Eternity of Future Punishment*, p. 82; Milles, *The Natural Immortality of the Soul*, p. 2; Shower, *Heaven and Hell*, p. 45; Venn, *Tracts and Sermons*, pp. 63–4.
79 Burnet, *A Treatise Concerning the State of Departed Souls*, p. 366.
80 Shower, *Heaven and Hell*, p. 6.
81 See Dawes, *Sermons*, p. 41.
82 See Lewis, *The Nature of Hell*, pp. 35–6.
83 See Richardson, *A Discourse*, pp. 103–4, 164.
84 [Van Helmont], *Two Hundred Queries*, pp. 117ff.
85 Huber, *The World Unmask'd*, p. 291.
86 [Pierre Cuppé], *Heaven Open to all Men* (London, 1743), p. 67.
87 Quoted by Beattie, *Crime and the Courts*, p. 556.

Bibliography

Ady, Thomas, *A Candle in the Dark: Shewing the Divine Cause of the distractions of the whole Nation of England and of the Christian World* (London, 1655).
Alger, W. R., *A Critical History of the Doctrine of a Future Life* (Philadelphia, 1864).
Allen, Don C., *Doubt's Boundless Sea: Skepticism and Faith in the Renaissance* (Baltimore, 1964).
Almond, Philip C., *Heretic and Hero: Muhammad and the Victorians* (Wiesbaden, 1989).
Althaus, Paul, *The Theology of Martin Luther* (Philadelphia, 1966).
Anon., *An Account of Mr. Asgil's Strange and Wonderful Translation which will happen upon the Twelfth of July next* (London, 1717).
Anon., *Annotations upon All the Books of the Old and New Testaments* (London, 1645).
Anon., *The Immortality of Mans Soule. Proved both by Scripture and Reason* (London, 1645).
Anon., *The Doctrine of Devils, Proved to be the grand Apostasy of these later Times* ... (London, 1676).
Anon., *The Scripture Account of the Eternity, or Endless Duration, of the Joys of Heaven, and the Torments of Hell, Stated, Explained, and Vindicated* (London, 1742).
Anon., *Seder Olam: or, The Order, Series, or Succession of all the Ages, Periods, and Times of the Whole World* (London, 1694).
Anon., *The Way to Heaven in a String: or, Mr. A—'s Argument Burlesqu'd. A Poem* (no place, 1701).
[Asgill, John], *An Argument proving that according to the Covenant of Eternal Life revealed in the Scriptures, Man may be translated from hence into that Eternal Life, without passing through Death, although the Humane Nature of Christ Himself could not be thus translated till he had passed through Death* (London, 1700).
A Collection of Tracts (London, 1715).
Atkins, Jonathan M., 'Calvinist Bishops, Church Unity, and the Rise of Arminianism', *Albion* 18 (1986), 411–27.
Aubrey, J., *Miscellanies*... (London, 1696).
Aylmer, G. E., 'The Religion of Gerrard Winstanley', in McGregor, J. F.

and Reay, B. (eds.), *Radical Religion in the English Revolution* (Oxford, 1984), pp. 91–120.
B., N., *The Resurrection founded on Justice: or, a vindication of this great standing reason assigned by the ancients and moderns* (London, 1700).
Barrow, Isaac, *Sermons and Fragments attributed to Isaac Barrow, D. D....* (London, 1834).
Barth, Karl, *Dogmatics in Outline* (New York, 1949).
Bates, William, *The Four Last Things: viz. Death, Judgment, Heaven, Hell, practically considered and applied, in several discourses*, 2nd edn, (London, 1691).
Baxter, Richard, *The Certainty of the World of Spirits. Fully evinced by unquestionable histories of apparitions and witchcrafts, operations, voices, &...* (London, 1691).
The Practical Works of the late Reverend and Pious Richard Baxter, 4 vols. (London, 1707).
The Saints' Everlasting Rest: or, a Treatise of the Blessed State of the Saints in their Enjoyment of God in Glory... (London, 1846).
Beattie, J. M., *Crime and the Courts in England 1660–1800* (Princeton, 1986).
Bekker, Balthazar, *The World Bewitch'd; An Examination of the Common Opinions Concerning Spirits...* (London, 1695).
Beveridge, Henry (trans.), *Institutes of the Christian Religion by John Calvin*, 2 vols. (London, 1953).
Tracts... by John Calvin, 3 vols. (Edinburgh, 1851).
Beveridge, William, *Of the Happiness of the Saints...*, 3rd edn (London, 1698).
Biddle, John, *A Twofold Catechism: the one simply called A Scripture Catechism; the other, A brief Scripture-Catechism for Children, etc.* (London, 1654).
Biographia Britannica..., 2nd edn, 5 vols. (London, 1778–93).
Birch, Thomas (ed.), *The Works of the Honourable Robert Boyle*, 6 vols. (London, 1744–72).
The Works of Mrs. Catharine Cockburn..., 2 vols. (London, 1751).
Blackburne, Francis, *An Historical View of the Controversy concerning an Intermediate State and the Separate Existence of the Soul between Death and the General Resurrection*, 2nd edn (London, 1772).
The Works, Theological and Miscellaneous (Cambridge, 1805).
Blunt, Henry, *A Voyage into the Levant...* (London, 1664).
Blyth, Francis, *Eternal Misery: the necessary Consequence of Infinite Mercy abused...* (London, 1740).
Boleman, Babette A., 'Success: The Puritan Highroad to Hell', *Journal of Religion* 23 (1943), 206–13.
Bond, D. F., *The Spectator* (Oxford, 1965).
Bonner, Hypatia B., *The Christian Hell from the First to the Twentieth Century* (London, 1913).
Bourn, Samuel, *A Series of Discourses...*, 2nd edn, 4 vols. (London, 1768).
Bowler, P. J., 'Preformation and Pre-existence in the Seventeenth Century: A Brief Analysis', *Journal of the History of Biology* 4 (1971), 221–44.

Boylan, Michael, 'Henry More's Space and the Spirit of Nature', *Journal of the History of Philosophy* 18 (1980), 395–405.
Boyle, Robert, *Some Physico-Theological Considerations about the Possibility of the Resurrection* (London, 1675).
Brandon, John, Το πυρ το αἰώνιον: or Everlasting Fire no Fancy. Being an answer to a late pestilent pamphlet entituled 'The Foundations of Hell-Torments shaken and removed' (London, 1678).
Briggs, E. R., 'Pierre Cuppé's debts to England and Holland', *Studies on Voltaire and the Eighteenth Century* 6 (1958), 37–66.
Brokesby, Francis, *The Life of Mr. Henry Dodwell...* (London, 1715).
Bromhall, Thomas, *A Treatise of Specters. Or, an History of apparitions, oracles, prophecies, and predictions...* (London, 1658).
Bullinger, Heinrich, *An Holsome Antidotus of counter-poysen, agaynst the pestylent heresye and secte of the Anabaptistes...* (London, 1548).
Bulstrode, Whitelocke, *An Essay of Transmigration, in defence of Pythagoras...* (London, 1693).
Bunyan, John, *A Few Sighs from Hell, or, the Groans of a damned Soul...* (London, 1658).
  The Pilgrim's Progress from This World to That which is to come... (London, 1678).
  The Resurrection of the Dead, and Eternall Judgement, in McGee, J. Sears (ed.), *The Miscellaneous Works of John Bunyan* (Oxford, 1987), pp. 201–321.
Burgess, Daniel, *The Death and Rest, Resurrection and Blessed Portion of the Saints...* (London, 1692).
Burke, Joseph, and Caldwell, Colin, *Hogarth: The Complete Engravings* (London, 1968).
Burnet, Thomas, *The Sacred Theory of the Earth* (London, 1965).
  A Treatise Concerning the State of Departed Souls Before, and At, and After the Resurrection... (London, 1733).
Burns, Norman T., *Christian Mortalism from Tyndale to Milton* (Cambridge, Mass., 1972).
Burthogge, Richard, *An Essay upon Reason and the Nature of Spirits* (London, 1694).
Burton, Robert, *The Anatomy of Melancholy*, 3 vols. (London, 1893).
Butterworth, G. W. (ed.), *Origen: On First Principles* (Gloucester, Mass., 1973).
Bynum, Caroline Walker, 'Material Continuity, Personal Survival and the Resurrection of the Body: A Scholastic Discussion in its Medieval and Modern Contexts', *History of Religions* 30 (1990), 51–85.
C., T., *An Impartial Examination and Refutation of the Erroneous Tenents of Thomas Moor; in his dangerous Writings, intituled, Clavis Aurea, etc.* (London, 1698).
Calvin, John, *An Excellent Treatise of the Immortalytie of the soule* (London, 1581).
Camfield, Benjamin, *A Theological Discourse of Angels and their Ministries.*

Wherein their existence, nature, number, order and offices are modestly treated of ... (London, 1678).
Campbell, Archibald, *The Doctrines of a Middle State Between Death and the Resurrection: of Prayers for the Dead: and the Necessity of Purification; plainly proved from the Holy Scriptures* ... (London, 1721).
Camporesi, Piero, *The Fear of Hell: Images of Damnation and Salvation in Early Modern Europe* (Cambridge, 1990).
The Incorruptible Flesh: Bodily Mutation and Mortification in Religion and Folklore (Cambridge, 1988).
Casaubon, Meric, *A Treatise Proving Spirits, Witches, and Supernatural Operations by Pregnant Instances and Evidence* (London, 1672).
Caussin, Nicholas, *The Holy Court in Five Tomes* (London, 1650).
Cavendish, Richard, *Visions of Heaven and Hell* (London, 1977).
Chadwick, Henry (trans.), *Origen: Contra Celsum* (Cambridge, 1953).
'Origen, Celsus, and the Resurrection of the Body', *Harvard Theological Review* 41 (1948), 84–102.
Chishull, Edmund, *A Charge of Heresy, Maintained against Mr. Dodwel's late Epistolary Discourse, concerning the Mortality of the Soul* (London, 1706).
Churchill, F. B., 'The History of Embryology as Intellectual History', *Journal of the History of Biology* 3 (1970), 155–81.
Clark, Stuart, 'The Scientific Status of Demonology', in Vickers, Brian (ed.), *Occult and Scientific Mentalities in the Renaissance* (Cambridge, 1984), 351–74.
Clarke, Samuel, *A Discourse Concerning the Unchangeable Obligations of Natural Religion* ... (London, 1706).
A Letter to Mr. Dodwell (London, 1731).
Cohn, Norman, *The Pursuit of the Millennium* (London, 1970).
Coleridge, Henry N., *The Literary Remains of Samuel Taylor Coleridge*, 2 vols. (London, 1836).
Colie, Rosalie L., *Light and Enlightenment: A Study of the Cambridge Platonists and the Dutch Arminians* (Cambridge, 1957).
'Spinoza and the Early English Deists', *Journal of the History of Ideas* 20 (1959), 23–46.
'Spinoza in England, 1665–1730', *Proceedings of the American Philosophical Association* 107 (1963), 183–219.
Colliber, Samuel, *The Christian Religion Founded on Reason: Or Two Essays on Natural and Revealed Religion* (London, 1729).
Collier, Jeremy, *The Difference Between the Present and Future State of our Bodies* ... (London, 1686).
Collins, Anthony, *A Discourse of Free-Thinking, occasion'd by the rise and growth of a sect call'd Free-Thinkers* (n.p., 1713).
Conway, Anne, *The Principles of the most Ancient and Modern Philosophy* ... (London, 1692).
Cook, Keningdale, 'John Asgill; and the Cowardliness of Dying', *Fraser's Magazine* 4 (1871), 150–66.

Cope, Jackson I., *Joseph Glanvill: Anglican Apologist* (St Louis, Miss., 1956).
Coppin, Richard, *Divine Teachings*... (London, 1653).
Coudert, Allison, 'A Cambridge Platonist's Kabbalist Nightmare', *Journal of the History of Ideas* 36 (1975), 633-52.
 'Henry More and Witchcraft', in Sarah Hutton (ed.), *Henry More (1614-1687): Tercentenary Studies* (Dordrecht, 1990), pp. 115-36.
[Coward, William], *Second Thoughts Concerning Human Soul*... (London, 1702).
 Grand Essay... (London, 1704).
Crawford, Patricia, 'Attitudes to Menstruation in Seventeenth Century England', *Past and Present* 91 (1981), 47-73.
Crisp, Stephen, *A Faithful Warning and Exhortation to Friends* (London, 1684).
Cudworth, Ralph, *The True Intellectual System of the Universe*..., 3 vols., with the notes and dissertations of J. L. Mosheim (London, 1845).
Cullman, Oscar, *Immortality of the Soul or Resurrection of the Dead?* (New York, 1958).
[Cuppé, Pierre], *Heaven Open to all Men*... (London, 1743).
Damrosch, L. Jr., 'Hobbes as Reformation Theologian: implications of the free-will controversy', *Journal of the History of Ideas* 40 (1979), 339-52.
Davies, Paul C., 'The Debate on Eternal Punishment in Late Seventeenth- and Eighteenth-Century English Literature', *Eighteenth-Century Studies* 4 (1970-1), 257-76.
Dawes, William, *Sermons Preach'd Upon Several Occasions before King William, and Queen Anne* (London, 1709).
Defoe, Daniel, *An Enquiry into the Case of Mr. Asgil's General Translation* (London, 1704).
Denison, John, *A Three-Fold Resolution, verie necessarie to saluation. Describing Earths Vanitie, Hels Horror, Heauens Felicitie* (London, 1608).
Descartes, René, *Principles of Philosophy* (Dordrecht, 1983).
Digby, Kenelm, *Observations upon Religio Medici* (London, 1643).
 Two Treatises: In the one of which, the nature of bodies; in the other, the nature of mans soule, is looked into (London, 1645).
Disley, Emma, 'Degrees of Glory: Protestant Doctrine and the Concept of Rewards Hereafter', *The Journal of Theological Studies* 42 (1991), 77-105.
Dodds, E. R. (trans.), *Proclus: The Elements of Theology* (Oxford, 1933).
Dodwell, Henry, *An Epistolary Discourse, Proving, from the Scriptures and the First Fathers, that the Soul is a Principle Naturally Mortal* (London, 1706).
 The Natural Mortality of Humane Souls clearly demonstrated from the Holy Scriptures... (London, 1708).
 A Preliminary Defence of the Epistolary Discourse, concerning the Distinction between Soul and Spirit (London, 1707).
 The Scripture Account of the Eternal Rewards or Punishments of all that hear of the Gospel... (London, 1708).
Dodwell, William, *The Eternity of future Punishment asserted and vindicated. In Answer to Mr. Whiston's late Treatise on that Subject* (Oxford, 1743).

Donne, John, *Fifty Sermons* (London, 1649).
D'Oyly, Robert, *Four Dissertations*... (London, 1728).
Duffy, Eamon, '"Whiston's Affair": The Trials of a Primitive Christian 1709–14', *Journal of Ecclesiastical History* 27 (1976), 129–50.
[Dunton, John], *An Essay Proving We shall Know our Friends in Heaven*... (London, 1698).
 (ed.), *The Athenian Gazette* (London, 1691–).
Edwards, Jonathan, *The Works of President Edwards*, 4 vols. (New York, 1844).
Edwards, Thomas, *Gangraena: or a Catalogue and Discovery of Many of the Errours, Heresies, Blasphemies and Pernicious Practices of the Sectaries of this time*... (London, 1646).
Enright, D. J., *The Oxford Book of Death* (Oxford, 1987).
Estes, L. L., 'Reginald Scot and his *Discoveries of Witchcraft*: Religion and Science in Opposition to the European Witch Craze', *Church History* 52 (1983), 444–56.
Farrar, F. W., *Eternal Hope* (London, 1878).
Felton, Henry, *The Resurrection of the same Numerical Body, and its Reunion to the same Soul*... (Oxford, 1725).
Finamore, John F., *Iamblichus and the Theory of the Vehicle of the Soul* (Chico, Calif., 1985).
Fleming, Caleb, *A Survey of the Search after Souls, by Dr. Coward, Dr. S. Clarke, Mr. Baxter, Dr. Sykes, Dr. Law, Mr. Peckard, and others*... (London, 1758).
Fleury, A., *A Short Essay on the General Resurrection*... (Dublin, 1752).
Fontaine, Nicolas, *The History of the Old and New Testament*, 2nd edn (London, 1699).
Force, James E., *William Whiston: Honest Newtonian* (Cambridge, 1985).
Foucault, Michel, *Discipline and Punish: The Birth of the Prison* (Harmondsworth, 1979).
Fremantle, W. H. (trans.), *Letters and Select Works of St. Jerome* (New York, 1893).
Gearing, William, *A Prospect of Heaven: or, a Treatise of the Happiness of the Saints in Glory*... (London, 1673).
Gillespie, Neal C., 'Natural History, Natural Theology, and Social Order: John Ray and the "Newtonian Ideology"', *Journal of the History of Biology* 20 (1987), 1–49.
Glanvill, Joseph, *A Blow at Modern Sadducism in some Philosophical Considerations about Witchcraft*... (London, 1668).
 'A Letter on Preexistence from Dr. Joseph Glanvill to Richard Baxter', *Bibliotheca Platonica* 1 (1890), 186–92.
 Lux Orientalis; or an Enquiry into the Opinion of the Eastern Sages concerning the Praeexistence of Souls... in *Two Choice and Useful Treatises* (London, 1682).
 Saducismus Triumphatus: or, Full and Plain Evidence concerning Witches and Apparitions..., 3rd edn (London, 1689).

A Whip for the Droll, Fiddler to the Atheist: Being Reflections on Drollery and Atheism (London, 1668).
Goddard, Peter, *The Intermediate State of Happiness or Misery between Death and the Resurrection, proved from Scripture*... (London, 1756).
le Goff, Jacques, *The Birth of Purgatory* (Chicago, 1981).
'The Learned and Popular Dimensions of Journeys in the Otherworld in the Middle Ages', in Kaplan, S. L. (ed.), *Understanding Popular Culture* (Berlin, 1984), 19–37.
Goodwin, Thomas, *A Discourse of the Punishment of Sin in Hell; Demonstrating the Wrath of God to be the immediate Cause thereof* (London, 1680).
Greene, William Chase (trans.), *Saint Augustine: The City of God against the Pagans*, 7 vols. (London, 1958–72).
Gregg, Tresham D., *An Argument to Prove that Death is not Obligatory on Christians by the celebrated John Asgill, esq., M. P.*... (New York, 1875).
Hall, Rupert A., *Henry More: Magic, Religion and Experiment* (Oxford, 1990).
Halley, Edmond, 'An Account of the cause of the Change of the Variation of the Magnetic Needle with an Hypothesis of the Structure of the Internal parts of the Earth', *Philosophical Transactions* 16 (1692), 563–78.
[Hallywell], Henry, *Deus Justificatus: Or, The Divine Goodness Vindicated and Cleared, against the Assertors of Absolute and Inconditionate Reprobation*... (London, 1668).
A Private Letter of Satisfaction to a Friend... (London[?], 1667).
Hammond, Henry, 'Αξια Θεου κρίσις. *Iudgment Worthy of God. Or an Assertion of the Existence and Duration of Hell Torments* (Oxford, 1665).
Hardwick, Charles, *A History of the Articles of Religion*... (London, 1884).
Harrison, Peter, *'Religion' and the Religions in the English Enlightenment* (Cambridge, 1990).
[Hartliffe, John], *A Discourse against Purgatory* (London, 1685).
Hay, Douglas, *et al.*, *Albion's Fatal Tree: Crime and Society in Eighteenth-Century England* (London, 1975).
Helmont, Franciscus Mercurius, van, *The Paradoxical Discourses of F. M. van Helmont, concerning the Macrocosm and Microcosm*... *Set down in Writing by J. B.* (London, 1685).
Two Hundred Queries moderately Propounded concerning the Doctrine of the Revolution of Humane Souls... (London, 1684).
Henry, John, 'Atomism and Eschatology: Catholicism and Natural Philosophy in the Interregnum', *The British Journal for the History of Science* 15 (1982), 211–39.
'A Cambridge Platonist's Materialism: Henry More and the Concept of Soul', *Journal of the Warburg and Courtauld Institutes* 49 (1986), 172–95.
Henry, Nathaniel M., 'Milton and Hobbes: Mortalism and the Intermediate State', *Studies in Philology* 48 (1951), 234–49.
Herbert, Thomas, *Some Yeares Travels into Divers parts of Africa and Asia the Great* (London, 1665).
Hick, John, *Evil and the God of Love* (London, 1985).

Hickes, George, *Some Discourses upon Dr. Burnet and Dr. Tillotson, Occasioned by the Late Funeral Sermon of the Former upon the Later* (London, 1695).
Hill, Christopher, *The Experience of Defeat* (London, 1984).
Milton and the English Revolution (London, 1979).
The Religion of Gerrard Winstanley (Oxford, 1978).
A Tinker and a Poor Man: John Bunyan and his Church 1628–1688 (New York, 1989).
The World Turned Upside Down (Harmondsworth, 1975).
Hill, Christopher, Reay, Barry, and Lamont, William, *The World of the Muggletonians* (London, 1983).
Hills, Henry, *A Short Treatise Concerning the Propagation of the Soul* (London, 1667).
Hoard, Samuel, *Gods Love to Man-kinde. Manifested by Dis-proving his Absolute Decree for their Damnation* (London, 1656).
Hobbes, Thomas, *Leviathan* (London, 1983).
Hodson, William, *Credo Resurrectionem Carnis: A Tractate on the eleventh Article of the Apostles Creed*... 2nd edn (Cambridge, 1636).
Hody, Humphry, *The Resurrection of the (same) Body Asserted*... (London, 1694).
Holdsworth, Winch, *A Defence of the Doctrine of the Resurrection of the Same Body*... (London, 1727).
A Sermon preach'd before the University of Oxford on Easter-Monday 1719... (Oxford, 1720).
Holmes, Geoffrey, *The Trial of Dr. Sacheverell* (London, 1973).
Hookyas, R., 'The reception of Copernicanism in England and the Netherlands', in Wilson, C. H. et al. (eds.), *The Anglo-Dutch contribution to the Civilization of Early Modern Society* (London, 1976), 33–44.
Horbery, Matthew, *An Enquiry into the Scripture-Doctrine Concerning the Duration of Future Punishment*... (London, 1744).
Huber, Marie, *The World Unmask'd: or, the Philosopher the greatest Cheat*... (London, 1736).
Hughes, Robert, *Heaven and Hell in Western Art* (London, 1968).
Hull, John, *Saint Peters Prophesie of these Last Daies. Discovering the Iniquity of the Time, and Atheisme of the Age*... (London, 1610).
Huxley, Aldous, *The Devils of Loudon* (New York, 1952).
Jackson, Samuel M., *The New Schaff-Herzog Encyclopaedia of Religious Knowledge* (Grand Rapids, Michigan, 1963).
Jacob, James R., *Henry Stubbe, Radical Protestantism and the Early Enlightenment* (Cambridge, 1983).
Jacob, Margaret C., 'Millenarianism and Science in the Late 17th Century', *Journal of the History of Ideas* 37 (1976), 335–41.
The Newtonians and the English Revolution 1689–1720 (Hassocks, Sussex, 1976).
Jacob, Margaret C., and Lockwood, W. A., 'Political Millenarianism and Burnet's *Sacred Theory*', *Science Studies* 2 (1972), 265–79.

Jenks, Richard, *The Eternity of Hell Torments Asserted and Vindicated...* (London, 1707).
Jobe, Thomas H., 'The Devil in Restoration Science: The Glanvill–Webster Witchcraft Debate', *Isis* 72 (1981), 343–56.
Johnson, Francis R., *Astronomical Thought in Renaissance England: A Study of the English Scientific Writings from 1500–1645* (New York, 1968).
Johnson, Samuel, *The Resurrection of the Same Body, as Asserted and Illustrated by St. Paul* (London, 1741).
Johnston, David, *The Rhetoric of Leviathan: Thomas Hobbes and the Politics of Cultural Transformation* (Princeton, 1986).
Jones, Rufus M., *Spiritual Reformers in the 16th and 17th Centuries* (Boston, 1959).
The Journals of the House of Commons, vol.15 (25/10/1705–1/4/1708).
Kargon, Robert H., *Atomism in England from Hariot to Newton* (Oxford, 1966).
Katz, David S., 'Henry More and the Jews', in Sarah Hutton (ed.), *Henry More (1614–1687): Tercentenary Studies* (Dordrecht, 1990), pp. 174–88.
Keynes, Geoffrey (ed.), *The Works of Sir Thomas Browne*, 4 vols. (London, 1964).
Kieckhefer, Richard, *European Witch Trials: Their Foundations in Popular and Learned Culture, 1300–1500* (London, 1976).
King, Peter, *The Life of John Locke*, 2 vols. (London, 1830).
Kocher, Paul H., *Science and Religion in Elizabethan England* (San Marino, Calif., 1953).
Kors, Alan C., and Peters, Edward, *Witchcraft in Europe, 1000–1700: A Documentary Study* (London, 1972).
Lamprecht, S. P., 'The Role of Descartes in Seventeenth-Century England', *Studies in the History of Ideas* 4 (1935), 181–240.
Law, Edmund, *Considerations on the Theory of Religion...*, 5th edn (Cambridge, 1765).
Layton, Henry, *Arguments and Replie in a Dispute Concerning the Nature of the Humane Soul...* (London, 1703).
Lewis, Thomas, *The Nature of Hell, the Reality of Hell-Fire, and the Eternity of Hell-Torments, explained and vindicated...* (London, 1720).
Locke, John, *An Essay Concerning Humane Understanding* (London, 1690).
Mr. Locke's Reply to the Right Reverend the Lord Bishop of Worcester's Answer to his Second Letter... (London, 1699).
Loptson, Peter (ed.), *The Principles of the Most Ancient and Modern Philosophy by Anne Conway* (The Hague, 1982).
Love, Christopher, *Hell's Terror: Or, A Treatise of the Torments of the Damned, as a Preservative Against Security* (London, 1653).
Lupton, William, *The Eternity of Future Punishment Proved and Vindicated* (Oxford, 1708).
Lye, Thomas, *Death the Sweetest Sleep* (London, 1681).
Macaulay, Thomas Babington, *The History of England from the Accession of James II*, 6 vols. (London, 1913–15).

Macdonald, Michael, *Mystical Bedlam: Madness, Anxiety, and Healing in Seventeenth-Century England* (Cambridge, 1981).
Mackenna, S. and Page, B. (trans.), *Enneads* (Chicago, 1952).
Mackie, J. L., 'Evil and Omnipotence', in Mitchell, B. (ed.), *The Philosophy of Religion* (Oxford, 1971), pp. 92–104.
Manchester, Henry Montagu, *Contemplatio Mortis & Immortalitatis*, 7th edn (London, 1658).
Manuel, Frank E., *Isaac Newton Historian* (Cambridge, Mass., 1963).
  The Religion of Isaac Newton (Oxford, 1974).
Marshall, P. J., and Williams, Glyndwr, *The Great Map of Mankind: British Perceptions of the World in the Age of Enlightenment* (London, 1982).
Matar, N. I., 'Heavenly Joy at the Torments of the Damned in Restoration Writings', *Notes and Queries* 33 (1986), 466–7.
McDannell, Colleen, and Lang, Bernhard, *Heaven: A History* (New Haven, Conn., 1988).
McGregor, J. F., 'Seekers and Ranters', in McGregor, J. F. and Reay, B., *Radical Religion in the English Revolution* (Oxford, 1984), pp. 121–40.
McGuire, J. E., 'Boyle's Conception of Nature', *Journal of the History of Ideas* 33 (1972), 523–42.
McManners, John, *Death and the Enlightenment: Changing attitudes to death among Christians and unbelievers in eighteenth-century France* (Oxford, 1981).
Milles, Thomas, *The Natural Immortality of the Soul asserted, and Proved from the Scriptures and First Fathers* (Oxford, 1707).
Milton, John, *Paradise Lost*, 6th edn (London, 1695).
Mintz, Samuel, *The Hunting of Leviathan: Seventeenth-century Reactions to the Materialism and Moral Philosophy of Thomas Hobbes* (Cambridge, 1962).
Molesworth, William (ed.), *The English Works of Thomas Hobbes*, 11 vols. (New York, 1839–45).
More, Henry, *Annotations upon the Two Foregoing Treatises, Lux Orientalis, or, An Enquiry into the Opinion of the Prae-existence of Souls; and the Discourse of Truth*... (London, 1682).
  An Antidote against Atheisme, or An Appeal to the Natural Faculties of the Minde of Man, whether there be not a GOD (London, 1653).
  ΑΝΤΙΨΥΧΟΠΑΝΝΥΧΙΑ, *or a Confutation of the Sleep of the Soul after Death* (Cambridge, 1642).
  Apocalypsis Apocalypseos; or the Revelation of St. John the Divine unveiled... (London, 1680).
  A Collection of Several Philosophical Writings..., 2nd edn (London, 1662).
  Conjectura Cabbalistica in *A Collection of Several Philosophical Writings*, 2nd edn (London, 1662).
  Divine Dialogues... (London, 1668).
  An Explanation of the Grand Mystery of Godliness... (London, 1660).
  An Exposition of the Seven Epistles to the Seven Churches; together with a Brief Discourse of Idolatry... (London, 1669).
  An Illustration of Those Two Abstruse Books in Holy Scripture, the Book of Daniel and the Revelation of St. John (London, 1685).

The Immortality of the Soul, so farre forth as it is demonstrable from the Knowledge of Nature and the Light of Reason (London, 1659).
A Modest Enquiry into the Mystery of Iniquity... (London, 1664).
Paralipomena Prophetica... (London, 1685).
Philosophicall Poems..., 2nd edn (Cambridge, 1647).
A Plain and Continued Exposition of the Several Prophecies of the Divine Visions of the Prophet Daniel... (London, 1681).
Psychodia Platonica; or a platonicall song of the soul, consisting of foure severall poems... (Cambridge, 1642).
Morley, Henry (ed.), *Table Talk of Samuel Taylor Coleridge* (London, 1884).
Morton, A. L., *The World of the Ranters* (London, 1970).
Moulin, Lewis du, *Moral Reflections upon the Number of the Elect, proving plainly from Scripture Evidence, &c...* (London, 1680).
Muggleton, Lodowick, *The Acts of the Witnesses of the Spirit...* (London, 1699).
Mullett, Charles F., 'A Letter by Joseph Glanvill on the Future State', *The Huntington Library Quarterly* 1 (1937), 447–56.
N., N., *A Letter to a Gentleman Touching the Treatise Entituled Two Hundred Queries concerning the Doctrine of the Revolution of Humane Souls, and its Conformity to the Truths of Christianity...* (London, 1689).
Napier, Alexander (ed.), *The Theological Works of Isaac Barrow*, 9 vols. (Cambridge, 1859).
Nathanson, Leonard, *The Strategy of Truth: A Study of Sir Thomas Browne* (Chicago, 1967).
Nicolson, Marjorie H., *Conway Letters...* (New Haven, 1930).
'Milton and the *Conjectura Cabbalistica*', *Philological Quarterly* 6 (1927), 1–18.
'The Spirit World of Milton and More', *Studies in Philology* 22 (1925), 433–52.
Norris, John, *A Letter to Mr. Dodwell, Concerning the Immortality of the Soul of Man...* (London, 1709).
A Philosophical Discourse concerning the Natural Immortality of the Soul... Occasion'd by Mr. Dodwell's late Epistolary Discourse (London, 1708).
Notestein, Wallace, *A History of Witchcraft in England from 1558 to 1718* (Washington, D. C., 1911).
Oakley, Francis, 'Christian Theology and the Newtonian Science: The Rise of the Concept of the Laws of Nature', *Church History* 30 (1961), 433–57.
[Orchard, N.], *The Doctrine of Devils, Proved to be the grand Apostasy of these later Times...* (London, 1676).
[Overton, Richard], *Man Wholly Mortal: Or, a Treatise Wherein 'Tis proved, both Theologically and Philosophically, That as whole man sinned, so whole man died; contrary to that common distinction of Soul and Body: and that the present going of the Soul into heaven or hell, is a meer Fiction: And that at the Resurrection is the beginning of our immortality; and then actual Condemnation and Salvation, and not before* (London, 1655).
Owen, D. D. R., *The Vision of Hell* (New York, 1971).

P., C., *A Dissertation Concerning the Prae-existency of Souls*... (London, 1684).
Pace, George B., 'Adam's Hell', *Proceedings of the Modern Language Association* 78 (1963), 25–35.
Pagitt, Ephraim, *Heresiography*, 6th edn (London, 1661).
Park, Katharine, and Daston, Lorraine J., 'Unnatural Conceptions: The Study of Monsters in Sixteenth and Seventeenth-Century France and England', *Past and Present* 92 (1981), 20–54.
Parker, Samuel, *An Account of the Nature and Extent of the Divine Dominion and Goodnesse, especially as they refer to the Origenian Hypothesis Concerning the Pre-existence of Souls* (Oxford, 1666).
P[atrick], S[imon], *A Brief Account of the new Sect of Latitude-Men Together with some reflections upon the New Philosophy* (London, 1662).
Patrides, C. A. (ed.), *The Cambridge Platonists* (Cambridge, 1980).
'"Paradise Lost" and the Mortalist Heresy', *Notes and Queries* 102 (1957), 250–1.
'Psychopannychism in Renaissance Europe', *Studies in Philology* 60 (1963), 227–9.
'Renaissance and Modern Thought on the Last Things: A Study in Changing Conceptions', *The Harvard Theological Review* 51 (1958), 169–185.
'The Salvation of Satan', *Journal of the History of Ideas* 28 (1967), 467–78.
Patterson, Frank A. (ed.), *The Works of John Milton*, 18 vols. (New York, 1931–8).
Pearson, John, *An Exposition of the Creed* (London, 1659).
Peckard, Peter, *Farther Observations on the Doctrine of an Intermediate State, in Answer to the Rev. Dr. Morton's Queries* (London, 1757).
Observations on the Doctrine of an Intermediate State between Death and the Resurrection (London, 1756).
Perronet, Vincent, *An Earnest Exhortation to the Strict Practice of Christianity*..., 2nd edn (London, 1750).
Pinto, Vivian de Sola, 'Peter Sterry and his Unpublished Writings', *Review of English Studies* 6 (1930), 385–407.
Peter Sterry: Platonist and Puritan 1613–1672 (Cambridge, 1934).
Pocock, J. G. A., 'Time, History and Eschatology in the Thought of Thomas Hobbes', in Elliott, J. H., and Koenigsburger, H. G. (eds.), *The Diversity of History* (Ithaca, New York, 1970), 149–98.
Prideaux, Humphrey, *The True Nature of Imposture Fully Displayed in the Life of Mahomet*... (London, 1697).
Pringle, William (ed.), *Commentary on the Book of Isaiah by John Calvin* (Grand Rapids, Michigan, 1984).
Prior, Moody E., 'Joseph Glanvill, Witchcraft, and Seventeenth-Century Science', *Modern Philology* 30 (1932–3), 167–93.
Quistorp, Heinrich, *Calvin's Doctrine of the Last Things* (London, 1955).
Rattansi, P. M., 'Paracelsus and the Puritan Revolution', *Ambix* 11 (1964), 24–32.

Raven, Charles E., *John Ray Naturalist: His Life and Works* (Cambridge, 1950).
Ray, John, *Miscellaneous Discourses concerning the Dissolution and Changes of the World*... (London, 1692).
Reay, Barry, 'Introduction', in McGregor, J. F. and Reay, Barry (eds.), *Radical Religion in the English Revolution* (Oxford, 1984).
Redwood, John, *Reason, Ridicule and Religion: The Age of Enlightenment in England, 1660–1750* (London, 1976).
Reeve, John, and Muggleton, Lodowick, *Joyful News from Heaven*... (London, 1658).
Richardson, Samuel, *A Discourse of the Torments of Hell*... (London, 1660).
Richetti, John J., *Popular Fiction before Richardson: Narrative Patterns 1700–1739* (Oxford, 1969).
Roberts, Alexander, and Donaldson, James (eds.), *Ante-Nicene Christian Library*, 25 vols. (Edinburgh, 1867–97).
Robinson, Thomas, *New Observations on the Natural History of this World of Matter and this World of Life*... (London, 1698).
Roe, Shirley A., *Matter, Life, and Generation: Eighteenth-century embryology and the Haller–Wolff debate* (Cambridge, 1981).
Rollins, Hyder E., *The Pack of Autolycus* (New York, 1969).
Ross, Alexander, *The Philosophicall Touch-Stone*... (London, 1645).
Rowe, Elizabeth Singer, *Friendship in Death, in Twenty Letters from the Dead to the Living*, 3rd edn (London, 1733).
Rowell, Geoffrey, *Hell and the Victorians: A Study of the Nineteenth-Century Theological Controversies Concerning Eternal Punishment and the Future Life* (Oxford, 1974).
Rupp, Gordon, *Religion in England, 1688–1791* (Oxford, 1986).
Russell, Jeffrey Burton, *The Prince of Darkness: Radical Evil and the Power of Good in History* (Ithaca, New York, 1988).
Russel, Robert, *Seven Sermons*..., 13th edn (London, 1705).
Rust, George, *A Discourse of Truth*... (London, 1682), in *Two Choice and Useful Treatises* (London, 1682).
A Letter of Resolution concerning Origen and the Chief of his Opinions (London, 1661).
Sabine, George H., *The Works of Gerrard Winstanley* (Ithaca, New York, 1941).
Salmon, Joseph, *Heights in Depths* (London, 1651).
Salter, Samuel (ed.), *Moral and Religious Aphorisms* (London, 1753).
Sanctorius, *Medicina Statics: or, Rules of Health, in Eight Sections of Aphorisms* (London, 1676).
Schaff, Philip, *The Creeds of Christendom*, 4th edn, 3 vols. (New York, 1919).
Schaffer, Simon, 'Newton's Comets and the Transformation of Astrology', in Curry, Patrick (ed.), *Astrology, Science and Society: Historical Essays* (Woodbridge, Suffolk, 1987), 219–43.

Schär, Max, *Das Nachleben des Origenes im Zeitalter des Humanismus* (Basel and Stuttgart, 1979).
Scholem, Gershom, *Major Trends in Jewish Mysticism* (New York, 1961).
Scot, Reginald, *The Discovery of Witchcraft, proving that the Compacts and Contracts of Witches with Devils and all Infernal Spirits or Familiars, are but Erroneous Novelties and Imaginary Conceptions* (London, 1665).
Scott, John, *The Christian Life, from its beginning to its consummation in glory...*, 2nd edn (London, 1683).
Seager, John, *A Discovery of the World to Come according to the Scriptures* (London, 1650).
Shaftesbury, Anthony Ashley, 3rd Earl of, *Characteristics of Men, Manners, Opinions, Times...*, 3 vols. (London, 1900).
Sharpe, J. A., *Crime in Seventeenth-Century England: A County Study* (Cambridge, 1983).
Sharrock, Robert, *De Finibus Virtutis Christianae...* (Oxford, 1673).
Sharrock, Roger (ed.), *The Miscellaneous Works of John Bunyan* (Oxford, 1976–).
Sheed, F. J. (trans.), *The Confessions of St. Augustine, Books I–X* (New York, 1942).
Sherlock, William, *A Practical Discourse Concerning Death*, 9th edn (London, 1696).
Shower, John, *Death a Deliverance; Or, a Funeral Discourse, Preach'd (in Part) on the Decease of Mrs. Mary Doolittle...* (London, 1693).
  Heaven and Hell; or the Unchangeable State of Happiness or Misery for all Mankind in another World (London, 1700).
Shumaker, Wayne, *The Occult Sciences in the Renaissance* (Berkeley, 1972).
Sinclair, George, *Satans Invisible World Discovered* (Edinburgh, 1685).
Smith, Nigel (ed.), *A Collection of Ranter Writings from the Seventeenth Century* (London, 1983).
South, Robert, *Twelve Sermons upon Various Occasions* (London, 1718).
Southey, R., *The Doctor*, 7 vols. (London, 1834–47).
Spencer, Theodore, 'Chaucer's Hell: A Study in Mediaeval Convention', *Speculum* 2 (1927), 177–200.
Spierenburg, Pieter, *The Spectacle of Suffering: Executions and the Evolution of Repression: from a preindustrial metropolis to the European experience* (Cambridge, 1984).
[Stafford, Richard], *A Discourse of the Misery of Hell...* (London, 1697).
Steadman, John M., 'Milton and Patristic Tradition: The Quality of Hell-Fire', *Anglia* 76 (1958), 116–28.
Steffe, John, *Two Letters on the Intermediate State...* (London, 1758).
  Five Letters... (London, 1757).
[Stegmann, Joachim], *Brevis Disquisitio: or, a Brief Enquiry touching a Better Way... To Refute Papists, and Reduce Protestants to Certainty and Unity in Religion* (London, 1633).
[Sterry, Peter], *A Discourse of the Freedom of the Will* (London, 1675).

The Rise, Race, and Royalty of the Kingdom of God in the Soul of Man (London, 1683).

'That the State of wicked men after this Life is mixt of evill, and good things', MS 291, Emmanuel College Library, Cambridge.

Stevens, Joseph, *The Whole Parable of Dives and Lazarus, Explain'd and Apply'd* (London, 1697).

Stillingfleet, Edward, *The Bishop of Worcester's Answer to Mr. Locke's Second Letter...* (London, 1697).

Stone, Lawrence, *The Family, Sex and Marriage in England 1500–1800* (Harmondsworth, 1979).

Stromberg, Roland, *Religious Liberalism in Eighteenth-Century England* (Oxford, 1954).

Strong, William, *The Worm that Dyeth Not, or, Hell Torments in the Certainty and Eternity of Them* (London, 1672).

Stroumsa, Gedaliahu G., '*Caro Salutis cardo*: Shaping the Person in Early Christian Thought', *History of Religions* 30 (1990), 25–50.

Stubbe, Henry, *An Account of the Rise and Progress of Mahometanism with the Life of Mahomet* (London, 1911).

Sturmy, Daniel, *Discourse on Several Subjects, But Principally on the Separate State of Souls* (Cambridge, 1716).

Sutton, Christopher, *Disce mori, learn to dye* (London, 1662).

Swinden, Tobias, *An Enquiry into the Nature and Place of Hell*, 2nd edn (London, 1727).

Taylor, Jeremy, *The Great Exemplar of Sanctity and Holy Life according to the Christian Institution*, 2nd edn (London, 1652).

Thomas, Keith, 'The Puritans and Adultery: The Act of 1650 Reconsidered', in Pennington, Donald, and Thomas, Keith (eds.), *Puritans and Revolutionaries* (Oxford, 1978), 257–82.

Religion and the Decline of Magic (Harmondsworth, 1980).

Thomson, John A. F., *The Later Lollards 1414–1520* (Oxford, 1965).

Tillotson, John, *Of the Eternity of Hell-Torments. A Sermon Preach'd before the Queen at White-Hall, March the 7th, 1689–90* (London, 1708).

A Sermon Preached at the Funeral of the Reverend Benjamin Whichcot D. D. (London, 1683).

The Works of the Learned Isaac Barrow, D. D., 2 vols. (London, 1716).

Tindal, Matthew, *Christianity as old as the Creation* (London, 1730).

Trapp, Joseph, *Thoughts upon the Four Last Things: Death, Judgment, Heaven, Hell* (n.p., 1734).

Turner, John, *A Brief Vindication of the separate Existence and Immortality of the Soul from a late Author's 'Second Thoughts'...* (London, 1702).

Justice Done to Human Souls... (London, 1706).

Turner, Ralph V., 'descendit ad inferos. Medieval Views on Christ's Descent into Hell', *Journal of the History of Ideas* 27 (1966), 173–94.

Tyacke, Nicholas, and White, Peter, 'Debate: The Rise of Arminianism Reconsidered', *Past and Present* 115 (1987), 201–29.

Tyson, Edward, 'A Relation of two Monstrous Pigs, with the resemblance of Humane Faces, and two young Turkeys joined by the Breast...,' *Philosophical Transactions of the Royal Society* 21 (1699), 431–5.
Underhill, John (ed.), '*The Athenian Oracle.*' *A Selection* (London, 1896[?]).
Ussher, James, *The Principles of Christian Religion* (London, 1678).
Velikovsky, Immanuel, *Worlds in Collision* (Garden City, New York, 1950).
Venn, Richard, *Tracts and Sermons on Several Occasions* (London, 1740).
Vincent, Thomas, *Fire and Brimstone From Heaven, From Earth, in Hell...* (London, 1670).
Walker, D. P., *The Ancient Theology* (New York, 1972).
 The Decline of Hell: Seventeenth-Century Discussions of Eternal Torment (London, 1964).
 'The Astral Body in Renaissance Medicine', *Journal of the Warburg and Courtauld Institutes* 21 (1958), 119–33.
 'Origène en France', in *Courants Religieux et Humanisme à la fin du XVe et au début du XVIe siècle* (Paris, 1959).
Wallace, D. D., 'From Eschatology to Arian Heresy: The Case of Francis Kett', *Harvard Theological Review* 67 (1974), 459–73.
 'Puritan and Anglican. The Interpretation of Christ's Descent into Hell in Elizabethan Theology', *Archiv für Reformationsgeschichte* 69 (1978), 248–87.
Walwyn, William, *The Power of Love* (London, 1643).
Ward, Richard, *The Life of the Learned and Pious Dr. Henry More* (London, 1710).
W[arren], E[dward], *No Praeexistence. Or a Brief Dissertation against the Hypothesis of Humane Souls, Living in a State Antecedaneous to This* (London, 1667).
Watson, Thomas, *A Body of Practical Divinity...* (London, 1692).
Watts, Isaac, *Death and Heaven; or The Last Enemy Conquer'd, and Separate Spirits made perfect* (London, 1722).
 The World to Come: or Discourses on the Joys or Sorrows of Departed Souls at Death (London, 1739).
Weber, Max, *The Protestant Ethic and the Spirit of Capitalism* (London, 1930).
Webster, C., 'Henry More and Descartes: Some New Sources', *The British Journal for the History of Science* 4 (1968–9), 181–240.
Webster, John, *The Displaying of Supposed Witchcraft. Wherein is affirmed that there are many sorts of Deceivers and Impostors, and Divers persons under a passive Delusion of Melancholy and Fancy* (London, 1677).
Wheeler, Michael, *Death and the Future Life in Victorian Literature and Theology* (Cambridge, 1990).
Whiston, William, *The Accomplishment of Scripture Prophecies* (Cambridge, 1708).
 Astronomical Principles of Religion, Natural and Reveal'd (London, 1717).
 The Cause of the Deluge Demonstrated: Wherein it is proved that the famous Comet of AD 1680, came by the Earth at its Deluge..., 2nd edn (London, 1714).

The Eternity of Hell Torments Considered: or, a Collection of Texts of Scripture, and Testimonies of the Three First Centuries, relating to Them (London, 1740).
Historical Memoirs of the Life and Writings of Dr. Samuel Clarke, 3rd edn (London, 1748).
Memoirs of the Life and Writings of Mr. William Whiston ..., 3 pts. (London, 1749).
A New Theory of the Earth, from its Original to the Consummation of all Things ... (London, 1696).
Sermons and Essays ... (London, 1709).
Whitby, Daniel, *Reflections on Some Assertions and Opinions of Mr. Dodwell* ... (London, 1707).
[White, Jeremiah], *The Restoration of All Things* (London, 1712).
White, Peter, 'The Rise of Arminianism Reconsidered', *Past and Present* 101 (1983), 34–54.
White, Thomas, *The Middle State of Souls. From the hour of death to the Day of Judgment* (London, 1659).
Whitehall, Robert, *Hexastichon hieron, sive Jconum* ... (Oxford, 1677).
Willey, Basil, *The Seventeenth Century Background* (London, 1953).
(ed.), *Thomas Burnet: The Sacred Theory of the Earth* (London, 1965).
Williams, George H., *The Radical Reformation* (London, 1962).
Williamson, George, 'Milton and the Mortalist Heresy', *Studies in Philology* 32 (1935), 553–79.
Wilson, Walter, *Memoirs of the Life and Times of Daniel de Foe*, 3 vols. (London, 1830).
Wind, Edgar, 'The Revival of Origen', in Milner, Dorothy (ed.) *Studies in Art and Literature for Belle da Costa Greene* (Princeton, 1954).
Wise, Thomas, *A Confutation of the Reason and Philosophy of Atheism; Being in a great measure either an Abridgment or an Improvement of what Dr. Cudworth offer'd to that Purpose in his True Intellectual System of the Universe* (London, 1706).
The True Intellectual System of the Universe, A Confutation of the Reason and Philosophy of Atheism (London, 1658).
Wolfe, Don M., 'Unsigned Pamphlets of Richard Overton: 1641–1649', *Huntington Library Quarterly* 21 (1957–8), 167–201.
Wolfson, Harry A., *Religious Philosophy* (Cambridge, Mass., 1961).
Wollheim, Richard (ed.), *Hume on Religion* (London, 1963).
Yates, Frances A., *Giordano Bruno and the Hermetic Tradition* (London, 1964).
The Sun-Centred World, audio (London, n.d.).
Younge, Richard, *A Serious and Pathetical Description of Heaven and Hell, According to the Pencil of the Holy Ghost* (London, 1658).
Zagorin, Perez, 'The Authorship of Mans Mortalitie', *The Library* (1950–1), 179–82.

Index

Adam 5, 8, 18, 50, 55, 136
Addison, Joseph 151–2
Ady, Thomas 169 n. 141
Alford, Joseph 186 n. 17
Allen, Don C. 10
Anabaptists *see* mortalism
angels 31, 34, 36, 73, 101, 107, 112, 118, 120, 126, 128, 130
Anglican Church 4, 39, 40, 149
Annesley, Samuel 184 n. 108
annihilationism 43, 44, 45, 50, 56–7, 62–3, 130, 145, 147, 148, 150, 153, 160
   demise of 53
   Ranters and 53
Anselm 85
Anti-Christ 120
Aquinas, Thomas 97
Arianism *see* Trinity
Aristotelianism 178 n. 146
Arminianism *see* Calvinism
ascension 55, 107, 112
Asgill, John 54–9
astrology 127
astronomy 15, 16, 47, 125, 126
atheism 16, 34, 41, 66, 129, 156
Augustine 11, 15, 74, 78, 97, 101

baptism 66
Baptist church 147
Barrow, Isaac 148
Bates, William 86, 90, 100, 132, 150, 152, 154
Bauthumley, Jacob 47
Baxter, Richard 82–3, 85, 97, 101–2, 103, 104, 144
Bekker, Balthazar 169 n. 141
Beveridge, William 89
Bible, authority of 53
   see also Bible, interpretation of; reason; science
Blackstone, William 161

Blyth, Francis 98, 145, 151, 153
body 45, 136–40
   aethereal 30, 138, 139, 140
   aerial 32, 36, 93, 138, 139
   heavenly 105–8
   a partner in sin 95–6
   punishment of 90–5
   of resurrection 131–43
   resurrection of 95–6, 131–43
Boehme, Jacob 46
Bourn, Samuel 151
Boyle, Robert 35, 133–5
Brandon, John 88, 147, 150
Brokesby, Francis 174 n. 91
Bromhall, Thomas 24, 34, 87
Browne, Thomas 10, 21, 41–2, 70, 101, 132–3, 134
Bullinger, Henry 40, 101
Bunyan, John 53, 84, 85, 95, 97
Burgess, Daniel 95
Burnet, Thomas 99, 106, 107, 119–23, 127, 153, 154, 160
Burns, Norman T. 40
Bynum, Caroline Walker 189 n. 85

Cabbalism 5, 16, 118
   Christianised form of 17, 20
   Lurianic 17, 18
   millennium and 20–1
   transmigration of souls and 17–21
   see also universalism
Calamy, Edmund 38, 43
Calvin, John 8, 10, 25, 68–9, 90, 92, 101
   mortalism and 39
   see also Calvinism
Calvinism 25, 49, 130
   American 98
   Arminianism and 25, 74
   divine goodness and 26
   earthly authority and 49
   God's sovereignty and 25, 26

heavenly bodies and 101
immortal soul and 41
punishment and 39
reprobation and 130
see also Calvin, John; predestination
Cambridge, University of 7, 119, 129, 148
Camfield, Benjamin 34
Campbell, Archibald 77–9, 153
Camporesi, Piero 110
Casaubon, Meric 169 n. 141
Catholicism 49, 92
see also purgatory
Caussin, Nicholas 68, 93, 154
Chaucer, Geoffrey 89
children 8, 12, 19, 21, 85, 97, 102, 108
Chishull, Edmund 60, 62, 66
Christ 18, 45, 50, 102, 106
   ascension of 55, 107, 112
   death of 18, 20, 55, 59
   earthly reign of 112
   harrowing of hell and 64–5
   resurrection of 18, 38, 49, 55, 135
   second coming of 39, 41, 112, 114, 118, 120, 123, 129
Clarke, Samuel 63, 65, 150–1, 159
Clement of Alexandria 13, 15, 64
Clement of Rome 189 n. 91
Colie, Rosalie L. 166 n. 91
Coleridge, Samuel Taylor 173 n. 79
Collins, Anthony 149, 156
Coloreda, Lazarus and John Baptista 108
cometology 127
   Newton and 127
   Whiston and 127–9
conflagration 111–30
   Descartes and 113–14
   hell and 121
   of the world 113–14
   repetitions of 117
   second coming and 114, 118, 120, 129
   see also fire
conscience 92
Conway, Anne, Lady 16, 17, 20, 22–3, 27, 29, 153
Copernicus *see* astronomy
Coppin, Richard 46
Corpus Hermeticum 5
   see also Hermes Trismegistus
cosmology
   Descartes and 113, 127
   Swinden and 126
Coudert, Allison 164 n. 56
Counter-Reformation 91
Coward, William 62
Creation 127, 128

biblical account of 9, 13, 18, 51
literal understanding of 15
philosophical Cabbala and 16
pre-existence of the soul and 9–10, 26–7
see also immediate creationism
Crisp, Stephen 56
Cromwell, Oliver 102
Cudworth, Ralph 21, 30, 35, 93, 119, 138–40
Cuppé, Pierre 73, 160–1
Curry, Patrick 188 n. 67

daemonology 48
damned 50, 69, 71, 73, 78, 81–95
   numbers of 72–4
Dante Alighieri 90
Dawes, William 70, 86, 98, 145, 150, 160
death 58–9, 79
Defoe, Daniel 55, 58–9
deism 14, 106, 156
deluge 128
demonology *see* demons
demons 34–6, 112
   Beelzebub and 121
   Browne, Thomas and 41
   destruction of 114, 128–9
   excesses of 35
   salvation of 6, 130
   torture and 85–7
Denison, John 181 n. 45
depravity *see* original sin
Descartes, René 12, 22, 33, 113, 117, 120, 121
Determinism 24
   Hobbes and 24
   see also predestination
Digby, Kenelm 70–1, 131
Diggers 53
Dillingham, Theophilus 7
Dodwell, Henry 60–7
Dodwell, William 90, 145, 151
Donne, John 132
D'Oyly, Robert 191 n. 34
Drexelius 73
Du Moulin, Lewis 73
Dunton, John 97, 102–4, 107–8

Earbery, Matthias 122
Edward VI 41
Edwards, Jonathan 98, 150, 151, 154–5, 157
Edwards, Thomas 43
Elizabeth I 41
embryology 9, 13
empiricism 132

Enlightenment 69
Erasmus 6
eschatology 52, 71
  Asgill, John and 54–9
  Dodwell, Henry and 60–7
  Hobbes, Thomas and 48
  Platonism and 119
  Whiston, William and 129
  see also Christ, second coming of; last day; judgement, day of
Ezekiel 132, 134

Fall of Man 51
  and loss of immortality 61
  Platonic view of 14–17
  and transmigration 22–3
  see also Adam
Family of Love 46
Felton, Henry 191 n. 34
Ficino, Marsilio 5
Fifth Monarchists 44, 53
fire 75, 78
  in hell 87–90
  punishment of the body and 92–3
  see also conflagration
Fleury, A. 191 n. 34
forgiveness 75, 153
Foucault, Michel 99–100
free will 8, 16–17
  beyond the grave 76, 153
  divine 24–8
  human 24–6, 76, 152
  see also determinism

Galen 133
Gearing, William 85, 95, 102, 106, 107, 108, 108–9
Gehenna 129
Glanvill, Joseph 4, 7, 12, 14, 22, 26, 26–7, 29, 34
  Calvinism and 26
  conflagration and 113–14, 117–19
  demons and 35
  Platonism and 5
  soul, journey of and 30–2
  soul, pre-existence of and 5
  soul, transmigration of and 22
  soul, vehicles of and 30, 31, 32, 36
God 15
  attributes of 16, 18, 27, 50, 73, 74, 88, 95, 115, 132, 133, 148–54
  authorship of sin 25
  focus of heaven 101–2
  free will of 24–28

goodness of 10, 18, 23, 26, 76, 77, 117, 130, 150, 150–1, 153
grace of 75
Kingdom of 49–50
knowledge of 42
severity of 27
sovereignty of 25–6
vengefulness of 83, 84
see also theodicy
Goodwin, Thomas 87, 89, 149–50
guilt 84

Hades 61, 64, 65, 77–78, 79, 129, 131
  see also hell
Halley, Edmond 129
Hallywell, Henry 26, 27, 29, 76–77, 153
Hartliffe, John 194 n. 78
heathen 62–3
  see also pagans
heaven 108–10
  bodies in 105–8
  friends in 101–5
  happiness in 97, 100–5
  location of 42, 46
  translation to 54–60
  women in 101–5
hell 64–5
  bodies in 106–8
  darkness of 87–90
  location of 42, 46, 73, 119–23
  terrors of 73
  see also conflagration; damned; fire; Gehenna; Hades; judgement, day of; punishment; torment
Helmont, Francis Mercurius van 5, 17–20, 22, 29, 153, 154, 160
Helmont, J. B. van 17
Herbert, Thomas 105
Hermes Trismegistus 5, 125
  see also Corpus Hermeticum
Hickes, George 193 n. 60
Hill, Christopher 47, 53
Hill, Nicholas 10
Hills, Henry 11, 12
Hoard, Samuel 25
Hobbes, Thomas 14, 22, 36, 53, 67, 150
  determinism of 24
  eschatology of 47–51, 147
  libertinism and 34
  materialism of 12, 24, 33, 47
  mortalism of 47–50, 56
Hody, Humphrey 96, 135
Holdsworth, Winch 96
Horbery, Matthew 69, 74, 144, 146, 152, 153

Huber, Marie 98–9, 148, 160
Hull, John 41
Hume, David 158
Huxley, Aldous 2

Iamblichus 5
immediate creationism 10–13
interpretation of Bible 15, 17, 49, 52, 55
    allegorical 127, 137
    cabbalistic 16–17
    exoteric and esoteric 15, 122, 148
    four levels of 15
    literal 15, 127, 148
    mystical 14
intolerance *see* toleration
Irenaeus 139
Islam 105–6, 145

James II 119
Jenks, Richard 69, 157
Jerome, Saint 6, 101
Jesus *see* Christ
Jews *see* Judaism
Johnson, Samuel 191 n. 134
Judaism 18, 106, 145
judgement 39, 67, 99–100
judgement, day of 32, 38, 41, 48–50, 62, 69, 112
justice 99
    see also God; judgement; penal systems; probation; punishment
justification by faith 90

Kabbala Denudata 5, 20
Kant, Immanuel 76
Kett, John 41
King, Peter 188 n. 75
Kingdom of God *see* God
Kircher, Athanasius 134

last day 111–30
    see also Christ, second coming of; judgement, day of
last judgement *see* judgement, day of
law 66, 150, 155, 156, 157
Layton, Henry 62
Lead, Jane 186 n. 17
Le Clerc, Jean 157
le Goff, Jacques 9, 67
Leveller 51, 53
Lewis, Thomas 145, 160
liberalism 100
libertinism 66
limbo 74
Locke, John 50, 129, 130, 132, 140–2, 147

Love, Christopher 83, 84, 85, 86
Lupton, William 70
Luria, Isaac 17
    see also Cabbalism
Luther, Martin 38–9, 68, 90, 101
Lutheran Church 39
Lye, Thomas 95

Macaulay, Thomas Babington 60
Marketman, John 81
marriage 104–5
materialism 12, 33
Mead, Richard 122
Mede, Joseph 25
metempsychosis 24
    see also soul, transmigration of
millennium 18–19, 20–1
Milles, Thomas 64
Milton, John 11, 25, 56, 89, 91
More, Henry 4, 6, 7, 12, 14, 15–17, 22, 25, 29, 32, 35, 67, 86, 98, 102, 107, 119, 146–7
    Cartesianism and 33
    conflagration and 112–14
    God and 27, 28, 29
    Platonism and 5
    predestination and 25–6, 44
    pre-existence and 5, 9
    resurrection of the body and 96, 138
    second coming and 112–14
    transmigration and 21
    vehicles of the soul and 30, 31, 31–2, 106
mortalism 32, 106, 147
    Anabaptists and 39, 40, 55, 56
    annihilationism and 43, 44, 45, 50, 56–7, 62–3
    Asgill, John and 56–7
    in English Reformation 40
    Hobbes, Thomas and 47–50
    libertinism and 76
    in Luther 38–9
    Milton, John and 51–2
    Overton, Richard and 51–2, 56
    radical 43–7
    Zwingli and 40
    see also annihilationism; soul, in intermediate state; soul, sleep of; soul, vehicles of
Moses 5, 16, 18, 55, 101, 125, 127
Muggleton, Lodowick 44–5
mysticism 15, 46, 125

natural theology 7, 14
naturalism 52, 87

neo-Platonism 5, 30, 42, 93, 112, 125
  see also More, Henry; Plato; Platonism;
    Plotinus; soul, vehicles of
Newton, Isaac 127
Nicholas, Henry 46
Norris, John 63

Orchard, N. 90
Origen 7, 11, 13, 15, 92, 117, 121, 133,
  139
  journey of the soul and 5–6
  pre-existence and 5–6, 24
  soul, vehicles of and 30, 137, 139
  transmigration and 21–2
  universalism and 6
original sin 7–8, 11
Oxford, University of 60, 88

pagans 64
pantheism 46, 56, 57
paradise 16, 56, 68, 69, 78, 79, 105–6, 121
Parker, Samuel 14, 27, 28
Pascal, Blaise 174 n.81
Pearson, John 95, 131
penal systems 84, 154
Philo 5
philosophy, mechanical 71, 113
Pico della Mirandola 6, 17
Plato 5, 21, 30, 125
  see also neo-Platonism; Platonism;
    Plotinus
Platonism 4, 6, 7, 9, 14, 15, 22, 24, 26,
  36–7, 76, 106, 132, 148
  see also Conway, Anne; Glanvill, Joseph;
    More, Henry; neo-Platonism; Origen;
    Plato; Rust, George
Plotinus 5, 21
prayers for the dead 41, 78–9
predestination 26, 44–5, 75, 129
  see also Calvinism
pre-existence 4–11, 26–7
Presbyterian Church 49
Prideaux, Humphrey 106
Protestantism 92, 93, 99
punishment 19
  as deterrent 158–61
  of body and soul 90–5
  eternal 144–61
  eternal or temporary 23, 65, 144–61
  for infinite offence 154–5
  natural and inevitable 151–2
  Platonic view of 6
  proportionate to sins 90–1, 155
  Puritan view of 82
  reformative 23, 74–5, 87, 153

retributive 84, 87, 90, 150
sadistic 84
scholasticism and 91, 93
of soul 90–5
transmigration and 17–23
  see also conflagration; fire; hell;
    judgement, day of; suffering; torment
purgatory 9, 48, 67–72, 147
  Anglican church and 69
  Calvinism and 68–9
  English Protestantism and 69
  Luther and 68
  Protestant version of 74–80
  purpose of 72

Quakers 56

racism 107
Ranters 46, 47, 53
Ray, John 123–5, 154, 159
reason
  faith and 141
  revelation and 147–9
  Scripture and 145, 147–8, 149
  as source of truth 14
  see also Bible; science
Reay, Barry 43
Reeve, John 45
Reformation, English 40
Renaissance 5, 6, 10, 17, 134
reprobation 130
Restoration 53, 56, 155
  see also revolution, English of 1688
resurrection 18
  see also body; translation
revolution, English of 1688 53, 119
rewards 65, 100, 156
  after final judgement 94
  degrees of 91
  in intermediate state 76, 94
Richardson, Samuel 88, 147, 160
Roach, Richard 114
Robinson, Thomas 187 n.54
Rogers, John 44
Rosenroth, Christian Knorr von 5, 17, 20,
  22
Ross, Alexander 52
Rowe, Elizabeth Singer 104, 108
Russel, Robert 189 n.96
Rust, George 4, 6, 7, 11, 13, 14, 27, 29,
  137–8
  conflagration and 116–17
  divine free will and 27
  Platonism and 5
  predestination and 26

pre-existence and 9
punishment and 116–17
vehicles of the soul and 30, 137

Salmon, Joseph 46
salvation 118
  of demons 6
  orthodox view of 64
  second chance at 18, 116, 122, 129
Sanctorius 133, 135, 139
Satan *see* demons
Schaffer, Simon 127
science 111–30
  philosophy and 15
  Scripture and 15
  see also astronomy; Bible; cometology;
    conflagration; cosmology; creation;
    deluge; last day
Scot, Reginald 36
Scott, John 152
Seager, John 131
Seder Olam 19–21
Seekers 47
sexuality 11–12
  Catholic view of 11
  in heaven 103, 107
  Platonic view of 12
  Protestant view of 12
Shaftesbury, Anthony Ashley Cooper, 1st
  Earl of 159
Sharrock, Robert 85, 89, 131–2, 144, 158
Sherlock, William 69, 105
Shower, John 73, 81, 98, 107, 132, 160
Sinclair, George 34
Society for the Reformation of Manners
  66
Socinianism 67, 156
soul
  existence of 33, 48
  immediate creation of 10–13
  immortality of 12, 48
  indivisibility of 12
  in intermediate state 39, 41, 56, 61, 76
  mortality of 38–41
  sleep of 40, 43, 76
  transmigration of 10, 14, 17–23
  see also mortalism; pre-existence; soul,
    vehicles of; traducianism
South, Robert 158
Spierenburg, Pieter 99
Spinoza 22
Stafford, Richard 83, 89
Stegmann, Joseph 67
Sterry, Peter 74–6
Stevens, Joseph 97

Stillingfleet, Edward 141–2
Stone, Lawrence 82
Strong, William 69, 92
Stubbe, Henry 106
suffering 23
  curative 23
  public 99–100
  previous lives and 7–9, 18, 24
  see also demons; pain; penal systems;
    punishment; theodicy; torments
Swinden, Tobias 69, 73, 92, 125–6

Taylor, Jeremy 6
Tertullian 10, 97, 99, 131
theocracy 154
theodicy 5, 28
  Christian Platonism and 24–9
  free-will defence and 24–9
  pre-existence and 7–9
Thomas, Keith 163 n.33, 169 n.141
Tillotson, John 96, 116, 155–7
Tindal, Matthew 151
Toland, John 14
toleration 53
torments
  eternality of 115–16, 144–61
  graded 90–1
  in hell 81–7
  mental 90–5
  physical 90–5
  temporary 23, 65, 129
  see also conflagration; fire; hell; justice;
    punishment; suffering
traducianism 10, 12, 13
Traherne, Thomas 97–8
translation 54–9
transmigration *see* soul
transubstantiation 129
Trapp, Joseph 88
Trinity 129
Turner, John 60, 65, 66
Tyson, Edward 163 n.34

universalism 6, 18, 19, 20, 41, 75, 115,
  119, 146, 147, 148, 160

vehicles of soul 29–32, 36, 92, 106, 137,
  138
Venn, Richard 157
Vincent, Thomas 83, 85, 88–9, 89–90

Walker, D. P. 2, 5, 98, 99, 130, 152
Warren, Edward 4, 27, 28, 29, 69–70,
  115, 146
Weber, Max 74

Webster, John 36
Wesley, Samuel 184 n. 108
Whiston, William 54, 127–30, 145, 146, 147, 152, 153
Whitby, Daniel 64, 65
White, Jeremiah 166 n. 87
White, Thomas 70, 71–2, 93
Winstanley, Gerrard 186 n. 17
Wise, Thomas 139

Wolseley, Charles 34
women 101–5
Writer, Clement 172 n. 49

Yates, Frances 187 n. 59
Younge, Richard 83, 95, 105

Zanchius, Hieronymus 131
Zwingli, Ulrich 40, 101